The Insider

The Insider

Trapped in Saddam's Brutal Regime

ALA BASHIR

with LARS SIGURD SUNNANÅ

ABACUS

First published in Great Britain in July 2005 by Abacus

Photographs on pp. 96, 204, 234, 252, 280 and 294 are from
Saddam's picture archive.

Quote from J. A. Chamier on p. 35 is taken from the *Journal of the
Royal United Services Institute*, February–November 1921, 210. Extract
from work of Arthur Harris also on p. 35 is from his book *Bomber
Offensive*, 1990 edition (originally published in 1947), courtesy of
Greenhill Books.

A CIP catalogue record for this book
is available from the British Library.

ISBN 0 349 11935 X

Typeset in Monotype Baskerville by M Rules
Printed and bound in Great Britain by
Clays Ltd, St Ives plc

Abacus
An imprint of
Time Warner Book Group UK
Brettenham House
Lancaster Place
London WC2E 7EN

www.twbg.co.uk

To those innocent, decent and honest children, women and men, wherever they be, who have lost and still are losing their lives, and to those who have suffered and continue to suffer mental and physical torture in events directed by others under shadows of hate, ignorance and revenge.

CONTENTS

Contents

PART III THE COLLAPSE

PART IV ENCLOSURE

PREFACE

by Ala Bashir

Sheikh Hassan bin Muhammad bin Ali al-Thani of Qatar loves art and possesses one of the world's largest collections of classic and modern oriental art. His book collection too is outstanding. In December 2002 he invited me for a week's stay in Doha, where a large studio and guesthouse were put at my disposal. During those days, while I was working in the studio, he hovered around me constantly, and I knew why. In accordance with Bedouin tradition he was waiting for me – as his guest – to tell him of my plans for the future, now that I was under his protection.

The Sheikh had made sure my invitation to Qatar was an official one. But I had not been invited to Qatar simply to paint. My wife and four grown-up children were in Europe. In Iraq regulations stipulated that I would therefore not be given permission to leave the country. My wife and I were not allowed to be out of the country at the same time; at any given moment one of us had to remain in Baghdad. But the official invitation from Qatar changed things. I was allowed to leave.

Thus Sheikh Hassan had opened the door for me to defect – to refrain from returning to Iraq to a war I knew was coming. Now he was waiting to hear what my decision would be.

For a painter to be a guest of Sheikh Hassan was a dream come true. In the large studio I found all the brushes and canvases I could want. The oil colours came from a family firm in the Netherlands. They were worth a small fortune, but then they had been mixed according to the same methods as those used in the days of Rembrandt. I had never worked with more beautiful colours.

I painted the severed head of a beautiful young woman. The head was wrapped in see-through plastic and lying on a chair.

Nine men were standing round the chair; they looked like animals and held knives in their claws. They symbolised ignorance, greed, egoism, hate, revenge and abuse of power: the deadly sins from which we Iraqis have suffered since time immemorial, squeezed between lesser and greater despots in Baghdad and powers from the outside who wanted to conquer the fertile land areas between the Tigris and the Euphrates, where once rocked the cradle of civilisation.

Saddam Hussein al-Tikriti conformed naturally to Iraq's bloody history. That history is full of brutal masters who have fallen victim to their own absolute power. Nor is it difficult to find parallels in the past to the suppression and cruelty which the President and his henchmen will soon have to answer for, after their thirty-five years in power.

Abu Jaafar al-Mansour, the Caliph who founded Baghdad in AD 762, would often throw carpets over his enemies after he had cut them down. Then he would invite family, friends and acquaintances to a feast – on top of the carpets. Festivities usually started before the fallen enemies' death-throes had ended. Meals with the Caliph were often turbulent!

Saddam was just as extraordinary. None of his Baghdad predecessors has to the same degree fascinated, upset and, from time to time, frightened the international community. Following the invasion of Kuwait in 1990 Western politicians, journalists and authors competed with each other to describe how dangerous he was and how serious the threat his regime posed to world peace.

That threat increased after al-Qaeda's attack on the World Trade Center in New York and the Pentagon in Washington on 11 September 2001. Although the regime in Baghdad could not be associated with Osama bin Laden and his network, the die seemed to have been cast by George W. Bush in the White House: Saddam needed to be removed because, contrary to UN Security Council resolutions, he had allegedly stored away weapons of mass destruction.

The choice for me was not an easy one. It was tempting to stay with Sheikh Hassan in Qatar. I had been witness to the revolution and the fall of the monarchy on 14 July 1958, the bloody settlements between Communists and pan-Arab nationalists in 1959,

the even bloodier coup on 8 February 1963, and the start to the Baath Party's final assumption of power on 17 July 1968. I had survived the war between Iran and Iraq from 1980 to 1988, as well as the bombing of Baghdad during the Gulf War of 1991 and the rain of missiles during Operation Desert Fox in 1998.

Now a new war was imminent.

'I'll return to Iraq,' I told Sheikh Hassan when the agreed week-long visit to Doha was nearing its end.

I could not defect. I ran three hospitals and employed three hundred colleagues in Baghdad. They would need me when the rumoured war became a reality. To jump ship now that the storm was brewing would go against everything I believed in and I would lose all respect. My love for my country was far greater than my dislike for Saddam's regime.

I also wanted to experience the fall of Saddam and his regime.

Without having been asked and without being able to decline, I had been pulled into his team of doctors as a specialist more than twenty years before. As an artist he had known me even longer. I had gained his confidence and he often asked my advice. In the shadow of high-level politics I had observed the play of power and intrigues, the purges, corruption and bloody family feuds from the inside. Without betraying my professional code of conduct or any patient confidentiality I wanted to train a spotlight on my observations of this tragic and frightening era of Iraq's modern history. My report would not be complete unless I returned to Baghdad, I told the Sheikh.

Ala Bashir
Doha, March 2004

FOREWORD

by Lars Sigurd Sunnanå

'The history of modern Iraq tells us that the road to democracy is almost closed. The Americans and the British should know better than to think they can make it blossom now that they're about to remove Saddam Hussein and his regime,' said Ala Bashir.

I was sitting with him in my correspondent's flat in Amman. It was New Year's Eve 2002 and our topic of conversation, naturally, was the approaching war. He had phoned me from Sheikh Hassan's art centre in Doha the previous evening. I was in Jerusalem on assignment for the Norwegian Broadcasting Corporation (NRK), but immediately cancelled all planned stories and interviews. When Ala was passing through, either to or from Baghdad, I always dropped everything I was doing in order to meet him. It would be good to see him again. I had some Norwegian smoked salmon in the freezer and a decent white Burgundy in the fridge.

'For the last forty-five years we have been living under an everlasting shadow of hatred, revenge and aggression,' he continued. 'The minority who have been fighting for honesty, integrity and humanity amongst the rulers of our country were sidelined a long time ago; there are increasingly fewer of them. Now they are so few I can't see how they can assert themselves in the new society which must rise after the war.'

That evening and night in the Jordanian capital was a long one. We had a lot to talk about. The new year, 2003, did not look promising.

I can thank Dr Bashir's cousin, the American oil analyst Faleh Aljibury, for having introduced me to the Iraqi doctor and artist when I arrived in Amman in May 1999. Before becoming correspondent in the Middle East I had, since 1975, covered for NRK the majority of the meetings of the ministers of the Organization of Petroleum Exporting Countries (OPEC). Aljibury, who was also present at the meetings, together with other international analysts and the press corps, had become one of my friends. His cousin in Iraq was told not to come to Amman without dropping by.

I met Ala several times in Baghdad during my travels as a reporter before the war broke out on 20 March 2003. My employer chose to pull me out of Iraq before hostilities began, but I went back again on 11 April, two days after the fall of Baghdad. I had difficulty in finding Ala, but heard that he had survived, thank God.

Four months later Faleh Aljibury phoned me from San Francisco, where he lives. He was with Ala Bashir and they were wondering whether I might help him write a book about his experiences as Saddam's confidant. Bashir wished the book to be initially published in Norway, a democratic welfare state which he had always admired. Would I be able to find a Norwegian publisher?

The last six months have been the most exciting of my forty years as a journalist. Yet at the same time they have been the most depressing. In Sheikh Hassan's guesthouse in Doha Ala Bashir introduced me to a dark and mad world which I would not have believed existed, until he started to turn over the leaves of his diary and talk.

Lars Sigurd Sunnanå
Amman, March 2004

CAST OF CHARACTERS

Line of Kings

KING FAISAL   1921–33
KING GHAZI   1933–39
ABDUL ILAH (Regent)   1939–53
FAISAL II   1953–58

Important politicians under the monarchy

NURI PASHA AL-SAID
Born 1888. Pro-British. Dominant character in Iraqi domestic
and foreign policy from the formation of Iraq in 1920 to the fall
of the monarchy in 1958. After his death his body was dragged by
a car through the streets of Baghdad.

Heads of state following the fall of the monarchy

ABDUL KARIM KASSEM, Prime Minister 1958–63
AHMED HASSAN AL-BAKR, Prime Minister February 1963–
November 1963
ABDUL SALAM AREF, President November 1963–66
ABDUL RAHMAN AREF, President 1966–68

*Heads of state following the Baath Party's final assumption
of power*

AHMED HASSAN AL-BAKR, President 1968–79
SADDAM HUSSEIN AL-TIKRITI, President 1979–2003

Closest family

SADDAM HUSSEIN AL-TIKRITI
Born 1937(?) Iraq s President and dictator from 1979. Went into hiding when American forces took control of Baghdad on 9 April 2003. Arrested by American soldiers on 13 December 2003.

SAJIDA KHAIRALLAH TULFAH
Saddam's cousin and first wife. He later took a second wife.

UDAY SADDAM HUSSEIN AL-TIKRITI
Saddam's elder son, born 1964. Head of Iraq's Olympic Committee. Killed in a shoot-out with American forces outside Mosul in Northern Iraq on 22 July 2003.

QUSAY SADDAM HUSSEIN AL-TIKRITI
Saddam's younger son. Inter alia, head of the President's special forces. Killed together with his brother outside Mosul on 22 July 2003.

RAGHAD SADDAM HUSSEIN AL-TIKRITI
Saddam's oldest daughter. Married to Hussein Kamel al-Majid.

RANA SADDAM HUSSEIN AL-TIKRITI
Saddam's middle daughter. Married to Saddam Kamel al-Majid.

HALA SADDAM HUSSEIN AL-TIKRITI
Saddam's youngest daughter. Married to Jamal Mustafa al-Tikriti.

SAMIRA SHAHBANDAR
Saddam's second wife. No children by the President.

Close family

SABAAWI IBRAHIM AL-HASSAN AL-TIKRITI
Saddam's oldest half-brother. Born 1939(?). Was for a period head of the secret police. Arrested and handed over to the Iraqi authorities in February 2005.

BARZAN IBRAHIM AL-TIKRITI

Saddam's middle half-brother and brother-in-law. Born 1951. Was for a period head of Iraq's intelligence service. Later UN ambassador in Geneva. Arrested in Baghdad 17 April 2003. Married to the late AHLAM KHAIRALLAH TULFAH, Sajida Khairallah Tulfah's half-sister.

WATBAN IBRAHIM AL-TIKRITI

Saddam's youngest half-brother and brother-in-law. Born 1953. Minister of the Interior from 1991 to 1995. Arrested 13 April 2003 whilst fleeing to Syria. Married to ILHAM KHAIRALLAH TULFAH, Sajida Khairallah Tulfah's half-sister.

Other family members

KHAIRALLAH TULFAH

Saddam's uncle, foster-father and later father-in-law. President Ahmed Hassan al-Bakr's cousin. Was mayor of Baghdad for some years. Removed owing to his corrupt practices.

BADRA TULFAH

Sister to Khairallah Tulfah and SUBHA TULFAH, Saddam's mother. Called 'Hajia Badra' as she had completed the pilgrimage to Mecca: the haj. Hypochondriac.

ALI HASSAN AL-MAJID

Saddam's cousin and one of the dictator's most trusted men. Born 1941. Led the Anfal operations in Northern Iraq in 1987/88 when tens of thousands of Kurds were killed. Nicknamed Chemical Ali.

ADNAN KHAIRALLAH TULFAH

Saddam's cousin and brother-in-law. Sajida Khairallah Tulfah's brother. Minister of Defence from 1977 to 1989. Killed in a helicopter crash.

HUSSEIN KAMEL AL-MAJID

Saddam's son-in-law. Born 1950(?). Lieutenant-General. Head

of Iraq's weapons development programme until he fled to
Jordan with his family in 1995. Returned in February 1996. Shot
and killed during a family showdown, led by his uncle, Ali Hassan
al-Majid.

SADDAM KAMEL AL-MAJID
Saddam's son-in-law. Lieutenant-Colonel. Was head of the
President's bodyguards when he fled to Jordan together with his
brother, Hussein Kamel, in 1995. Shot and killed during the same
family showdown after having returned from Jordan in February
1996.

JAMAL MUSTAFA AL-TIKRITI
Saddam's son-in-law. Distant relation. Born 1949(?). His brother,
Kamal Mustafa al-Tikriti, was head of the President's elite
forces – the Republican Guard and the Special Republican
Guard. Both arrested and imprisoned following the fall of the
regime.

LUAI KHAIRALLAH TULFAH
Saddam's brother-in-law. Sajida Khairallah Tulfah's half-brother
and Ali Hassan al-Majid's nephew. Same age as Uday Saddam
Hussein; often acted as Uday's drinking companion. Arrested
and imprisoned by the Americans.

The inner circle

ABED HAMOUD AL-TIKRITI
Distant relation and Saddam's private secretary from 1991.
Together with Ali Hassan al-Majid, Izzat Ibrahim al-Douri, Taha
Yassin Ramadhan and Tareq Aziz, one of the regime's most pow-
erful and most trusted men. Arrested 16 June 2003.

IZZAT IBRAHIM AL-DOURI
Born near Tikrit in 1942. Son of an ice-block seller. Deputy
Chairman of the Revolutionary Command Council, Iraq's high-
est executive body. One of Saddam's most trusted colleagues.
Not yet arrested (March 2004).

TAHA YASSIN RAMADHAN AL-JAZRAWI

Born in Mosul in Northern Iraq in 1938. Father was a bank clerk. Member of the Revolutionary Command Council and Vice-President of the Republic from 1991. Arrested by Kurdish guerrilla soldiers in Mosul on 19 August 2003 and handed over to American forces.

TAREQ AZIZ

Born in Mosul in 1936. Journalist. Member of the Revolutionary Command Council. Deputy Prime Minister. As Foreign Minister from 1983 to 1991 was Iraq's face to the world. Surrendered to American forces on 24 April 2003.

Other protagonists

FATIQ AL-SAFI

Landowner and retired member of Iraq's Baath Party. Saddam's friend and sparring partner. Brave enough to contradict the President.

FAWZI FARMAN BASHIR

Opposition politician. Spent time in prison. My cousin.

ZAFER MUHAMMAD JABER

Schoolfriend of Uday Saddam. One of Uday's secretaries. Fell into disgrace and imprisoned in 1998. Lives in Amman in Jordan.

KHAUDIR ABDUL AZZIZ AL-DOURI

An early member of the Iraqi Baath Party. General Ahmed Hassan al-Bakr's bodyguard when Abdul Karim Kassem was overthrown in the coup of February 1963. Member of the Revolutionary Command Council. Fell into disgrace and was placed under house arrest in 1993. Arrested by the Americans when Baghdad fell.

NAJI SABRI AL-HADITHI

Saddam's last Foreign Minister. For many years Iraqi ambassador in Vienna.

NIZAR AL-KHAZRAJI
Saddam's Chief of the General Staff 1989 to 1990. Fled to
Turkey in 1995.

RIYADH IBRAHIM
One of the first Baath Party members. Minister of Health.
Dismissed and executed in 1983.

SAMIR AL-SHAIKHLI
Baath Party pioneer. Member of the Revolutionary Command
Council since 1968. Interior Minister 1987 to 1991. Dismissed
following a disagreement with Ali Hassan al-Majid concerning a
whorehouse and because he disapproved of the Kuwait invasion.

Lilies that fester smell far worse than weeds.

William Shakespeare

PART ONE

The Regime Expands

Faisal I (1885–1933) Iraq's first king. (Hulton-Deutsch Collection/Corbis)

CHAPTER 1

The Monarchy

A kingdom is established and then
toppled. A statesman is disgraced.

'Saddam wants you in his office,' the bodyguard said when he
came to fetch me at the al-Wasiti hospital in Baghdad.

The war between Iraq and Iran was nearing its end. The
President wanted to thank me for my efforts, saving life and limb
of soldiers and officers wounded at the front. I was director of
Saddam's Centre for Plastic and Reconstructive Surgery; since
the senseless bloodbath began in 1980, eight years earlier, we had
treated more than twenty thousand patients.

Saddam was housed on the second floor of the Majlis building,
a few hundred yards from the Republican Palace in the centre of
the Iraqi capital. The fenced-in and strictly guarded palace complex on the banks of the River Tigris covered two and a half
square kilometres and contained a large and partly intercon-
nected complex of offices, guesthouses, residences and quarters
for the presidential bodyguards. Bin-Sina, the presidential family's
private hospital, was also attached to the palace. It had been built
by King Faisal II, before he and almost his entire family had been
shot and killed during the uprising against and subsequent aboli-
tion of the monarchy in 1958.

I was frisked and as usual relieved of my watch and wedding ring.
In a familiar routine, all my pockets were emptied. Even my handkerchief was stuffed into a plastic bag together with the rest of my
possessions before I was given leave to enter the President's office.

The interior decoration was not exactly lavish. A large and exquisite blue Persian carpet covered the floor, but the overall impression of the office was rather sober and plain. Two sofas, one on each side of the room, were covered in a pinkish material with a white pattern. The curtains too were a faint purple. In the corner, to the right of the desk, was an Iraqi flag. On two walls were framed quotations from the Holy Koran.

One read: 'If we had caused this Koran to descend upon a mountain, thou (O Muhammad) verily hadst seen it humbled, rent asunder by the fear of Allah' (Sura 51. 25). The second took the form of an admonition. 'Nay, but we hurl the true against the false, and it doth break its head and lo! it vanisheth. And yours will be woe for that which ye ascribe (unto Him)' (Sura 21. 18). It was probably aimed at some of Saddam's visitors.

The President was sitting behind his mahogany desk. It was neat and tidy; on it lay a closed case file, probably containing the latest intelligence about the hospital and myself, a glass dish with Muslim prayer beads made of ivory and a crystal ashtray with a silver cigar-cutter. A regiment of black telephones covered the table-top. The President was engrossed in a book.

'Sit down and wait a moment,' he said. 'This book is incredibly exciting and interesting. It's a thesis about Nuri al-Said. I've got it on approval and want to finish the chapter.'

When I was a student at Baghdad's Central High School between 1954 and 1956 I sometimes threw stones at Nuri al-Said. The school had been established in the thirties and I was lucky enough to have been accepted. A large majority of Iraq's intelligentsia and academic elite were educated there. During my time it was a veritable cauldron of heated political opinions; the mood was defiantly anti-imperial and anti-colonial.

Of all the Arab countries Iraq had been the first to gain independence in 1932. However, in every field we were still heavily influenced by Great Britain. Iraq was a virtual dependency. Tempers rose to boiling point in 1956 when Great Britain, France and Israel attacked Egypt and closed the Suez Canal. As the crisis developed, both those that were Communists and the other students, like me, who envisaged a free Iraq based on solidarity and close cooperation with other Arab countries, gave free vent to our feelings. But the fury and frustration was not aimed solely at the two European colonial powers and the new Jewish state. It was equally directed at members of the Iraqi National Assembly.

The National Assembly was housed in a magnificent old building, built by the Abbasid Caliph Haroun al-Rashid for his sisters twelve hundred years ago. In those days the Muslim empire reached from Africa to present-day Iran, and the capital Baghdad, with more than one million inhabitants, was the second largest city in the world, second only to Constantinople. If any parliamentary building could be said to be historic, it was ours. It overlooked the Tigris, next door to the high school; only a narrow path separated the two buildings.

The road and car park used by MPs was less than a stone's throw away from the roof of our school. Our favourite target was Nuri al-Said's black American Chevrolet. As soon as it was spotted we ran up on to the roof with stones, bricks and anything else that could be used as a projectile.

The missiles rained down over him while we screamed 'agent' and 'traitor', accusing him of selling us down the river to the British. The Prime Minister wore a yellow shirt and sat in the middle of the back seat as he ran the gauntlet of our shower of stones. But he always smiled and waved. I remember thinking his face radiated warmth.

It was above all monumental political misjudgement in Constantinople that led to British suzerainty of one-time Mesopotamia. Before the fateful shots in Sarajevo which triggered off the First World War, Iraq, as we know it today, consisted of three underdeveloped and not very highly esteemed provinces of Turkey: Mosul, Baghdad and Basra. The Great War plucked the provinces out of oblivion and deposited them into the crucible of strategic power play in the Middle East. The Ottoman rulers had backed the wrong horse; they chose to join forces with the Central European Powers, Germany and Austria/Hungary, instead of throwing in their lot with France and Great Britain. When the Central Powers capitulated four years later a large part of the Ottoman Empire – including Mesopotamia – was already in dissolution.

Iraq was about to take shape.

The consequences of the war which had started in the Balkans took immediate effect in the Middle East. In London the government feared that Turkish forces in the region would threaten the newly discovered oilfields in Persia – which supplied the British navy with a large amount of fuel – and in November 1914, an Anglo-Indian expeditionary corps disembarked in Basra to, amongst other things, safeguard the strategic Persian oilfields.

Having captured Basra the troops moved northward. In November 1915 they had reached a point eighty kilometres south of Baghdad. There they were met by a Turkish counter-offensive which drove the invasion forces back to Kut, where it was surrounded, suffered very heavy losses and in the end surrendered. London immediately despatched reinforcements from India. Under the leadership of General Sir Stanley Maud, they once again drove the Ottoman army back. 'We arrive as liberators, not occupiers,' he said when the British and Indian troops captured Baghdad in March 1917.

Chaos reigned in the city when the general arrived. Public buildings, libraries, shops and the houses of well-heeled Jews and Christians were being looted of anything the mob could lay its hands on. In the Kazimiya district a caravan of camels was attacked and the animals slaughtered by the mob. Maud reacted with all speed. In the course of a few hours peace and order were restored; many of the bands of robbers and thieves fled the city, leaving behind what they had plundered.

The general enjoyed widespread popularity and after his death influential tradesmen raised money for a memorial to him. The statue, which represents Maud mounted on a horse, was created by an Italian artist and erected in 1923.

The Turks encountered increasingly serious problems. On the Arabian peninsula, too, their large empire was starting to show signs of breaking up. In the province of Hijaz the Grand Sharif of Mecca, Hussein, revolted in the summer of 1916. His army was soon swelled by young Arab officers who had been educated at the Constantinople Military Academy. Amongst them was the twenty-eight-year-old Nuri al-Said. In time al-Said was promoted to Chief of Staff of the Arabian rebel army which set out towards the north. Their leaders were the Sharif's son Faisal, and T. E. Lawrence, the famous British adventurer and intelligence officer.

Prince Faisal and Lawrence of Arabia's greatest triumph was the conquest of the port of Aqaba at the head of the Red Sea. But the acts of sabotage and military pinpricks they inflicted on Turkish lines of supply and garrisons in the area made it easier for General Edmund Allenby and his British, Australian and Indian soldiers to advance on Palestine from Egypt. Allenby captured Jerusalem in December 1917 and continued the campaign up the coast towards Syria and Damascus. The Arab rebels followed suit in the interior of the country.

Prince Faisal, Lawrence and Nuri al-Said won the race by the skin of their teeth. After General Allenby's soldiers had put the remainder of the Ottoman army out of action in the decisive battle of Megiddo in September 1918, they halted on the outskirts of Damascus to await orders from London.

The night of 1 October the Arabian rebel army rode in to the historic town on their horses and camels to a hero's welcome. Allenby and his army marched in two days later without much ado. Further east General Maud contracted cholera a mere six months after having taken Baghdad and promised the inhabitants self-government. He died shortly afterwards and never lived to see the decisions that were taken in the corridors of power in post-war Europe, the defeat of the Central Powers and the breakdown of the Ottoman Empire.

On 18 January 1919 the victorious superpowers gathered in Versailles outside Paris to sign the peace treaty. It was soon made clear that there would be no talk of self-government either for the three liberated Turkish provinces in Mesopotamia or in Syria, where Prince Faisal had proclaimed himself king (after he rode into Damascus with Lawrence and Nuri al-Said).

The border lines were already drawn in the sand.

The First World War had made it crystal clear to the superpowers that modern, motorised warfare demanded oil. Neither planes, battleships, tanks nor lorries were of any use without fuel. In London the geology of the three Ottoman provinces in Mesopotamia was compared to the areas in Persia where oil had already been found. The similarities were striking. Iraq, too, might possess large resources under the sand dunes.

Great Britain and France, with tacit agreement from Russia, had already in May 1916 decided how much of the Ottoman Empire should be divided amongst themselves when the war was over. The Sykes–Picot Agreement, named after the two negotiators, Sir Mark Sykes and Georges Picot, was accurately adhered to.

At a conference in San Remo at the end of April 1920 Iraq and Palestine became, with the blessing of the new League of Nations, British mandates. Syria and the Lebanon fell to Paris. French troops were thus immediately on the spot in the Levant and threw the self-appointed King Faisal out of Damascus.

After only a few months rebellion broke out in Iraq. Dissatisfaction with British military rule spread, both in the central areas of the new nation and in the Kurdish regions in the north. While the battles raged and the rebels gained ever more ground the British commander-in-chief, Sir Aylmer Haldane, sent for poison gas to try and turn the fortunes of war. In London he found an attentive colleague in the then Colonial Minister: 'I cannot understand this extreme sensitivity with regard to the use of gas. I totally agree in the use of gas against uncivilised tribes,' Winston Churchill is reported to have said.

However, it is uncertain whether Sir Aylmer actually used the supply of chemical weapons which he had ordered. Unlike the rebels General Haldane had an air force at his disposal: bombing raids and guns sufficed to mow down the insurgents. About six thousand Iraqi and five hundred British and Indian soldiers lost their lives in the hostilities before the General forced the rebels to their knees in the autumn of 1920.

But it was costly to suppress a rebellion. London got worried. Led by Churchill, the British government therefore started to investigate a more flexible and less provocative alternative to the unpopular direct military rule. It was concluded it would be better for them to rule themselves, but under full British control.

An Iraqi 'government' was formed, with British advisers, and in March 1921 Churchill and Lawrence travelled to Egypt where they met with envoys from this 'government'. Together they worked out new guidelines for the control of the mandates. At the Cairo Conference it was decided to create a kingdom in Iraq and offer the throne to Prince Faisal, whom the French had thrown out of Syria. The thirty-six-year-old Prince accepted and during the summer a highly questionable general election was held. No less than ninety-six per cent of the population said 'yes' to the new monarch.

On 23 August 1921, with due pomp and circumstance, King Faisal was crowned King of Iraq. Yet it was soon obvious that it was Nuri al-Said, and not the new King, who played the most important political role in the semi-democratic British dependency. He started off as Chief of Staff, advanced to Minister of Defence, then Prime Minister, then Foreign Minister, Minister of Defence and Prime Minister again, and so on in an endless circle. In the, to put it mildly, uncertain political waters he navigated – there were sixty changes of government between 1920 and 1958 – al-Said usually avoided total capsize. With much political shrewdness and unfailing effort he dragged the country's successive kings, mighty officer corps, government, and the elite of landowners and tradesmen with him in building a nation with one ultimate goal: Iraq would develop into a modern welfare state based on the large oil resources in which, as was becoming ever more clear, the nation was literally wallowing. New schools, universities, hospitals, waterworks, roads and power stations were built in rapid succession. Scholarships gave bright students the possibility of studying at universities and high schools abroad, principally in Great Britain. The oil revenue, which increased in step with greater extraction, gave the country freedom of action. The economic growth muffled any conflicts.

The undercurrents of ethnic and religious conflict and the often ungovernable tribal, clan and family networks which characterise life in Iraq, al-Said managed to deal with year after year thanks to a well-developed secret police and security forces which were not always known for their humanity. His authority was unshakeable. When, after the Suez crisis, we pelted him with stones, he had been Iraq's strongman for more than thirty-five years.

One day Nuri al-Said had had enough of our pestering. There was one exit only at our school and when we were returning home after yet again having demonstrated our opinion from the rooftop, a row of policemen, shoulder to shoulder on both sides of the road, batons raised, formed a long corridor which led to the police station a few hundred yards away. There were about 150 of us that afternoon who were forced into the police station to have our names registered and told that our schooldays were over if we persisted in throwing stones. I myself, together with a friend (Lalib Samarria, who later became an American citizen and a prominent plastic surgeon), managed to escape through a gap between two policemen, but a baton caught me in the knee and I can still remember the pain.

The Cold War cast long shadows over Iraq too in the fifties. The illegal Communist Party was becoming ever more popular, especially amongst students. The most zealous risked being expelled from school or university. Nuri al-Said continued his unflinching pro-Western and pro-British stance: he regarded the increasing influence of the Soviet Union in the Middle East to be the greatest threat to Iraq's interests. At the beginning of 1955 the government had suspended diplomatic relations with Moscow, and before the year was out the Baghdad Pact had seen the light of day. Iraq, Turkey, Iran, Pakistan and Great Britain agreed to a joint defence policy to counter the red menace.

But in the end it was the Iraqi Army and not the red menace which ultimately toppled Nuri al-Said and the royal family.

A group of young officers in Cairo had had enough of the corrupt King Farouk after his ignominious military defeat at the hands of the Israelis in 1948. In 1952, The 'Free Officers', as they liked to be called, rebelled. Farouk was sent off to sea in his yacht and never returned. The British Army was told it was not welcome and by 1954 the last British soldier had left the young republic. In March 1956 the President, Gamal Abdul Nasser, nationalised the Suez Canal, thereby turning himself into a hero and role model for the rest of the Middle East. The Iraqi army was about to follow suit.

In Baghdad young Free Officers were starting to organise themselves along the same lines. Defeat in Palestine had insulted their honour and dissatisfaction with the monarchy and Nuri al-Said's pro-British attitude was increasing. Recruitment gathered momentum when Great Britain and France, with the aid of Israel, intervened and took back control of the Suez Canal in October 1956.

This intervention provoked strong reactions all over the Middle East. In Iraq schools and universities were closed to try and stem the wave of demonstrations and riots which swept over the city in protest against the colonial powers and Israel's attack. Nuri al-Said was forced to introduce a state of emergency which lasted until May 1957.

Following strong pressure from America, British, French and Israeli forces withdrew from Egypt with their tails between their legs. Gamal Abdul Nasser emerged as the supreme victor. His popularity reached new heights.

During the autumn of 1957 the forty-three-year-old Brigadier Abdul Karim Kassem was contacted by one of Iraq's Free Officers and asked to lead the revolution they were preparing. He agreed and included his adjutant, thirty-six-year-old Colonel Abdul Salam Aref, in the preparations.

It was unbearably hot when I awoke early on the morning of 14 July 1958. The radio announced that a military coup had taken place during the night. The King and the Government had been deposed. Colonel Aref appealed to everyone to demonstrate in the streets in favour of the revolution. Corruption and people's shameful living conditions would come to an end; imperialism and its agents would be defeated. The colonel encouraged every-one to go to the Rihab Palace.

Faisal II was twenty-two years old when the mob caught him. In the short Iraqi line of kings, he was the third. His grandfather, Faisal I, died from obscure causes in a Swiss hotel room in 1933. His father, King Ghazi, perished in a car accident in 1939. In this case, too, the circumstances were not quite straightforward. Up until the time when he himself was old enough to be installed as king in 1953, his uncle on his mother's side, Abdul Ilah, had ruled the country as regent.

Abdul Ilah and the young King were both shot when they emerged from the palace on 14 July 1958, despite the fact that they were holding a copy of the Koran over their heads. A young lieutenant, Abdul Sattar al-Abosi, became nervous when he thought he heard shots from inside the palace. He opened fire on the entire royal family without having been given orders to do so. King Faisal II did not die immediately. He was taken to the military hospital in al-Rashid, but his life could not be saved. Abdul Ilah's wife, badly wounded also, was taken there with him. She alone of the family survived the burst of fire.

Khaudir Abdul Azziz al-Douri has since told me what happened to the young lieutenant who fired the fatal shots. Al-Douri was one of the early members of the Baath Party. When the party came to power in 1968, he was sent to a military unit in Basra as political officer. Abdul Sattar al-Abosi was attached to the unit and had developed mental problems. 'Every night he was visited by Faisal the Second asking why he had shot him,' al-Douri told me. 'One day it just became too much for him to bear and we found him dead. He had taken his own life.'

Smoke was pouring out of the Rihab Palace windows when my cousin and I – his name was Muhammad Kassem – reached it on the morning of the coup in 1958. The surrounding areas were chock-a-block with crowds singing and dancing; looting was in full swing. A happy young man appeared clasping an armful of the King's shoes and shirts. Inside the palace it struck me how stark everything was. I had been to many a rich man's house in Baghdad which was far more sumptuous.

Abdul Ilah's body was lying on the ground outside the palace, naked. The mob had got hold of a piece of rope and a small lorry. He was hooked to the lorry and dragged through the streets – the laughing stock of everyone – to Martyr Square in the centre of town. My cousin and I ran after the lorry with the hollering mob.

On Martyr Square Abdul Ilah was hoisted up on to a lamp-post. A young woman wielding a knife was pushed up after him.

She cut a hand off the body, impaled it on the knife and waved to the crowd with her trophy. The next man up on to the lamppost cut the penis off the former regent. Several followed suit. Bit by grisly bit, Abdul Ilah was soon past recognition.

The Prime Minister himself had managed to escape by rowing up the Tigris in a small boat which had been tied up near his house. A friend gave him refuge in his house in the Kazimiya district of Baghdad but realised it would not be long before the coup leaders would arrive in search of the Prime Minister. Al-Said decided to leave and go to a relative of his in the Betaween district. He donned an abaya, the woman's black dress, and stole away through the streets of Baghdad. But at Nassir Square an urchin caught sight of pyjama trousers peeping out under the abaya. He raised the alarm and a crowd gathered around the man in woman's clothes.

According to some eyewitnesses al-Said drew a pistol and shot himself. Others report that he was shot by a soldier in the crowd. His body was left lying on Nassir Square. The coup leaders were informed, and Colonel Wasfi Taher arrived to verify that it really was the Prime Minister. Taher had been his trusted bodyguard for many years. Now he emptied his tommy gun into the head of his old boss – a final humiliation. The Colonel had already been appointed to his new job, that of personal bodyguard to the Republic's first Prime Minister, Abdul Karim Kassem.

As Nuri al-Said had been Iraq's first Chief of Staff and Minister of Defence Abdul Karim Kassem ordered a dignified funeral. But he too was dug up and dragged by a rope behind a lorry. Cars and buses were commandeered by the mob and driven over the corpse during its macabre journey through the streets of Baghdad. When I caught a glimpse of the madness only a bloody and filthy spinal column remained of the seventy-year-old statesman.

Afterwards we learnt that Nuri al-Said left no money either in Iraq or abroad. The house he lived in was not even his own.

After the coup only one politician refused to become a member of the newly formed Cabinet. Kamil al-Jaderji, despite personal pressure from Kassem himself, defied the coup leaders by saying that all officers who took part should return to their posts and Iraq should be declared a democracy. Al-Jaderji was the head of the Iraqi National Democratic Party. He died in 1967 in Baghdad. His request went unanswered.

I relived those tumultuous days in 1958 when, thirty years later, I was sitting in Saddam's office waiting for him to finish the chapter on Nuri al-Said. He took his time, but finally closed the book and put his reading glasses away.

'If I ever write a book about Iraq's recent history, I will vindicate Nuri al-Said. In contrast to what many say he was a great man and his efforts on behalf of our country were exemplary,' the President said.

Prime Minister Abdul Karim Kassem (left), Taha al-Sheik Ahmed
(right) and Fadhil al-Mahdawi. This was the picture seen by Iraqis
when the cameras were turned on in the TV studio where the three
generals had been executed during the coup which led to the Baath
Party assuming power on 8 February 1963. (Bettmann/Corbis)

CHAPTER 2

Street Fighting

Communists and Pan-Arabs shed blood.
The country's leaders are executed
in a TV studio.

'I must be off,' said my father. It was Friday, the Muslim holy day and yet another coup had erupted in Baghdad.

My father was Deputy Chief of Police of the Kazimiya district of Baghdad. This morning, 8 February 1963, he had been unable to contact his boss or any of his subordinates by phone.

'No, don't go,' my mother, my sisters and I said. 'You'll only be killed if you go to the police station now.' We could hear bombs falling and shots being fired, but it was useless to try and stop him.

Five years had passed since Abdul Karim Kassem had promoted himself to general and taken over as Prime Minister and Minister of Defence after the July revolution of 1958. But Iraq's new strongman had not had an easy ride. There had been several coups against him and his regime.

Iraq was seething with internal social and political unrest. Amongst a great many army officers, students and young people the dream of a pan-Arab superstate, 'from Tunisia to Bahrain', was asserting itself ever more powerfully. 'Cairo is our heart. When it beats, the whole Arab world beats with it', is a Middle Eastern saying.

In the Egyptian capital Gamal Abdul Nasser had taken an important step on the road to Arab unity. In February 1958 Syria and Egypt had formed a union: the United Arab Republic. The Egyptian President wanted Iraq to join them.

But Kassem hesitated. Iraq came first. In contrast to many of his young officer colleagues he saw no advantage in being ruled from Cairo.

'National unity is our one priority,' he repeated time and again. On the other hand, amongst the population in general, it was the Communist Party, rather than the pan-Arab ideal, which held greatest sway. In the countryside millions of smallholders lived in increasing poverty, poverty which approached serfdom, under the few, privileged sheikhs and families who owned the land. Many had fled the countryside for the towns in the hope of a better life. But here, too, it was difficult to find work. The slums grew and the social and economic gap between the classes increased.

The Communist Party promised far-reaching land reforms and a redistribution of social assets which would lift the masses out of their misery. In their tens of thousands the Iraqis flocked to the red banners whose message was 'a free county and a happy people'. From a foreign policy perspective the Communist Party demanded rapprochement with Moscow, not Cairo. It was not difficult to foresee that Abdul Karim Kassem would encounter problems.

In March 1959 Northern Iraq erupted. A group of Free Officers in Mosul initiated a rising against Kassem and what they considered was his Communist-friendly regime, in the hope that the revolt would spread to other parts of the country. The Communist Party reacted by drumming together 250,000 followers and dispatching them to Mosul. The rebellion didn't spread; instead the Mosul situation completely got out of hand. Street fights between pan-Arabs and Communists developed into a true orgy of aggression and brutality. In the end everyone was fighting everyone else. Communist attacked pan-Arab. Christian beat Muslim. Kurd fought Turcoman and Arab, tribe stood against tribe, clan against clan, and the poor looted the rich. Any weapon, knife or stick was used.

The battles between Kurdish Communists and pan-Arabs raged fiercest. The pan-Arabs were supported by Sunni Muslims who had grouped into brotherhoods along the lines of similar organisations in Egypt and Syria. To the Muslim brotherhoods the Communists were the devil: atheists who worshipped Marxist ideology.

The Communists were in the majority and well organised, and as long as the street fighting went on in Mosul Abdul Karim Kassem gave them free rein to handle the rebellious officers, the Arab nationalists and the supporters of the Muslim brotherhoods as they saw fit. Street justice ruled. Only after five or six days did the government forces intervene and re-establish peace and order.

Five months later, in July 1959, another bloodbath took place in the oil town of Kirkuk. On the anniversary of the military coup and the fall of the monarchy a large demonstration through the streets of the town was organised to express its support for Abdul Karim Kassem. Before the organisers could react, the demonstrators ran amok. In blind fury the masses pounced on the large Turcoman middle class who dominated Kirkuk's trade and business life. Their houses, shops and businesses were looted and torched. Fathers and sons were fetched out, tortured and shot. Many fared worse. I had a doctor colleague called Widad, who grew up in Kirkuk. From her parents' flat in Almaz Street she saw lorries pulling humans along by ropes attached to the back. Most of them were alive when the journey started.

'I will never forget the bodies swinging up and down, up and down,' she said.

One day she saw a man whose legs were tethered to two lorries. The lorries turned and drove off in different directions. 'He was a Turcoman and it was Kurd Communists who tied him up and drove the lorries.'

The bloodbaths in Mosul and Kirkuk further antagonised Iraqi factions. The new Baath Party, which had seriously started to increase in membership, decided to kill Abdul Karim Kassem at the first opportunity.

The Baath Party was also based on the ideal of Arab unity. It had become the most important opposition to the Communist Party in the increasingly complex political minefield. This pan-Arab, secular, socialist party was founded in Syria in 1940. Eleven years later an Iraqi offshoot appeared but initially support for the new party was only moderate. Only a few ardent souls were members the first years. Only when the Suez crisis and President Nasser brought feelings in the Middle East to boiling point in 1956 did thousands of young Iraqis embrace the Baath Party and its ideology, inspired by the slogans 'unity, freedom and socialism'.

One of them was Saddam Hussein al-Tikriti, and in October 1959 he was asked by the party leadership to take part in an assassination attempt against Kassem.

Officially Saddam's age at this point was twenty-two. But Saddam's birth date, 28 April 1937, is, in my opinion, pretty uncertain. Having treated and examined him many times over a period of twenty years, I am convinced that he is at least four years older.

His start in life was uncertain too. He was born in the tiny village of al-Ouja, which stands where the Tigris makes a sharp bend eight kilometres south of Tikrit. His father, Hussein al-Majid, seems to have disappeared from his son's life even before he was born. His mother, Subha Tulfah, then married Ibrahim al-Hassan, who became the father to Saddam's three half-brothers, Sabaawi, Barzan and Watban.

Neither his father nor stepfather were amongst the most esteemed in this impoverished village, to put it mildly. They called his stepfather 'Hassan the liar'. He maintained that he had completed the haj, the pilgrimage to Mecca, but everyone in al-Ouja knew that he had never set foot in the Saudi kingdom or any of its holy places.

Saddam's youth was spent at the bottom of the social ladder in extreme poverty, with a mother and stepfather who could not even afford to buy him underwear. Schooling was unheard of. Only when he went to live with his uncle, Khairallah Tulfah, who lived in Tikrit, did he have an opportunity to learn to read and write.

The uncle was a bitter man. He had been an officer in the Iraqi army but had been kicked out following a failed Nazi-friendly coup in 1941. Tulfah was an ardent pan-Arabist. He hated Communists, but he hated the British even more. The fact that he was imprisoned for five years probably had something to do with it.

Now he became foster-father to his nephew and he took him to Baghdad in the early fifties with the rest of the family when he got a job teaching in an elementary school in Karkh.

The assassination attempt against Abdul Karim Kassem failed. Saddam and fellow Baath Party conspirators opened fire on the cortège on its way down al-Rashid Street in Baghdad late one afternoon on 7 October 1959; the head of state's chauffeur was killed but he himself was only wounded – but badly. He survived, however, and after eight weeks in hospital was discharged.

Most of the assassins were arrested, but not Saddam. Together with landowner Fatiq al-Safi he managed to escape, first to Tikrit, and then further, over the desert to Syria and Damascus. He too had been wounded in the exchange of fire: a bullet had entered his left leg. But when he sought help from doctors he knew belonged to the Baath Party, they refused.

'I therefore cut it out myself with a razor blade,' he told me later. He often reminded me of this story whenever he needed medical assistance and was suffering a bit. 'Don't worry, I can bear it,' he used to say with a smile.

More than fifty Baathists and pan-Arab officers connected to the party were arrested and stood trial. I remember sitting glued to the TV during the court proceedings; on the whole only Communists were allowed in to witness them. They applauded loudly whenever the public prosecutor spoke, but they hollered, whistled and shouted abuse whenever the Baathists or officers were permitted to defend themselves. Seventeen of the accused were sentenced to death. To the others were awarded long prison sentences. The court also condemned Saddam Hussein al-Tikriti to death, in absentia. That was the first time I had heard his name.

Abdul Karim Kassem's problems were by no means over. It became an ever more difficult balancing act to placate the Communists on one side and the pan-Arab officers and Baathists on the other. The pan-Arabs saw him resisting an alliance with Nasser in Cairo, the Communists criticised him for not doing enough to cooperate with Moscow, in spite of his having withdrawn from the Baghdad Pact immediately after assumption of power. Another coup might materialise – and succeed – at any time.

The coup happened on 8 February 1963, and before long fighting raged in the streets and blood flowed in large parts of Baghdad. On one side were the coup leaders: pan-Arab officers, soldiers and members and supporters of the Baath Party. On the other side were officers and soldiers loyal to Kassem, and the Communists.

My father, Deputy Head of Police in Kazimiya, was caught in the middle.

Muhammad al-Wardi and I usually got on well. We both studied medicine at Baghdad University and as he lived close to us he often came over for supper. I had realised he was heavily involved with the Communists but we never talked about it. My father did not trust the Communists. As a Muslim believer it was difficult for him to tolerate people's lack of belief. He steered clear of all political activity.

A few hours after he had gone off to the police station in Kazimiya, where he took command in the absence of the Chief of Police, Muhammad al-Wardi and a large gang of armed friends banged on our gate.

'Everyone likes and respects your father, but he is in big trouble now,' said al-Wardi, who reported that the police station was surrounded by many thousands of Communists. They were short of weapons and ammunition, in contrast to the Baath Party fighting groups who seemed to be well equipped with weaponry. The Communists were demanding that my father open the arsenal to give them access to machine guns, rifles and pistols. My father refused.

'You must phone him,' said al-Wardi. 'If he doesn't open up I don't know what will happen.'

I phoned. 'Muhammad al-Wardi is standing beside me saying there is no point refusing access to the arsenal,' I said. 'There are thousands of Communists outside the police station. They're mad. Give them what they want.'

'No,' said my father. 'It is our duty to maintain law and order. Not to hand out machine guns and automatic weapons so they can kill each other.' And he slammed down the receiver.

Abdul Salam Aref, Abdul Karim Kassem's companion from the 1958 revolution, was the key man behind the fighting. Aref had fallen out with Kassem over the latter's refusal to join Nasser's Arab nation and had failed twice already to oust him. Once again he was leading a coup, this time in tandem with General Ahmed Hassan al-Bakr. The General was from Tikrit and a cousin of Saddam's uncle and foster-father, Khairallah Tulfah, a zealous anti-Communist and Baath Party member.

I remember hearing loud shooting from the direction of my father's police station. Then a gang of boys came running up and they stopped in front of our house. 'All the policemen have been killed. They were dragged through the streets!' they called. One of them handed me a pistol. It was my father's.

But he was neither dead nor had he been dragged through the streets. The Communists had handcuffed him and many of his colleagues and taken them to the main police station, where they were told they would soon be executed. One of my uncles got through to the rebellious forces, who were starting to gain control of Baghdad, and asked for help. At five the next morning the Communists who had captured the police station were neutralised. My father was freed. He returned home, beaten up and bloody; a bullet had hit his left shoulder. But what had upset him most was the behaviour of an old, retired colleague. The pensioner had had little to live on when he retired but still had to provide for his wife and several under-age children. My father therefore arranged for him to set up a tiny café in the general reception hall and earn a few pennies serving tea and coffee to staff and visitors.

'He was the first person to hit me after I had been shot and handcuffed by the mob,' my father said. 'I imagine it was important for him to show the Communists that he was no friend of mine.'

Iraq's air force chief, Brigadier Jalal al-Awqati, was a Communist. He was attacked and killed and Kassem's air force neutralised, before the first rebellious military units made a move to capture radio and television stations and other strategic targets.

Abdul Karim Kassem had barricaded himself in the ministry of defence together with bodyguards, loyal officers and soldiers. Tens of thousands of Communists arrived, hoping to lay their hands on weapons so that they could take part in street fights against the rebellious forces who were advancing on the ministry accompanied by the far better-armed Baathists. Kassem refused to give them weapons; he feared that the clash would unleash a massacre in Baghdad. Most probably he also thought that loyal army units would soon come to his rescue.

No army units came to his rescue. On the other hand, four fighter planes appeared from the Habbaniya base about seventy kilometres west of Baghdad and bombed the ministry of defence.

One of the pilots was a Lieutenant Fahad al-Saadoun. In Arabic Fahad means cheetah. In his private life and as a fighter pilot, he lived up to his name. He was fearless, and when I got to know him during my military service in 1964, I realised that he was also honourable through and through. Al-Saadoun flew low, lower than the other three and placed his bombs with deadly accuracy. But during one of the sorties over the ministry of defence his plane was hit by anti-aircraft artillery. He parachuted out before the plane crashed, landed in the Mansour area, hailed a taxi and drove back to the base. He continued the fight in a new plane.

Kassem's back was against the wall. It was not least this low-level precision-bombing that forced him and his closest generals and supporters to surrender to the rebels on 9 February.

An armoured personnel carrier fetched the beaten Prime Minister, the Defence Minister and the two generals, Taha al-Sheik Ahmed and Fadhil al-Mahdawi. The two generals had presided over the court in the old parliament building after the assassination attempt against Kassem in October 1959. They were driven to the radio and TV station where Ahmed Hassan al-Bakr and Abdul Salam Aref waited for them. Khaudir Abdul Azziz-al Douri, al-Bakr's bodyguard, was there too. He told me that Kassem was impeccably dressed in a general's uniform when he stepped out of the personnel carrier. His trouser-creases could not have been sharper.

'Be careful,' Kassem shouted as he waved to the masses who had gathered to watch. 'This coup won't benefit Iraq. It is an imperialist plot.'

Kassem, Ahmed and al-Mahdawi sat down beside al-Bakr and Aref, who had already been proclaimed Prime Minister. Khaudir al-Douri has given me an account of the short conversation which took place before the three generals were executed.

'Which one of us planned the 14 July revolution?' Aref started the conversation. 'Was it you or me?'

'It was I, as history will confirm,' said Kassem.

'You are a scoundrel. You executed nineteen innocent officers in nineteen-fifty-eight. Why?' the new President continued.

'Because they were criminals. They conspired against me. They confessed and were executed in accordance with the law. I myself am prepared to be tried in a court of law,' Kassem said.

'That is out of the question. I must act on the orders of the coup leaders.'

'Then expel me from Iraq, as I did to you once.'

'That's not possible; I do not have the authority.'

Nothing more was said and Kassem, Ahmed and al-Mahdawi were taken to an adjoining television studio where they were shot. They refused to be blindfolded before being killed.

The studio containing the corpses was then floodlit and the cameras turned on. During the broadcast, which was repeated time and again in the course of the afternoon and evening, we saw a soldier walk over to Abdul Karim Kassem, lift him up by the hair and spit in his face. Kassem's bodyguard, Wasfi Taher, did not accompany his boss to the radio and TV station. He committed suicide.

The colonel, who had emptied his machine-gun magazine into the head of Nuri al-Said (after the Prime Minister's death on Nassir Square during the July revolution in 1958), was himself exposed to the same humiliating treatment. Taher was taken from the defence ministry and his body thrown on to the lawn in front of the radio and TV station. A soldier ran up, pointed his machine pistol at the head and pulled the trigger.

Kassem was laid to rest in an unmarked grave south of Baghdad. Some of his adherents dug him up and reburied him, but the new Baath government dug him up yet again, fastened large, heavy stones to his legs and dumped the body in the Diyala, a tributary of the Tigris.

One day at the end of 1998 Fahad al-Saadoun dropped by at my private clinic in the Mansour district. He had retired from the air force with the rank of brigadier. He was furious and needed someone to talk to.

His son, who was doing his national service as a soldier, had fallen out with his sergeant over some trifling matter. His punishment was to go for a swim in a cesspool behind the camp. The son phoned his father and now the brigadier had come straight from Saddam's office where he had gone to complain.

'Is this the reward I get after having helped remove Abdul Karim Kassem from power in February 1963?' he had asked, having informed Saddam about the son's extremely unpleasant punishment. The President asked him to calm down and had made it clear that no soldier should be treated like that.

'I'll let your son serve out his time here in my office,' Saddam promised him.

But the brigadier was still indignant. 'When I see how things have turned out in Iraq I bitterly regret my role in the coup of 1963,' he said.

'It is for reasons of hatred, and revenge, that I joined the coup,' he added.

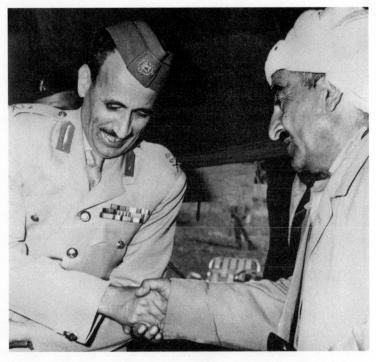

The Kurdish leader Mustafa Barzani (right) and President Abdul
Rahman Aref agreeing upon a ceasefire in September 1966.
The agreement was short-lived. The Kurds' struggle for independence
and their own state in Northern Iraq continues unabated
to the present day. (Bettmann/Corbis)

CHAPTER 3

The Stab

The Baath Party seizes power, loses it and ultimately regains it.

Many rumours circulated about the CIA's role in the coup which toppled Kassem. When I was on national service there in 1964, two air-traffic controllers told me how American military transport planes had arrived at the Habbaniya base after the coup. They had landed and taxied to the end of the runway, weapons were unloaded, the planes tanked up and took off again. Kassem's rapprochement with Moscow had caused concern in Washington, not least because the withdrawal from the Baghdad Pact was followed by an Iraqi/Soviet agreement on technical and economic cooperation.

'We came to power on the back of the CIA,' a content and frank Baath Party general secretary, Ali Salih al-Saadi, confirmed the rumour when he became Deputy Prime Minister and Minister of the Interior after Abdul Karim Kassem's fall. The party's clear anti-Communist stance had paid off.

A sixteen-member national revolutionary administration was set up and chose Abdul Salam Aref as President and Ahmed Hassan al-Bakr as Prime Minister. Twelve of the members belonged to or sympathised with the Baath Party. The remaining four, led by the President, were primarily pan-Arabs.

It soon became obvious that internal tension and disagreement were rife, although the entire administration agreed on one thing – the old regime's supporters must be called to account

and removed: in the first instance the members of the
Communist Party and its sympathisers.

The cargo of weapons which had been offloaded from the
American transport planes in the dead of night now came into
their own. Thousands of young Baathists were given weapons
and green armbands. Equipped with lists of names they trawled
the neighbourhoods, street by street, house after house, in a comprehensive witch-hunt of Communist leaders, members and
sympathisers. I later read in foreign newspapers and books that
CIA agents had helped make up the lists.

It was impossible for many of the Communists to hide away.
They had been able to hold down high-profile jobs at schools and
universities, in trade unions and other organisations during Abdul
Karim Kassem's rule. Then it had not been illegal to be a
Communist as was the case before the monarchy and Nuri al-
Said had been toppled. Now the familiar faces were hauled in,
executed or thrown into prison by the new Baath regime.

The militia took the name National Guard and adopted King
Faisal II's residence in Rihab as a torture and interrogation centre.
The palace was already the subject of public gossip – it was called
'The Final Palace' as this was where, in 1958, the royal family had
met its cruel fate. Few people escaped alive from the interrogation
centre. If one was unfortunate enough to get into the clutches of
Nazim Kazzar, a Shia who had joined the Baath Party as a student
in the fifties, the palace might well be one's last stop in this life.

Kazzar never smiled. His brutality and sadism were, even by
Iraqi standards, exceptional. A host of new torture methods,
accompanied by aids and special instruments, were developed
personally by Kazzar while his career blossomed in the palace's
basement. He was later handpicked by Saddam and promoted to
head of the security police.

Many thousands of Communists and their sympathisers lost
their lives during street fighting in the coup of February 1963.
The cleansing which took place in the weeks and months afterwards also claimed thousands of lives. Many more were
imprisoned. But the numbers are vague and it is not clear what
role Saddam played when the blood was flowing most copiously.

Following the failed assassination attempt on Kassem in 1959 he had fled to Syria and thence to Cairo. With the aid of a scholarship from President Nasser he was able to continue his schooling while waiting for events to settle down so he could return to Baghdad.

Now he was back. But no one talked about him, not my many friends from amongst the persecuted Communists nor from the National Guard with the green armbands. I am sure Saddam was implicated in the bloodbath, but I doubt that he played a central role.

Most of the Communists who had attacked the police station in Kazimiya and who had beaten up and shot at my father when he refused to hand out weapons were arrested. He recognised their faces when he was asked to testify against them in the summary court cases the National Guard organised.

'I'm sorry,' he said. 'I don't recognise any of them.'

Mustafa al-Wardi was in hiding at our home. His second cousin and my fellow student, Muhammad al-Wardi, was captured by the Baathists. He jumped off the lorry and tried to escape when en route to prison. He did not succeed: he was shot and died in the attempt. Mustafa, also a medical student, turned up at our house fearing what would happen if he was taken. Like Muhammad he had held a position of trust in the Communist Party. Three days after he had taken refuge with us, two armed Baathists, wearing green armbands, knocked on our door. They had Mustafa's sister with them. His father's life had been threatened if he failed to reveal his son's whereabouts, and he had given in to the threats. The sister had come to show the way. One of the Baathists recognised me.

'Why have you sheltered this Communist?' he asked.

Before I had time to answer, Mustafa rushed in. 'Ala is not hiding me. I dropped by to ask about university tomorrow.'

He must have thought he had nothing to lose.

It worked. The Baathists left me alone and took Mustafa to prison. He was freed after a month and continued his studies. Today he is one of Iraq's foremost heart specialists.

The National Guard established its headquarters in a large house in the Azamiya neighbourhood; Mukdad al-Ani became one of its leaders. He studied medicine too and was in my year. Our

physiology professor, Sadiq al-Hilali, was arrested and imprisoned when some of our fellow students spread the rumour that he
was pro-Communist. I therefore went to Azamiya to ask al-Ani to
help. Surely it should be possible to free the professor?

'I'll do what I can,' Mukdad al-Ani said. 'Sit down and wait.'
He started to make phone calls.

There were many chairs in al-Ani's office but only one was
empty. I sat down and realised I had a green armbanded Baathist
on each side. While I was waiting a former classmate walked in
through the door. He was an engineer and we had not seen each
other for a long time.

I got up and was about to embrace him, as is the custom
amongst good friends in my country, when he stiffened and pretended not to see me. Immediately it struck me that he thought I
had been arrested and brought in to HQ. Why would I otherwise
sit between two guards?

After a while al-Ani – who today is professor of urology and
dean of the medical faculty at Hadhdramout University in
Yemen – succeeded in getting hold of the head of the secret
police.

'OK,' he said when he put the phone down. 'You can go and
fetch our professor. I'll get you a car and a driver.'

I thanked him profusely and he got up to accompany me out.
Then – as if by magic – my old classmate came running, exuber-
ant with joy at seeing me.

It was my turn to pretend I had not seen him. He might have
said hello, and even helped me, if in fact I *had* been arrested by
the National Guard. He knew perfectly well that I had never
flirted with politics of any persuasion or colour. I would meet
many of his type later in life.

The daggers hung loosely in the revolutionary government
during that summer and autumn of 1963. The Baath Party was
divided over many issues. Ministers stabbed each other in the
back on all imaginable and even unimaginable occasions. The
differences reflected deep divisions in the party's leadership.
Should Iraq continue to back an Arab superstate in line with
pan-Arab ideals? Scepticism reigned. The Syrian/Egyptian

United Arab Republic was dead in the water – it had collapsed in 1961. How far should they go to the left? The Secretary General, Ali Salih al-Saadi – he was deposed as Minister of the Interior during the summer for his radical beliefs – went as far as to suggest that Marxism should be the Baath Party's new ideology. The conservative Baathists, mostly army officers, fumed when the suggestion was raised.

The situation was no less confused at street level. The National Guard grew unchecked. Bullying young Baathists menaced the street. Summary arrests and abductions continued on a grand scale. The militia was a pest and a nuisance, not just for ordinary people, but also for the President Abdul Salam Aref himself and the officer corps who supported him.

In November the internal conflicts came to a head. The right-wingers in the Baath Party dismissed Ali Salih al-Saadi. The Secretary General and his closest collaborators were asked to leave the country and put on a plane to Spain. The young National Guard Baathists – al-Saadi's supporters – answered by swarming on to the streets of Baghdad, with their machine guns and green armbands.

Anarchy was just round the corner when the President and the army said enough was enough. On 18 November, yet again, the tanks rolled out on to Baghdad's streets. Military units loyal to the President took up positions all over the capital. The National Guard HQ was fired at and orders given to arrest and disarm its members. In the course of the day, all over the country, the unruly militia was put out of action and the Baathists in the revolutionary council shown the door.

President Abdul Salam Aref had succeeded – a coup within a coup. With help from the army it was now he, and not the Baath Party, who ruled Iraq. It would take five years for the Baathists to regroup.

It was a relief to leave the chaos and bloodshed in Baghdad behind me when, as a young, newly qualified doctor, I left to serve my time at the Habbaniya base, early in 1964. But not even there was I spared the brutality that has left its sad scars on a country which was once the cradle of civilisation.

Imad al-Mashat was a lieutenant, newly married and one of the pilots at the airbase. His quarters were next door to mine. One morning, while out on a sortie in a British-built Vampire, the plane crashed between Samarra and Fallujah, near Lake Thirtar, and he was unable to eject. When the alarm was raised we set off in a helicopter to the lake. Imad al-Mashat was lying in the burning wreckage on the shore; he was dead.

I can still see him. He was lying face down and smoke was pouring out of his back. The villagers were standing around watching. When I turned the newly married lieutenant over I realised that his ring finger had been cut off. They had taken his watch too.

One of the Habbaniya pilots' tasks was shelling the Kurds. In 1961, in the mountains of Northern Iraq, the Kurds had risen again. Their legendary leader, Mullah Mustafa Barzani, demanded autonomy – a demand that had its roots in the past.

When the Ottoman Empire fell apart after the First World War, the Allied superpowers promised the Kurds an independent state. But the 1920 agreement did not last. Only three years later the Sèvres Treaty was replaced by the Lausanne Treaty and here the new state was not even mentioned. Having made the mistake of supporting Germany and suffering the consequences, the Turks were starting to recover under Kemal Atatürk. The President in Ankara saw no reason to give away the fertile Kurdish agricultural areas in the south-east of the Republic.

Nor were Great Britain and France, on second thoughts, especially interested in establishing a new Kurdish state. There just might be, as was quickly established, a large amount of oil in the Kurdish part of old Mesopotamia, round the towns of Mosul and Kirkuk. It was therefore markedly to the two European colonial powers' advantage to stick to the League of Nations mandate.

The Kurds were knifed in the back. The territory which had belonged to them from time immemorial was now in the hands of Turks, Iranians, Iraqis and Syrians. 'Only the mountains are our friends', is a saying among the around thirty million Kurds who live in this area today, still in the hope that one day the country might be theirs.

The struggle which Mullah Mustafa Barzani and his guerrilla soldiers – the peshmerga – initiated in Northern Iraq in 1961 was just one in a long line of similar sad uprisings. The first one saw the light of day in 1919 and was brutally put down from the air.

The history of the RAF is full of stories of its excellence at this time: 'The most efficient way to demoralise the local population is to concentrate the bombing on the most inaccessible village belonging to the dominant tribe we want to punish. All available planes must attack together with bombs and machine guns. The attacks must continue relentlessly and incessantly day and night and target houses, inhabitants, crops and animals,' wrote an enthusiastic Wing Commander J. A. Chamier in London in 1921.

Squadron Leader Arthur Harris expressed it equally clearly a few years later: 'The Arabs and the Kurds now understand what proper bombing is. An entire village can be erased within forty-five minutes, and one-third of its inhabitants be killed or wounded. Only four or five planes are needed. They do not allow them to escape. And the planes themselves do not appear as targets that will bestow on them hero status as warriors.'

Harris's spirit was hovering around Habbaniya during the two years I spent there. Barzani's Kurdish rebellion took its course, interrupted by sporadic ceasefires and negotiations in Baghdad which never led anywhere. The generals and colonels who led Abdul Salam Aref's government forces in the north demanded frequent bombing of entire Kurdish villages if they thought Barzani's guerrilla soldiers had sought refuge there.

One tearful pilot after another came into my clinic. They knew what they were doing to innocent old women and children who had not been able to reach the safety of the mountains.

Abdul Salam Aref was killed in a helicopter accident in 1966 and his brother succeeded him as president. But while Abdul Salam had enjoyed considerable trust and was highly respected amongst army officers, Abdul Rahman Aref was considered weak. The small trust he did enjoy amongst Iraqis completely evaporated after the Six Day War in June 1967.

We had all been indoctrinated with the belief that it was only a matter of time before the Zionist intruders in Palestine would be thrown into the Mediterranean by Egyptian, Syrian and Jordanian forces working together with our own soldiers. In Cairo President Nasser had risen to new rhetorical heights and suited his actions to his words by closing the approach from the Red Sea to all shipping to and from the Israeli town of Eilat at the head of the Bay of Aqaba.

Only an Arab will understand the disaster and degradation we all felt when the announcement was made that Defence Minister Moshe Dayan had made a clean sweep of it. It was unbelievable that our Egyptian, Syrian and Jordanian brothers had been so emphatically beaten as they were during the six days the war lasted. In disbelief we heard that the Israeli flag was flying over the Sinai Peninsula, on the Golan Heights and the West Bank of the Jordan. In East Jerusalem the Old Town, with its many Christian and Muslim sacred places – the al-Aqsa Mosque and the Dome of the Rock – was under the control of our arch-enemy.

Worst of all, we thought, was the failure of the Iraqi army to come to the rescue of our Arab brothers. The small and few units that were sent to Jordan never really saw battle. Fury over such weakness was directed towards the President, Abdul Rahman Aref.

'There'll be a coup soon,' said my cousin Fawzi Farman Bashir. It was 1968, spring was approaching and I was en route to Great Britain to specialise as a plastic surgeon.

Fawzi had a nose for such things. He was an ardent supporter of the Baath Party, and had been a member since 1957. He believed in the party's founding ideas, like Arab unity, freedom and socialism and fought for democracy and human rights. He never refrained from airing his opinions.

He had been arrested by Abdul Karim Kassem's security police in 1959 and imprisoned for a couple of months for having spoken out against the general's authoritarian style of government. The same thing happened in 1964. Then Abdul Salam Aref threw him into prison, with General Ahmed Hassan al-Bakr and a host of other leading Baathists, accused of plotting a coup.

Abdul Rahman Aref however, decided to free al-Bakr and most of the other Baathists when he took over after his brother's death in 1966. Reconstruction of the party, which to a large extent had been directed by al-Bakr, also from prison, shot ahead.

The reorganisation was in the hands of the general's young relative, Saddam, who had been recruited to the party in 1964 as party secretary. He too had been arrested and imprisoned but managed to escape after a few months in prison. His case was coming up before the judge, and he was en route to the courthouse with a few gaolers when he got away. They can't have been of the brightest; either that or they had been bribed. Saddam invited them to a coffee and slipped out of the back door while his guards enjoyed their free meal.

'I think we'll seize power in the course of the summer,' my cousin said.

It went off smoothly. Saddam's half-brother, Barzan Ibrahim al-Tikriti, has told me what went on after al-Bakr and the Baath Party leadership had decided to remove President Abdul Rahman Aref and his weak and increasingly unpopular military regime. 'It was no problem. The officers responsible for his safety stabbed him in the back.'

Ibrahim Abdul Rahman al-Daud was a brigadier and head of the President's security force, the Republican Guard. Colonel Saadoun Ghaidan commanded the Guard's tank regiment. The President trusted them both implicitly. When they were asked to be part of the coup, they jumped at the chance.

It was planned for 17 July 1968, but it was nearly a disaster. Brigadier al-Daud was a close friend of the head of the military intelligence service, General Abdul Razzaq al-Nayif, and had been told by the coup leaders not to mention the plans to his friend.

'He did so anyway, and on the night before we were ready to go,' Barzan told me. 'It was a bit of a shock when a messenger arrived from Abdul Razzaq al-Nayif with an ultimatum to the effect that either he was appointed Prime Minister after the coup or he would tell the President and trigger off a full alarm.'

Al-Bakr and the party leadership said yes; al-Nayif could be Prime Minister.

'Saddam said all we had to do was remove him as soon as we came to power. It wouldn't be more difficult than that.'

Samir al-Shaikhli, the future Minister of the Interior, was a leading member of the party. The coup leaders, including Ahmed Hassan al-Bakr, Saddam and Barzan met in his parents' house before taking action on 17 July. They had got hold of military uniforms and two lorries with which to drive to the presidential palace. There they would be met by Brigadier al-Daud and Colonel Ghaidan and a wide-open door.

'Just after we had set off, of all things, a policeman stopped us,' al-Shaikhli told me one evening when we were talking about what really happened that historic night. 'But Saddam quickly managed to gag the policeman, tie his hands behind his back and bundle him on to the back of the lorry, and we continued.'

The assumption of power took place according to plan and without any bloodletting. Abdul Rahman Aref soon realised that he had been betrayed by his most trusted officers and that there was no use resisting. The broadcasting station, ministry of defence and most important civilian and military institutions in Baghdad were already in the hands of the coup leaders.

The President was allowed to leave Iraq, having been told he was no longer welcome there. He was put on a plane to Turkey. He later went on to London where his seriously ill wife was undergoing medical treatment.

General Ahmed Hassan al-Bakr was made Iraq's new President. Abdul Razzaq al-Nayif got the job he wanted, that of Prime Minister, while Brigadier al-Daud and Colonel Ghaidan became respectively Minister of Defence and Interior Minister in the new government.

A few days after the coup al-Bakr suddenly remembered the policeman who had stopped them en route to the presidential palace. He had been imprisoned and forgotten in all the commotion.

'Al-Bakr ordered him to be found and brought to his office. When he arrived he was promoted. The general thoroughly enjoyed that episode,' Samir al-Shaikhli told me.

Barzan Ibrahim al-Tikriti was seventeen years old that summer. He followed closely on Saddam's heels wherever he

went, including the time when Abdul Razzaq al-Nayif, as
planned, was kicked out after less than fourteen days as Prime
Minister.

Al-Nayif's good friend, Defence Minister al-Daud, had gone to
Jordan to inspect Iraqi troops who were serving time in the
Hashemite kingdom. This was a hang-over from the catastrophic
Six Day War against Israel the previous year. No sooner had the
Defence Minister arrived in Amman than Saddam, Barzan and
Salah Omar al-Ali – one of the party leaders – struck.

'We walked into al-Nayif's office, pulled our guns and handcuffed him,' Barzan said. 'Then we packed him off to Morocco.
He was better suited as ambassador in Rabat.'

The Defence Minister did not fare much better. He heard a
radio report that he had been dismissed and was no longer
wanted in Baghdad. The cleansing had started and there would
be much, much more.

In high spirits: Iraq's President and Vice-President in November 1978. Eight months later Ahmed Hassan al-Bakr (right) withdrew for reasons of 'health', and Saddam took over the presidency. (AP/Scanpix)

CHAPTER 4

Purges

A torturer attempts a coup, but fails.
Saddam consolidates his power.

Nazim Kazzar smoked like a chimney and it was said that one of his specialities was to stub out his cigarette in the eye of his torture victim. He was hand-picked by Saddam to lead the security police after the Baath Party coup and assumption of power on 17 July 1968. At the end of June 1973 he tried to become President.

I returned to Baghdad a year earlier, having completed my training as a plastic surgeon in Great Britain, and I soon realised that a great deal had happened in Baghdad during my four-year absence. My cousin, Fawzi Farman Bashir, told me that although General Ahmed Hassan al-Bakr was President and Prime Minister, Saddam was really the nation's new strongman.

Not only was he Vice-President but he was also Deputy Chairman of the Revolutionary Command Council, which had been established as the country's most powerful body after the 1968 coup. The general's young protégé was not given a ministerial position, but his was the responsibility for the republic's security, a position he exploited fully, without hesitation.

Carefully, but systematically, he got President al-Bakr to accept changes in the party, the army and the civil service. Out with officers, undersecretaries and assistant secretaries he did not know or could not trust. In with cousins and other relatives with tribal and clan connections from Tikrit and the surrounding areas. Hashem

Hassan al-Majid, one of Saddam's cousins, was part of a committee set up to oversee the process.

'I remember him continually coming in and asking to see the suggestions we had worked out. "We won't change that under-secretary yet; we'll show that major the door immediately; and we'll give this department head another six months, so we can replace him with someone we've trained," he used to instruct us. Nothing was left to chance,' al-Majid said. He was proud of his cousin.

Traditionally, well-educated Shia Muslims from the privileged upper and middle classes had held some of the top political, army and government positions. Now, more and more, they were pushed to the side and replaced with far less well-off Sunni Muslims from Saddam's own region. Many of the newly appointed lacked schooling worth mentioning, if they had any at all.

Nazim Kazzar regarded this development with ever-increasing scepticism. He himself was a Shia from Amara in southern Iraq and a trained engineer from the Technical Institute in Baghdad. Not only was he no longer one of Saddam's favourites in the battle for power and positions, but – according to one of his officers in the secret police – he suspected that al-Bakr and Saddam were in league with America and the CIA.

Kazzar chose to strike one afternoon when President al-Bakr was expected back from a state visit to Poland. In line with protocol Saddam, as Vice-President, was to go to the airport to welcome the President home. Kazzar could thus kill two birds with one stone. He sent a gang of fellow conspirators to the airport to carry out the mission.

Earlier in the day his men had arrested and taken into custody the Minister of Defence, General Hammad Shihab and the Interior Minister, Saadoun Ghaidan. As soon as al-Bakr and Saddam had been killed the radio and TV stations would be seized, and the end of the 'Tikriti regime' would be proclaimed by Kazzar himself.

Al-Bakr's plane was delayed. It had taken off late from Warsaw and landed in Sofia to refuel. The Bulgarian government had decided to give the Iraqi President a decent reception as he was there anyhow. That took time, so it was eight in the evening before the plane landed in Baghdad, four hours late.

It emerged later in the court case that Saddam's colleagues and bodyguards had noticed that several officers in attendance from the secret police were getting visibly restless and nervous as time passed by without al-Bakr's plane turning up. The Vice-President was informed of their suspicious behaviour and reacted at once.

Soldiers were sent off to arrest Kazzar. The dreaded Chief of Police, realising that the assassination attempt had come to nothing, fled towards Iran, taking Defence Minister Shihab and Interior Minister Ghaidan with him as hostages. Saddam pursued them with planes and helicopter gunships; the cortège was overtaken and stopped at Badrah, by the border. In the ensuing fight Shihab was shot and killed and Ghaidan severely wounded. Kazzar was brought back to Baghdad, court-martialled and executed. The same fate befell more than thirty officers and civil servants in the secret police and Baath Party officials and committee members.

Many more were imprisoned. One was my cousin, Fawzi. He had had nothing to do with the unsuccessful coup, but as usual, he could not keep his bloody mouth shut.

In the summer of 1973 after Nazim Kazzar was executed an extraordinary general meeting was called by the Baath Party. More than four hundred leading Baathists from all over Iraq filled the al-Khuld Hall near the Republican Palace. Fawzi was one of the delegates. The EGM had been drummed up to rubber-stamp the extensive cleansing operations which had been going on in party ranks in the wake of Kazzar's failed coup. But for Saddam it was also important to secure the grounds to rid himself of Abdul Khaleq al-Samarrai, a party founder and respected ideologist.

Al-Samarrai was a socialist and one of the few who might prevent the young Vice-President from climbing right to the top of the party tree. Al-Samarrai's thoughts and ideas on Arab unity, fundamental agricultural reforms and increased rights for the working classes made him extremely popular at grass-roots level. There was never talk of his exploiting his position to enrich himself. Many party members considered him to be a natural successor to al-Bakr.

'No one can match him,' said my cousin.

But that is not what the members of the conference were told when it opened in the al-Khuld Hall. They were told that al-Samarrai had just been arrested and thrown into prison. 'He supported Nazim Kazzar and is a traitor,' an indignant Taha Yassin Ramadhan al-Jazrawi shouted. He was chairman of the meeting. 'He's utterly corrupt and should be relieved of all his duties.'

Thirty-five-year-old Taha Yassin Ramadhan was one of Saddam's closest lieutenants. The former banker from Mosul had been invited to join the Revolutionary Command Council soon after the revolution in 1968. He always obeyed Saddam and never questioned his decisions.

Fawzi asked for the floor when Ramadhan had finished complaining about the ideologist's treacherous behaviour. 'These accusations against Abdul Khaleq are utter nonsense. We who know him can guarantee that. This is a conspiracy to try to gag him,' said my cousin.

You could have heard a pin drop. No one dared support him.

When Fawzi returned after the conference he was arrested.

I visited him shortly afterwards in 'Prison Number 1', as the establishment was called. Political prisoners were held here and it was strictly guarded. The cells were four by four metres and he shared one with six or seven other prisoners. They had no mattresses, but slept on the concrete floor. They covered themselves with small rugs. He had been badly beaten up.

'Why did you defend al-Samarrai?' I asked.

'He was my friend and a man who never thought of himself. We went to East Germany together once, as delegates, and when we got to Berlin I bought him some socks and a shirt. His were so holey and his shirt so worn, it was unbelievable. And this is the man they want us to believe is corrupt and represents a threat to Iraq?' Fawzi looked at me in despair.

I tried many times to obtain permission to visit Fawzi, but it was denied. Prisoners in Prison Number 1 rarely had visitors. They were either executed or quite simply disappeared without the families knowing what had happened to them.

Fawzi's wife Amel al-Janabi was politically active too. She was educated and well bred. She'd been a member of the Baath Party since 1959 and had risen to become Deputy Chairman of the organisation's women's department when her husband was jailed. The women's department had frequent meetings with Saddam.

'I never asked him to pardon my husband and he never raised the question,' Amel al-Janabi told me.

After a year the Vice-President wanted to know why she had never asked for her husband's release.

'I answered that he knew all the details and that he must have known that my husband was innocent. He had only voiced his opinion.'

'That's OK. Go to the prison and fetch him. He is free as from today,' Saddam said.

They both left the Baath Party when Fawzi, one of only a few, was let out of Prison Number 1 with life and limb intact.

There was no denying that Iraq was moving forwards under al-Bakr and Saddam. In June 1972 they nationalised IPC (Iraq Petroleum Company). This led to a huge increase in oil revenue. And the spin-off from yet another war between Israel, Egypt and Syria saw an economic bonanza which no one in Baghdad could have dreamt of.

The Jews were celebrating Yom Kippur on 6 October 1973 when Egyptian forces crossed the Suez Canal and made rapid progress through the Sinai Desert. In contrast to the Six Day War in 1967, this time it was the Israeli government who were caught napping.

On the Golan Heights the Syrian army was experiencing sim-ilar success during the opening phases of the war. Significant supplies of modern weapons from the Soviet Union gave President Anwar Sadat in Cairo and Hafez al-Assad in Damascus striking power which caught Tel Aviv off guard.

Only when massive American supplies had been flown in did the fortunes of war shift. The Egyptian and Syrian armies were slowly pushed back, but not without consequences for the world economy.

In reply to the Americans supplying weapons to Israel, and led by King Faisal in Saudi Arabia, a majority of the OPEC members agreed to boycott deliveries to the USA and the Netherlands and to reduce supplies to Western Europe. The oil price hit the roof on the New York and London stock exchanges. Before the Yom Kippur war Iraq and the other oil-producing countries were getting three dollars per barrel for crude, now they were getting eleven.

The nationalisation of oil production combined with the dizzy prices oil was fetching on the world market opened up a world of new possibilities for al-Bakr and Saddam. They had hit the jackpot. Suddenly all Baath Party promises could be honoured and we became quickly aware of the country's new-found prosperity. The construction of schools and universities, motorways, power, water and sewage plants, houses and apartment blocks gathered momentum. New hospitals and clinics opened their doors to provide free treatment, prescription medicines were free too. Electricity soon lit up village after village and refrigerators and TV sets were subsidised so most people could afford to buy them. Standards of living rose, unemployment fell. Illiteracy became public enemy number one: everyone would learn to read and write.

Suddenly Iraq was the model nation in the Middle East. People believed in the future and the Baath Party's popularity and support reached new heights. Saddam had his weak points, we all knew that, but after all the ups and downs, Iraq was heading in the right direction.

Taha Yassin Ramadhan was in charge of large parts of the economic planning. His banking experience from Mosul and the fact that he had managed to complete secondary school in his home town gave him a considerable professional advantage over Saddam's two mainstays, Izzat Ibrahim al-Douri and Ali Hassan al-Majid. Izzat Ibrahim, who was born in 1942, was the son of an ice-seller from Tikrit. With exception of the Koran, it is difficult to believe that he had ever read a book at all.

The same could be said of Ali Hassan al-Majid, Saddam's cousin from al-Ouja outside Tikrit. He was a year older than Izzat Ibrahim and the most he had achieved was to become an army motorcycle messenger, until he was pulled into his cousin's inner circle. Now, to all intents and purposes, he controlled Iraq and the country's huge oil revenue.

As the oil money started to flow we at al-Wasiti hospital in Baghdad were told to buy in all the technical equipment, medicines and instruments we needed. Health Minister Riyadh Ibrahim circulated a directive to all hospitals telling us to keep the pressure up; there was clearly no limit to what could be imported through the state's purchasing channels. However, not even then was there an overall health plan. Many hospital directors and doctors bought instruments and advanced analysis and laser equipment which were never used, because there were not enough laboratory technicians, bioengineers and qualified nurses to operate and maintain the equipment.

The fabric of society suffered in other areas as well. Staggering amounts of investment trickled away into the sand owing to bad planning; in many cases because key competent and knowledgeable personnel had been pushed out of their jobs and replaced by Tikritis whose only qualification was their family or tribal connection with or loyalty to Saddam. Saddam's half-brother, Barzan, had been given the job of developing and leading Iraq's intelligence service, the Mukhabarat. Adnan Khairallah, Khairallah Tulfah's son and Saddam's cousin on his mother's side, was appointed to the post of Defence Minister. He was also the Vice-President's brother-in-law, as his sister, Sajida, married Saddam early in the sixties after his return from exile in Egypt. Adnan Khairallah was on his part married to one of al-Bakr's daughters.

Thus the contours of the tribal-based family medley which would rule our country for the next thirty years were starting to take shape. Forces within the Baath Party thought it had gone too far and tried to stop Saddam. But they never managed to organise themselves before it was too late.

The Vice-President was also in charge of the army. The majority of the officer corps was favourably disposed towards Saddam and his Minister of Defence. The huge oil revenues, which continued to flow into the country at the end of the seventies, were not only paying for roads, power stations, electricity lines and

other infrastructure; on the contrary, the lion's share went to purchase weapons. Smiling generals and colonels noted how Saddam
and Adnan Khairallah armed the forces like never before in the
history of Iraq. From the Soviet Union tanks, armoured personnel carriers, missiles, fighter and bomber planes were purchased
as part of the friendship and cooperation treaty between the gov-
ernments in Baghdad and Moscow. France jumped on the
bandwagon and sold Baghdad fighter planes and helicopters.
Nor did Paris bat an eyelid or ask any questions when it supplied
the equipment needed to build Iraq's first nuclear reactor outside
Baghdad.

In the middle of the summer of 1979 Saddam struck.

On 16 July radio and TV broadcasts reported that General
Ahmed Hassan al-Bakr had resigned. He had withdrawn 'for
reasons of personal health' and Saddam Hussein al-Tikriti had
been installed as Iraq's new President and leader of the
Revolutionary Command Council. Izzat Ibrahim al-Douri was
Vice-President and the council's Deputy Chairman.

Saddam's next and decisive move has been immortalised on
TV. This shows a packed al-Khuld Hall a week later, where Baath
Party representatives and members of the Revolutionary
Command Council have gathered for another EGM. After
Saddam has asked him to speak, the party's General Secretary
Abdul Hussein Mashhadi 'confesses' that he and some colleagues
have conspired over a number of years to topple al-Bakr and the
regime. Their objective was to unite with Syria, and the Syrian
President Hafez al-Assad had advised them on how to proceed.

After the well-edited 'confession', the broadcast shows the
General Secretary being asked to name his fellow conspirators.
'Those who hear their name mentioned must get up and leave the
hall,' Saddam says.

Mashhadi starts to read. When he has finished more than fifty
leading representatives in the party have stood up. Some of them
try to protest their innocence before being led out; none of them
gets to speak. Many have to be carried out by force. Barzan,
Saddam's half-brother, has placed his Mukhabarat officers in
strategic places around the hall.

During the session Saddam smokes a cigar. From time to time, when one of the 'conspirators' who is close to him is removed, he takes out a handkerchief and wipes his eyes. Several of them are members of the Revolutionary Command Council and have been party members since its inception. At the end Ali Hassan al-Majid, the former motorcycle messenger, speaks out: 'You must cut the head off the snake, too!'

He is referring to the ideologist, Abdul Khaleq al-Samarrai, imprisoned since 1973 when Taha Yassin Ramadhan accused him of conspiring with Nazim Kazzar during the police chief's failed coup at the airport.

'Keep calm,' says Saddam. 'It will be done'.

More than sixty delegates were expelled from the al-Khuld Hall. Over twenty of them – amongst them General Secretary Abdul Hussein Mashhadi, despite presumably having been promised leniency if he said what he said – were sentenced to death and executed. The others were given long prison sentences. Al-Samarrai too was liquidated during the so-called 'democratic executions'.

Democracy was evident in the composition of the firing squads. Only leading party representatives who had been at the meeting were chosen. None of them said no to shooting old friends and party comrades.

PART TWO

Danse Macabre

Near Basra, July 1982. (Jacques Pavlovsky/Corbis)

CHAPTER 5

Danse Macabre

The war against Iran.
Soldiers tell their story.

About five in the morning on 23 September 1980, while spending the night at the al-Wasiti hospital in Baghdad, I was woken by a loud bang. I was the hospital director, chief surgeon and responsible for the department of plastic and reconstructive surgery.

I jumped out of bed and rushed to the window. Flames and black smoke rose from the residential area of Zaiuna, a few kilometres away. A few tentative rays of sun heralded daybreak. They glanced off the wings of the bombers as they dropped their fatal cargo over the city, making them glow in a golden light.

At first I thought this was a coup attempt, but I soon realised the planes were Iranian. The day before Saddam Hussein had dispatched his soldiers, tanks and air force into Iran, eastwards along a 500-kilometre-long front from south to north.

Tehran was responding.

Twenty minutes later ambulances carrying the dead and wounded started to arrive. The first victim was a five-year-old boy. He had spent the night on the rooftop of his house with his father, mother and siblings, enjoying the cool air. His head had been torn off. It hung by a few shreds of skin, covered in blood, sand and mud. His father and mother were dead too. They had died as soon as they hit the ground of their little garden, blasted off the roof by the air pressure from the bombs exploding in the neighbourhood. The coagulated blood, dust and mud made them look like Sumerian terracotta statues.

A Voice of America analyst from CIA was commenting on the outbreak of war – I had tuned in on my short-wave radio. I remember him saying it would be long and bloody; it would last for many years and neither party would emerge triumphant.

I wonder whether the CIA analyst realised how accurate his prediction was.

The war came as a complete surprise, although it shouldn't have. Six months earlier I had been appointed to a special committee whose task it was to discuss the improvement of imports of medicines, instruments and other medical equipment to public and military hospitals in Iraq. Half the committee had been appointed by the health ministry, the other half by the ministry of defence and consisted of doctors and officers. Not even when it was staring me in the face and we were asked to give very accurate indications of what surgical equipment, fluids, blood plasma, ointments for burns and antibiotics would be needed to enable us to treat tens of thousands during a so-called 'national catastrophe', did the penny drop. I had no idea that I was part of the preparation for war against our neighbour.

Allegedly Shatt al-Arab was the reason for Iraqi troops violating the Iranian border. North of Basra the Euphrates and the Tigris merge into one mighty river which flows another two hundred kilometres before pouring into the Persian Gulf. The last eighty kilometres of the river make up the border to Iran. Iraq's sole access to the Gulf is through Shatt al-Arab. Sindbad of *The Thousand and One Nights* sailed down the river when leaving on his legendary travels. Arabs to the west and Persians to the east have been fighting over the control of this strategic tidal waterway for hundreds of years.

The border ran along the river bank on the Iranian side. But in March 1975, during a meeting of OPEC ministers in Algeria, there was a surprising announcement to the effect that Saddam Hussein and the Iranian Shah Muhammad Reza Pahlavi had agreed to move the border. It would now run down the centre of the river, where the shipping lane was deepest. It was a piece of horse-trading, like so much in the history of the Middle East.

During this time Iran supported the Kurdish leader Mustafa Barzani and his guerrilla warriors, the peshmerga, with money and weapons. Barzani had again initiated an armed revolt against Saddam's forces in Northern Iraq in order to gain independence. It had up until now been relatively quiet in the mountain areas, not least owing to a deal brokered between Saddam and Barzani in 1970, whereby the Kurds were granted something approximating self-rule. But, as so often with Saddam, the promise was never kept. The deadline for establishing autonomy had passed in March 1974 without Saddam having done enough to grant the Kurds the independence promised in the agreement.

Initially, Barzani, when he realised he had been duped, found it easy to persuade the pro-American Shah to support him. Washington was wary of Iraq's rapprochement with the Soviet Union and unrest in Northern Iraq would weaken the Baghdad regime politically and economically – such was the thinking in the White House.

Now the Shah pulled the carpet from under Barzani. Supplies of weapons and money to the Kurdish insurgents dried up as soon as Saddam agreed to the new border down the centre of Shatt al-Arab. Barzani saw no alternative but to end the struggle – for the time being. He fled to Iran where he joined the more than one hundred thousand Kurdish refugees, most of them women, children and old men.

The Algeria agreement between Iraq and Iran was meant to 'completely end the conflict between the two sister nations', as the treaty so delicately puts it. But not many years were to pass before new accusations about border violations along Shatt al-Arab flowed between Baghdad and Tehran, where in the meantime the Shah, mortally ill with cancer, had been toppled, and where a Shia Muslim priesthood, led by Ayatollah Ruhollah Khomeini, had stepped into the power vacuum after the revolution of 1979.

The relations between the 'sister nations' did not improve after Khomeini resumed the supply of money and weapons to the Kurdish resistance in the North. Led by Mustafa Barzani's son, Masoud, the peshmerga had again started to stir in the Kurdish areas of North Iraq.

The summer leading up to the outbreak of war was marked by continuous reports of Iranian violations of Iraqi territory along Shatt al-Arab and the long border between the two countries. On its side the Iraqi army had carried out retaliatory attacks inside Iran. But like most Iraqis I had difficulty believing that the continuous pushing and shoving would lead to all-out war.

Now it was a fait accompli and the official line was that border violations had forced the military operations. But we suspected that there were other, more deep-rooted, reasons for the sudden war. It was not difficult to see that Khomeini and his followers could appear threatening to Saddam and the Sunni Muslim elite who surrounded him: a majority of Iraqis were Shia Muslims, as was the fundamentalist priesthood in power in Tehran. No one could predict whether the Islamic revolution might not also spread to secular Iraq.

One of my friends, Nizar al-Khazraji, belonged to the top echelon of Saddam's military leaders and was appointed Chief of the General Staff towards the end of the eight-year war. He never concealed from me that the President thought it absolutely vital to strike at Iran in order to forestall a future Iranian attack. 'We must strike first, before the Ayatollah and his priesthood have time to rebuild the Iranian army, which has been severely reduced in the chaos and purges of officers that followed the Shah's fall. The advice to Saddam from the military intelligence services was unambiguous.'

The relations between the two power-hungry men, one in Baghdad, the other in Tehran, had frozen solid when Khomeini was thrown out of Iraq and the Shia Muslims' holy town of Najaf in October 1978. The Ayatollah was then seventy-six years old. He had crossed the border fourteen years earlier and settled near the Imam Ali's grave after he had fallen out with the Shah and was forced into exile. The magnificent shrine that is built over the burial site of the prophet Muhammad's son-in-law and fourth Caliph ranks as one of Shia Muslims' most holy places.

The job of telling the Ayatollah that it no longer served Iraq's national security and interest to have him living in Najaf – the political situation was too fraught and unstable – fell to the respected poet and Culture and Information Minister Shafiq al-Kamali.

Al-Kamali guided a large delegation to Khomeini's flat in the holy city. Before they were let in they were met by his secretary who told them the Ayatollah had no wish to shake any hands. The traditional spoken Muslim greeting 'Salaam aleikum' – 'Peace be with you' – would have to suffice.

When they entered the room they found Khomeini sitting on the floor together with an interpreter. Al-Kamali said, 'Salaam aleikum,' and the Ayatollah answered but did not get up. The delegation was obliged to get down on the floor; the Culture and Information Minister stated his errand.

During the whole meeting Khomeini either looked up at the ceiling or at his interpreter. He did not look at the minister nor any of the other delegates from Baghdad. He answered no or yes to questions and otherwise left it to his secretary to reply.

When the meeting was over and al-Kamali had made it crystal clear that there was no alternative, Khomeini would have to leave Iraq as soon as possible, the Ayatollah at last looked the messenger in the eye.

'He looked at us, one by one, without saying a word. His charisma was tremendous,' I can remember al-Kamali telling me. 'It was like standing in the jet stream of an aeroplane, I started to shake, and so did everyone with me.'

Islam's holy month of fasting, Ramadan, had started when the Ayatollah and his entourage drove from Najaf to Basra to cross the border into Kuwait. He was initially denied entry owing to visa problems and had to return and spend the night in a hotel by the airport. The government's Health Director, Nizar Shahbandar, was a member of the committee looking after him during his stay.

'Khomeini was furious and upset,' Shahbandar told me. He talked to no one, and refused to partake in iftar, the meal eaten during Ramadan after the day-long fast from sun-up to sundown. Only after having crossed the border to Kuwait, while waiting for transit to France where he had been granted asylum, did the Ayatollah allow himself to eat or drink.

No wonder Saddam, who received detailed reports about the incident, knew that Khomeini, in the manner of the Bedouin, would sooner or later avenge himself. He had to forestall him.

When the war broke out in September 1980 al-Wasiti was quickly converted into a military hospital. Because of our superior expertise in plastic and reconstructive surgery, we were allocated the worst and most complicated cases. Hospital records show that we completed twenty-two thousand operations at the hospital during the eight years of war. Anyone who has not experienced such a vast and ongoing human tragedy at close quarters and over such a long period would find it hard to comprehend the sum total of sorrow and suffering and death.

Individual fates, like that of a twenty-one-year-old lieutenant who was admitted during the autumn of 1982, still have the power to keep me awake at night.

He was transported from the front to al-Wasiti together with fifteen other wounded officers and soldiers. They had taken cover under a large lorry as they were being shot at by Iranian artillery and the lorry took a direct hit. A large shell splinter had severed the lieutenant's arm.

As I examined him I couldn't help feeling he seemed a lot younger than twenty-one. His face showed how desperately he wanted to live the life of a normal youth but the amputated arm had robbed him of all hope for the future.

I tried to encourage him. 'Your brave war efforts will be recognised with a medal of valour which you can wear with pride for the rest of your life.'

The young lieutenant looked me in the eyes, then glanced down at his right arm; he could no longer hold back his tears.

I understood.

The Iraqi army made certain progress at the beginning of the war, but the Iranians pushed Saddam's forces back during 1982. Several Arab countries made diplomatic efforts to try and arrange a truce, but inflamed by success on several fronts Khomeini chose to continue. It turned into a war of attrition; losses inflicted on both sides were terrible.

In time all male, able-bodied Iraqi citizens who were not needed to keep the machinery of society going were mobilised. One family after another lost its breadwinner and in many cases fell into extreme poverty.

One of my relatives told me about a family from Basra who moved into his neighbourhood during the war: a young man and his wife and their three-month-old baby. They had only just arrived when the Baath Party representative in the area asked him to report for active service immediately.

'Please look after my wife,' the young man pleaded before he left. She knew no one in Baghdad. Two weeks later the neighbours saw her sitting on the steps of her house crying. There was neither food nor water in the flat and the baby was dead. She had been too frightened to go out and ask for help.

The neighbours paid for the funeral and took care of the young mother from Basra. A month later a coffin with her husband arrived from the front line.

Saddam understood that war was a bitter pill to swallow and needed sugaring. He therefore started handing out cars to the families of fallen soldiers. Every family got a new car and ten thousand dinars, worth at that time about thirty thousand dollars. The delivery of cars and payment of compensation was rarely unaccompanied by friction, however. If the soldier was married, according to the rules, the wife was the beneficiary, but his parents and brothers did not always agree. And if the cheated widow called on her father or brothers or cousins to help her, fights, armed attacks and killings followed.

One of my male colleagues at al-Wasiti also lost a son at the front. I can still see him, completely broken down by sorrow and inconsolable. But two weeks later he arrived at the hospital in a brand-new Toyota Corona. It was spattered in blood; a sheep had been sacrificed and the car sprinkled with the blood to protect it from evil powers. The father was smiling brightly.

Initially the car offered was a Toyota Corona from Japan, but as the losses increased the standard was lowered to a Volkswagen Passat, produced in and imported from Brazil. Delivery was usually made straight to the door but the majority of widows and families did not have any form of driving licence. Despite this, the cars were put to use immediately. The number of traffic accidents increased manifold, adding to the death toll. This was clearly one of the reasons Saddam stopped 'a car for a son' halfway through the war.

Early on in the war the so-called people's army was mobilised. A kind of militia under Baath Party control, it had been established in the 1970s to give party activists basic military training, but also to counterbalance the regular army should any of its officers be busying themselves with plans for a coup d'état.

In the autumn of 1981 Baath Party members all over Iraq were told to lead by example and report for active service in the people's army. The order applied to committee members too but many of them were unhappy about it; they felt they were unfit for the front and they cited various health and personal reasons in mitigation.

Dr Hashim Jaber was one of them. He was professor of odontology and chancellor of Baghdad University, and had suffered for many years with serious kidney problems and high blood pressure. His private dental surgery and my private offices were next door to each other; we were good colleagues and friends. In December 1981 he was ordered to report to the al-Khuld Hall, next to the Republican Palace, together with 420 other high-ranking Baath Party members.

Saddam's voice was mild and silky soft. 'I would like to ask those of you who aren't well enough, are too exhausted or have other compelling reasons for not joining the people's army on the front line, to stand to the left of the hall.'

Dr Jaber and about 230 Baathists followed his request.

'You have been relieved of your jobs and I do not want to see you in the Baath Party again.'

Then the 230 were sent to the front.

In 1982 a summit for heads of state of the Non-Aligned Movement (NAM) was to have taken place in Baghdad. Preparations were comprehensive and thorough and Saddam built a new hotel, al-Rashid, for the guests from more than a hundred countries. He also bought in a large number of Mercedes cars to cover transport requirements.

Owing to the war and the virtually impossible security situation – Baghdad was subject to continuous rocket and bomb attacks from Iran – the meeting was postponed for a year and moved to New Delhi. A bright spark on the presidential staff conceived the brilliant idea of rewarding selected architects, doctors, engineers, teachers, authors, actors, artists and cultural personalities who had made extraordinary contributions to the fatherland during the war, with the shiny new, unused Mercedes cars.

I was asked to turn up at one of Saddam's palaces to receive my mobile reward, as a doctor, not an artist. That surprised me as his then personal secretary, Arshed Yassin, who was married to Saddam's sister, Nawal, had on several occasions over the last few years phoned or dropped in to tell me how much the President appreciated my work, which he had got to know through TV reports and reviews in newspapers and magazines. Several of my paintings and sculptures had gone to Saddam following gallery exhibitions.

Yassin, who was a pilot and air marshal, was himself very interested in art and antiques. The papers published an article about the theft of thousand-year-old, irreplaceable Iraqi antiquities which had been smuggled out of the country and sold for millions on the international black market. The air marshal was named in connection with the scandal but the truth of the allegations was never established. He, however, was relieved from his post as personal secretary.

When the summit of the non-aligned countries was cancelled, about twenty of us turned up to be praised and given the surplus-to-requirement Mercedes cars as a reward for our war efforts. Saddam emphasised how important our jobs were 'for the frontline soldiers and officers and the families they have left behind to battle against the enemy. People like you will go down in Iraq's history,' he said, 'not businessmen or millionaires who think of nothing but money.' He then walked round and shook everyone's hand whilst being photographed. When he came to me he was taken aback by my name.

'Are you and the painter Ala Bashir one and the same?' he asked. 'That's unbelievable,' he went on when I answered in the affirmative. 'Do stay behind and we'll have a chat.'

When the other doctors had left Saddam extolled my paintings and sculptures. He was more interested in them than in the progress we had made within orthopaedic and plastic surgery, the operating techniques we had pioneered since the start of the war, or the fact that our scientific articles had been accepted and published by leading international medical journals.

'I have always read about doctors in Europe who were also famous authors, musicians and painters, but this must be the first time in the history of Iraq that one of our leading surgeons is at the same time an eminent artist. I am pleased and proud that we have people like you in Iraq.'

Three days later a colleague on Saddam's staff phoned to say that I was now a member of the President's team of doctors. When I joined the group consisted of about ten specialists allocated to him and his closest family. In time this number grew to twenty or twenty-five. Saddam was extremely vigilant about paying for all consultations and services; he was very careful not to owe anyone a debt of gratitude. I was the one exception. He never paid me a dinar for paintings and sculptures taken from my exhibitions. But he protected me from the jackals and that protection was worth its weight in gold. Anyone too close to the President was regarded by his inner circle with increasing distrust and aversion.

For others the sword of Damocles hung by a hair. Under cover of war the security agency and the secret police hunted down, ever more ruthlessly, anyone in opposition, or thought to be in opposition to the President and his regime. All political activity outside the Baath Party had already been outlawed in 1978. Membership or affiliation to any other party, if the person concerned served or had already served in the armed forces, was punishable by death. Three of my second cousins, Faiq, Laiq and Sadeq Abdul Rahman, all in their twenties, were rounded up one night and accused of sympathising with the illegal Islamic party al-Dawah. There was no talk of a court case, either for them or thousands of other Iraqis who disappeared into mass graves after their execution.

Culture and Information Minister Shafiq al-Kamali was one of the very few who tried to limit the purges. He was a Baath Party founder member and belonged to the central committee, the Revolutionary Command Council. At one of the committee meetings al-Kamali raised the question whether it was right that the secret police continued its established practice of torturing innocent fathers and brothers of suspected opponents of the government whom they could not get hold of.

'It damages the public's opinion of the party, and that hurts the government,' he said.

Saddam looked at him but said nothing until the meeting was over. Then the president walked over to al-Kamali. 'Listen to me, comrade. If we wish to continue to rule Iraq we must let our heads rule and not our hearts.'

Not long after Iraq got a new Culture and Information Minister. Al-Kamali went to gaol and by the time he was freed a few months later, his health had severely deteriorated. Just before he died he told me about the incident in the central committee.

The danse macabre and the persecutions hit high and low, even Riyadh Ibrahim. In my opinion he was Iraq's best ever Health Minister. He was one of the first to join the Baath Party and was arrested following the failed attempt to kill President Abdul Karim al-Kassem in Baghdad in 1959. Ibrahim had helped Saddam and his fellow conspirators hide the weapons which were used during the assassination attempt. He was arrested and tried but got away with imprisonment.

Like many others who had joined the Baath Party he was an honest and upright man. He believed in the movement's fundamental ideas of cooperation between Arab states and the importance of a just distribution of society's riches and resources. I knew him as a man who was genuinely engaged in the welfare of the Iraqi people. He had a medical degree from Great Britain and thus a solid professional basis on which to base his ministerial work. But he lived dangerously. He laughed at his cabinet colleagues' stupidity and ineffectiveness and he railed against the puppets in the national assembly, questioning the dubious means by which they had secured their seats.

One summer's day in 1982 I was asked to come to Ibrahim's departmental office. He did not say what it was about. When I got there he explained that two men were going to pick me up and take me to someone who wanted to discuss a very special matter with me. He gave me no further details, but stressed: 'When you meet him you must not hesitate to voice your opinion. It is your decision.'

I was fetched by a black Mercedes with soot-coloured windows and driven to a small, low house in the al-Jadiriya district near the Tigris. I was expected, was served tea and soon realised that my host was an Iraqi secret service agent who worked in Syria.

He got straight to the heart of the matter. 'We want to send a Syrian citizen here in Iraq back to Damascus to take part in an assassination. The problem is that he is well known by the Syrian authorities. We want you to change his face completely so he won't be recognised.'

I thanked him for his great confidence in me as a plastic surgeon. Then I begged his pardon. 'I don't feel I can do this. It would go against everything I believe in and my professional ethics.'

He said OK. 'But you must forget this meeting and never tell anyone about it.'

The next morning I reported straight back to Riyadh Ibrahim. 'Did you know what they were going to ask?'

'Yes,' he said, 'and I told them you would never agree. When you came here yesterday I was only making quite sure when I said it was your decision.'

We talked openly in his office. With other ministers scraps of paper were shoved back and forth when sensitive questions were discussed to avoid being overheard by bugging equipment.

I don't know who in the higher echelons of power ultimately got rid of Riyadh Ibrahim. Just before he was deposed in 1983 he told me that the President's staff wanted to send a veterinary surgeon abroad to qualify in the various methods of prevention of poisoning. The candidate had been promised a research scholarship at an American medical institute and all that was missing was a confirmation from the health ministry that he was a qualified doctor and not just a vet.

Dr Ibrahim refused. 'The ministry of health will lose all credibility if we agree to something like that,' he said when a furious executive officer phoned from the presidential palace wondering why it was taking so long to convert the man, who was ready to leave at a moment's notice, from a vet to a doctor.

The sword fell on Riyadh Ibrahim at once. Suddenly he was made the scapegoat for a number of hospital deaths. The patients concerned had allegedly been given intravenous injections with a solution of potassium chloride past its sell-by date. He was dismissed and an investigation was launched. Two weeks later he was arrested and thrown into gaol.

I visited him before he was imprisoned. He was making fun of the bodyguards who continued to guard his house. Normally they rushed to open the garage door every time he got in or out of his car. Now they sat like pillars of salt in their guardroom. 'I even used to carry meals out to them,' he said.

I told him not to be surprised at their behaviour. 'That's what they're like.'

Riyadh Ibrahim had a good laugh.

The investigating committee's findings cleared the Health Minister. The batch of potassium chloride from the French drug company had not, after all, passed its sell-by date. However, the concentration of potassium chloride in the solution was higher than normal and the hospital personnel had not realised that it needed diluting before being administered to patients.

But these results counted for nothing. Ibrahim was executed after a six-week prison stay. I visited his wife two days before the regime took his life. Her husband had managed to smuggle out a small piece of paper. He wrote that he was looking forward to seeing her and the children as it was now clear that the accusations against him were without foundation. As soon as the President had read the committee's report he would be freed, he wrote.

His brother took care of the funeral. He told me that Ibrahim's jaw had been crushed, his left arm broken and his body badly battered. He had been shot with a nine-millimetre bullet at close range, through the head, pelvis and thigh. His eyes had been removed.

Bin-al-Haytham hospital in Baghdad received a constant stream of Saddam's victims, and the eye unit was able to save the sight of many of its patients with cornea transplants.

Rumours have circulated in Baghdad as to who actually, physically killed Riyadh Ibrahim. The most far-fetched accuses Saddam himself of shooting him in a corridor after having asked him to step outside during a cabinet meeting. But as he had been dismissed as Health Minister many weeks before he was done away with – most probably in the prison where he was being tortured – it is unlikely he took part in the cabinet meeting referred to.

Another persistent rumour has it that Saddam's half-brother Barzan al-Tikriti shot him. He was head of the intelligence service in Iraq when the killing took place.

In 1985 Barzan dropped in to al-Wasiti for a minor operation. When it was over we talked for a while. I pointed out the modern state-of-the-art medical equipment we now had in the theatre. 'Dr Ibrahim was responsible for all this,' I said.

'It was a great mistake to have liquidated him,' said Barzan.

Neither then, nor at any other time during our many and long conversations, did Saddam's half-brother care to expand on the subject.

Dr Ibrahim was not the only one of my friends who paid with their lives for their frank opinions. My highly professional colleagues Hisham al-Salman and Ismail al-Tatr were both liquidated for not choosing their words with more care. Al-Tatr was a dermatologist and a member of the president's elite team; al-Salman was Iraq's leading paediatrician. During a high-spirited party they were careless enough to crack some foul-mouthed yet innocent jokes about Saddam and his pathetic efforts to introduce new and rigorous rules to combat AIDS. They were both known for their senses of humour and quick-witted tongues but what they had not realised was that one of the party-goers – obviously attached to the secret police – was filming them covertly. The recording was given to the President who immediately ordered the two doctors' execution for having made fun of him.

I used to note down conversations I had with young victims of the war. But in time I realised that I was playing with fire and burnt the notes to be on the safe side. If the notes got into the hands of the intelligence services or the secret police's numerous informers, it would mean certain death.

When official delegations arrived at al-Wasiti to decorate heroic patients, the press trailing behind, the men's fighting spirit and burning wish to return to the front to continue the fight against the Iranians was convincingly displayed. Otherwise morale was rock-bottom. During meetings with me, their doctor, alone, the wounded soldiers and officers were open, trusting and honest. In the hospital they were far from the horrors of the battlefield and felt confident that what was discussed would remain between doctor and patient, and go no further. They were virtually all against the war. They could not understand why they, Muslims, were fighting other Muslims.

In 1983 I operated on a photographer who was also a good friend. His left hand had been badly wounded. He recovered and was sent back to the front. During the summer of 1985 he took part in one of the bloodiest battles of the war inside Iranian territory, near Nafit-Khana. Hostilities broke out in the middle of the night and the photographer's unit suffered great losses. He and another soldier hid in a ditch and lay quiet as mice, hoping not to be discovered.

After a while two more soldiers jumped into the ditch, and they were followed by three more. It was pitch black and they could see no further than the ends of their own noses and dared not whisper. It was only when dawn arrived that they realised that two of the soldiers who had joined them in the ditch were Iraqi but the other three were Iranian.

'We're all Muslims and it's not right that we should kill each other,' they said.

'They buggered off, and so did we.'

In February 1984 I gave an exhibition in al-Riwaq, in the Sadoun Street in Central Baghdad. In those days it was Iraq's most prestigious gallery and the exhibition was widely publicised and given a lot of attention in the papers and on TV.

During surgery hours one day a patient at al-Wasiti, Karim I think his name was, asked if he could have a catalogue and would I be kind enough to sign it. I was taken aback; victims from the front did not often give much thought to art and certainly not modern art. But Karim had read the reviews in the paper and seen a photograph of one of the paintings. It was of an empty room with a tiny window which emitted a thin ray of sunshine, just strong enough to illuminate the head of a man, wrapped in a piece of cloth and hanging from the ceiling. At one end of the room was a door to another room; there was another door in that room, and further doors to more rooms, until the last door opened out on to a beautiful landscape and a cloudless sky.

Karim was a war hero, decorated with no fewer than five medals for his exploits, often far behind enemy lines. His leg was badly wounded and we transferred skin from his thigh and muscles from his back to try and patch it all together. The operations succeeded beyond all our expectations and after a stay of only three weeks he was mobile again and could be discharged. It was therefore a great surprise when I found him waiting for me outside the hospital gates a couple of months later.

'Is the leg troubling you?' I asked.

'No,' said Karim, 'but I'd be grateful if you could read this.' He handed me a piece of paper on which he had written a poem in my honour, praising me as doctor and artist. At the bottom a few lines were added asking whether he might talk to me in private. I said OK and took him into my office.

'When I saw your painting I just couldn't bear it any longer – the guilt and remorse. I felt physically sick. I don't mind what happens to me now.'

I said that what he wanted to confess would be between him and me and God.

In the end it had all been too much for him. Not that he was frightened of fighting, he was brave, as all his decorations could testify, but he just couldn't see any purpose in going on. He couldn't bear the thought of going on lying in the trench, struggling with himself, while his unit prepared for further attacks against the Iranian positions a few hundred metres away.

When the orders to advance were given and his comrades went over the top, everything unravelled.

'I climbed out of the trench and immediately shot myself in the leg with the Kalashnikov.'

Karim lost consciousness and woke up in the military hospital in Kut, midway between Basra and Baghdad. He was transferred to al-Wasiti and hailed as a hero.

'Go ahead and tell the authorities what I've told you,' he said.

The confession was like the bursting of a dam. I said that what he had been through was a normal human reaction and it was a good thing that he realised he could have acted differently.

'But only the two of us and God will know what we have been talking about. No one else. You can feel safe,' I promised.

In July 1984 a sergeant was admitted to the hospital suffering from serious bedsores. No one at the primitive field hospital where he had first been taken had thought of turning him. He was unable to move. A bullet to the spinal cord had paralysed him from the waist down. He was from a district in Central Iraq, twenty-four years old, powerfully built and fit, and belonged to one of the army's elite commando units.

When I asked him to tell me what had happened he said that he had been assigned a risky reconnaissance mission with four other commandos in a rubber dinghy on one of the large wetland areas in Southern Iraq. One of the other soldiers was his best friend. They came from the same village, had gone through primary and secondary school together, enlisted together and passed the rock-hard physical tests required to join the prestigious elite unit. Subsequently they found themselves in the same group, which just after midnight had set out on the perilous operation in the swamp close to the enemy's line.

They hid in the thick reeds but were eventually detected and fired upon. The sergeant was the first to be shot, and collapsed, unconscious. When he came to he realised he was paralysed from the waist down. Day had dawned and the dinghy had sunk. Four comrades floated in the reeds, dead, his best friend a mere arm's length away.

The sun rose and with it the temperature. It was fifty degrees in the shade, impossible to find cover from the sun and the sergeant ran out of water. His friend's water bottle, which he managed to get hold of with great difficulty as he could only use his arms, had been riddled by bullets and was empty. To survive he would have to drink the swamp water, which was coloured red by blood.

His thirst was intolerable; in the end he could resist no longer and drank, whilst feebly trying to push his friend and the blood away. 'No one prepared us for anything like this in training,' the sergeant said.

The young man was remarkable in many ways. Just before the war he had married a beautiful eighteen-year-old cousin. There had been no time to start a family, and when his father came to visit the sergeant said that his wife should now divorce him. 'If she won't sort it out, I will,' he added. He loved her and dreamt of her all the time. But he did not want her to visit. 'It would be wrong for her to have to nurse me for the rest of her life; that would be criminal.'

An attitude like this was unheard of in the tribal areas in Central Iraq from whence he came. No other patient, and thousands were admitted as the war ran its course, ever reacted in the same way.

From time to time Saddam too visited the front. But we never knew whether he actually got there or not. Like the rest of his family he was incredibly superstitious. A black cat crossing the road might result in him ordering the motorcade to return to Baghdad. Even a plastic bag blowing across the road might be considered a bad omen and cause a turnaround.

He constantly changed cars. Sometimes he would sit in the rear car, sometimes in the middle of the convoy. Sometimes he might be picked up by a helicopter halfway and taken to his destination.

At the front he never remained in the same place for long. Two different commando centres visited by him one night were bombed immediately after he had left them.

Usually Sabah Merza accompanied him to the theatres of war. Merza was head of his team of bodyguards and as a diversion from the daily grind he used to take off for a few hours to volunteer his expertise to the special death squadrons formed to stop and shoot soldiers who were retreating without permission, or deserters.

Saddam also visited field hospitals and wounded soldiers but had little time for the doctors who fought night and day, year in and year out, to save the life and limbs of war victims. He actually despised the medical profession, as did his three half-brothers Watban, Sabaawi and Barzan.

I suspect his dislike stems from the time in 1959, after the unsuccessful coup against Abdul Karim Kassem, when he himself was forced to remove a bullet from his leg with a razor blade.

'Doctors are utterly obsessed with their own importance, and compete with each other as to who can make most money,' I remember the President saying during one of our early, confidential conversations. 'And they're dishonest,' he continued. 'If they're friendly it's just to exploit you. If you're an important person with a high-ranking job and power, they'll use that as a bridge to make more money.'

One morning he arrived at the al-Karkh hospital in Baghdad, a quarter of an hour before the shift change. He asked the night staff to give him a list of the names of the incoming shift. Anyone who turned up late, be it only by five minutes, was told not to show themselves at the hospital for the next year. In all six or seven of my colleagues were affected. Most of them had legitimate reasons for being late: they were working at other Baghdad hospitals; to add insult to injury, the list given by the night staff was incorrect. They wrote to the President and explained the misunderstanding, but to no avail. That was Saddam. If he had made up his mind nothing would change it; whether it was right or wrong.

One of the senior registrars never forgot that day. He came up to the President in his white coat with the stethoscope dangling carelessly round his neck. If there was something Saddam hated it was sloppy behaviour. But it got worse. The young doctor greeted the President with the word 'Ustath'. Directly translated this means 'professor': teachers at all levels throughout the educational system are called 'Ustath' by pupils and students. But the word also expresses respect – ministers and party bigwigs are called 'Ustath' when addressed.

'Did you call me "Ustath" or "Sir"?' Saddam asked.

'I apologise, sir, I thought I had used the correct term.'

The young doctor was imprisoned for six months that very day.

In the middle of the eight-year war a young bride was killed on her wedding night during an Iranian attack in Mandili in Eastern Iraq: she had lost both arms and legs. She was discovered with her husband, the groom, who was also dead.

Saddam announced a competition amongst the republic's artists to reproduce the tragedy, and the mode of expression was to be purely figurative. The young woman was to be painted wearing her wedding-dress and without arms and legs. Future generations were to be left in no doubt about Iranian cruelty.

Night after night the various contributions to Saddam's competition were shown on Iraqi TV; the President was not pleased with any of them, something he made abundantly clear on screen. I was exhibiting at the al-Riwaq gallery during the competition. One of the pictures was called 'The Martyr': a desert landscape and a sky. Two feet protruded from the sand. They were cut off at the ankle and a little plant with a few green shoots had grown up between them. Two hands stood out against the blue sky. They were cut off at the wrist and the fingers were spread out. It looked like a human in the desert, stretching its arms to the sky, bodyless.

General Yassin was still his brother-in-law's secretary. The article about his commercial interest in Iraq's ancient monuments had not yet been published. He dropped in at the exhibition one day. He looked at 'The Martyr' and phoned me two days later saying the President wanted to see me.

The President was in a meeting with two generals back from the front and I kicked my heels in Yassin's office for an hour or so before he arrived. He apologised for the delay and then began to examine the painting. He remained standing in front of it for a long time.

'This is a strong and expressive work of art,' he said. 'You have left out the body and kept what the young bride lost.'

I tried to interrupt him to say that I had painted it long before the bride was killed and the competition announced but never got a chance.

'This is obvious, there is no need for an explanation,' he said.

I asked to be allowed to speak. I wanted to say something about the war and its martyrs. When Saddam nodded I said that what we see does not necessarily reflect reality. And what humans say is not necessarily true. 'What is important is that we understand what we neither see nor hear.'

I dared go no further in my careful attempt to tell him that what his generals said about the war's progress probably bore no relation to the reality I experienced every day at the hospital in my conversations with victims of the bloodbath.

'A martyr is someone who stands firm for what he or she believes in and who sacrifices himself for others. The martyr reaches up to heaven,' I said.

Saddam was silent and I did not think he was listening. But as I was leaving he looked straight at me. 'In the heat of war there's no time to count the killed and wounded. We have to concentrate on a single goal: to beat the enemy and emerge victorious. And when we have reached the goal and the victory is ours we can count our losses and look after the wounded in the best possible way.' Then he went back in to his generals.

General Yassin saw me out. When we said goodbye one of Saddam's bodyguards came running with a small packet: a cheap watch with a gilded picture of Saddam on the dial. He kept 'The Martyr'.

Someone, however, had to count the dead whilst the war raged on. In the border areas close to the Iranian town of al-Ebsaiteen the battle raged back and forth at the turn of the year 1983/84. A solder was admitted to al-Wasiti from this sector; his left ear had been completely torn off. I asked him how it happened; he explained that the soldiers and officers in his unit had been ambushed, surrounded and mown down indiscriminately.

'Even when we surrendered the Iranians continued to shoot.'

It was dark, three o'clock at night. He had feigned death and hidden under two of his dead comrades. The Iranian soldiers, who were expecting an Iraqi counter-attack, started to withdraw. One stayed behind. He had a torch in one hand and a knife in the other. A small bag hung from his belt.

'I saw him shining his torch and using his knife on one fallen soldier after the other. He stuffed the ears into his little bag.' One ear from every Iraqi corpse so they knew exactly how many had been killed in the successful ambush.

'Then he cut the ears off my two comrades. He was unaware that I was alive when he started on me. It was dark and he was obviously in a great hurry.'

One of my cousins was called out as a reservist and sent to work in the mortuary at the military hospital al-Rashid in Baghdad. Here dead soldiers and officers from the long and bloody front line came for their final rest. They arrived in lorries, usually shot to bits, heads, arms and legs in one tangled heap. It was my cousin's job to identify the victims, put them into coffins and deliver them to their families. But it wasn't all that simple. When a Muslim is buried the body is supposed to be whole. But to match body to head and get the remaining parts to fit was a time-consuming puzzle under great pressure.

'We did what we could before nailing down the lids. But sometimes the corpses had two right arms or two left legs. There was just too much to do before the next lorry unloaded its cargo.'

One day he asked me if I could pull some strings and get him sent off to the front, if necessary to the area where the fighting was heaviest. It was all too much for him. I got him transferred to a less depressing section at another military hospital. But he never really recovered and suffered serious mental problems when the war was over.

The victims, the martyrs, went to their place of burial in coffins draped in the Iraqi flag. In Baghdad, Basra, Nasiriya, Karbala, Hilla, Samarra, Tikrit, Mosul and all the other towns and villages in Iraq they were a daily sight. In nearly every quarter of every town relatives had erected tents of mourning so that family, both close and distant, neighbours and friends could come to express their sympathy and show their respect. Not a street was without the black pieces of cloth stretched along the house walls with the names of the families' fallen sons written in white letters.

I was driving through Baghdad one day with my wife and daughter. We got stuck behind two cars, both with coffins on the roofs. My daughter looked at them and said she wished she too were dead. 'I can't bear seeing this every day,' she said.

My wife started to cry. 'How can she think like that? She's only six!'

At the same moment a low-flying Iranian rocket skimmed the air above us. It struck something near the al-Rashid hotel. The blast from the explosion made the car shake.

In May 1985 a team from Iraqi TV arrived to interview me about my work as a painter and about surgical progress made at al-Wasiti during the treatment of the thousands of badly wounded men from the battlefields. The woman who interviewed me was Iraq's best-known TV personality and the recordings were made in my studio.

I had just painted a man fighting with a large bird and trying to stop it from biting his face. He was holding the bird by its wings over his head. The painting was red and black.

'What's the bird doing?' she asked.

I explained that the bird symbolised man's struggle with destiny. 'And destiny always gets the upper hand. The man cannot ward off the bird for ever.'

'So he's the loser?' said the interviewer.

'Yes, he loses when he dies, but life goes on. That's what makes life what it is.'

'You're not exactly optimistic.'

'There is always some bitterness in truth, whether we like it or not,' I said and reminded her of the great American boxer Muhammad Ali who was asked whether he still considered himself the 'world's fastest and strongest'. 'I have discovered that time is the fastest and strongest,' said the heavyweight champion.

I added that only time can teach us the realities of life, or at least some of them. 'When we are young, strong, rich and powerful we forget how fragile and weak and vulnerable we really are. That is mankind's tragedy.'

The interviewer instructed the photographer to pan over some of the other paintings in the studio. I was about to give another exhibition and there were a lot of them.

'When I ask people they say that your paintings depress them.'

'It's not my job to make people laugh or feel happy by covering up life's realities.'

'Do you read poetry? Can you recite one?' was the next question.

I answered that I always carried around a poem by the great Iraqi poet al-Mutanabbi, who died a thousand years ago. It suited my temperament. 'Humans find nothing more difficult than to befriend an enemy.'

Then it all went wrong.

'You're a plastic surgeon and carry out hair transplants. But what about you, you don't have a great deal of hair yourself?'

'I've never found that a problem. To be honest, I never think about it.'

'But you look at yourself in the mirror every day?'

'Yes, but only to shave. Not to admire myself, if that's what you think.'

The next morning the President's secretary phoned me. 'He thought it was a super interview and would like to see you.'

When I got to the ante-room I was told that Saddam had watched the programme from start to finish, something he rarely does. 'But he was pretty damn furious when the interviewer asked about the hair transplants and your lack of hair.'

I later discovered that the President had demanded retribution. The interviewer was taken off the air for six months.

Towards the end of 1987 one of Saddam's generals phoned and asked if I could come to the Republican Palace and look at his son who had been unfortunate enough to shoot his own foot with a Kalashnikov. By mistake I was ushered into the President's antechamber. Saddam was on his way out and apologised for the incorrect directions given to the bodyguards. 'But come into my office and have a cup of tea,' he said.

We talked about the war and the President asked whether there were many wounded at al-Wasiti.

I said that compared to some of the military hospitals in Baghdad we did not have a very large number, but that the worst cases came to us.

He wanted to know if many died amongst the soldiers and officers brought in. I answered that patients were rarely sent to us from the front unless there was a good chance they would survive the transport. 'Some, but not many, die en route.'

Saddam was quiet, then he said, 'It's sad that so many young men have to suffer, but there was no other way. We were forced to attack Iran. History would have judged us for ever if we had not gone to war.'

I dared not contradict him.

Very few dared speak up against the President, even face to face. Fatiq al-Safi, whom I had come to appreciate as a good friend, was one of them, however. He is a landowner and was a member of the Baath Party when the movement took root in Iraq in the fifties. He followed Saddam through the desert to Syria when he had to flee after the unsuccessful attempt to assassinate President Abdul Karim Kassem in Baghdad in 1959. The flight took a week. They hid during the day and walked or rode donkeys at night. Bedouins helped them on the way. When the Baath Party came to power Saddam offered him a string of ministerial posts. But al-Safi always refused. He wanted an Iraqi democracy, not an ever more despotic tribe- and family-oriented dynasty centred on the President's palaces along the Tigris.

But Saddam liked to talk to his old friend. Every Thursday over many years he had dinner with him in his home in the Mansour district of Baghdad.

'I always told him that the best solution for Iraq would be free elections and that the Iraqis be given democratic rights and the opportunity to practise them.' Initially Saddam was prepared to listen and discuss such ideas. 'But gradually I noticed he was beginning to look ill at ease when I raised this or other political matters.'

It came to a head one summer's evening in 1987 when the President arrived from an annual general meeting of the Iraqi

Law Association. After his speech judges and barristers joined in deafening and protracted applause. When the soup was served for dinner a comprehensive report from the session appeared on Iraqi TV evening news.

'Look,' said Saddam, 'do you think I asked them to applaud me? They reacted spontaneously, no one forced them.'

Al-Safi laughed. 'Honestly, do you really think so?'

'Yes.'

'In that case you're wrong. They are liars and hypocrites to a man.'

Saddam got up, threw the spoon down on the table and stormed out of the house. He broke off all contact with his old friend and never went to dinner again.

During the summer of 1988 it became clear that the CIA predictions from Voice of America when Khomeini's bombs dropped over Baghdad in 1980 had come true. No one would win the war. In spite of the Iranian army gaining certain advantages after the Iraqi invasion forces were pushed back over the border in 1982, Khomeini never succeeded in a decisive counter-offensive which led to Iraqi defeat and Saddam's fall.

Thanks to American help on the military espionage front, and the extensive weapons supplies from France and the Soviet Union, it was now Iraq who had a small edge, but no more. Both Saddam and Khomeini saw the writing on the wall.

The guns fell silent on 8 August. Saddam declared the war won but the border between Iran and Iraq remained exactly where it had been before the senseless bloodbath began – even in Shatt al-Arab where the shipping lane was as good as impassable owing to bombed-out and sunken wrecks.

Boys having fun. Uday and his friend Zafer Muhammad Jaber (right) on a beach holiday. (Photo courtesy Zafer Muhammad Jaber)

CHAPTER 6

Cease Fire

The war against Iran ends.
Saddam loses his valet.

A sigh of relief could be heard all over the Middle East when hostilities between Iraq and Iran finally came to an end in August 1988. Hosni Mubarak sent his wife Suzanne to Baghdad to congratulate Saddam. The two presidential wives, Egypt's and Iraq's, were bosom friends. They both stayed in one of the official residences close to the Republican Palace for the duration of the visit.

Close to the official residence – there were ten of them in all – on an idyllic island, where a small detour of the river Tigris formed a lagoon inside the river bank, was the 'wedding garden' al-Aras, laid out with lawns and trees. A bridge led over to the park which was encircled by about forty guesthouses. These could be hired for large festive occasions. A separate hall had been earmarked for wedding ceremonies.

Six additional guesthouses had been constructed on the far side of al-Aras. They were considerably more luxurious, each with an outdoor swimming pool, and were reserved for the President and his family, his closest collaborators, ministers and the Baath Party hierarchy, the so-called Revolutionary Command Council. Outside one of them, on an evening when Sajida Hussein and Suzanne Mubarak were in bed in the official residence just a few hundred yards away, was a large gathering. The atmosphere was highly unstable and growing ever more so. Kamel Hanna was throwing a birthday party for one of his family and alcohol was flowing freely among the approximately fifty guests.

Hanna was Saddam's Christian valet. He was not part of the presidential family, nor did he come from Tikrit, but no one could have been more loyal. He handled all the day-to-day chores, from dressing Saddam to cooking and organising his large staff of servants. The President valued Hanna enormously: the valet was one of the few he really could rely on. And this trust and respect were mutual.

Uday, Saddam's son, lived close to the Republican Palace: the twenty-four year old had settled permanently in one of the official residences. This evening, as usual, he was relaxing with a bottle of vodka and watching television with his friend Zafer Muhammad Jaber, when they were disturbed by the sound of shooting from al-Aras. A bodyguard was sent over to investigate and returned with the news that Kamel Hanna's party was out of control. Kalashnikovs had appeared from somewhere and there was now indiscriminate shooting going on, to the sheer delight of host and guests, who were having a terrific time in the increasingly boozy atmosphere.

'Get over there and tell them to stop,' Uday said. 'They'll wake my mother and Suzanne Mubarak!'

The bodyguard returned to the wedding garden and delivered the message but the shooting continued.

Zafer Muhammad Jaber and Uday were the same age and had known each other since sixth form. Zafer had become Uday's personal secretary and now the two of them, accompanied by a couple of bodyguards, threw themselves into a car and drove over to Kamel Hanna to try to make him see reason and stop the loud music and gunfire.

Uday was wearing a black dishdasha, the traditional tunic worn by Arab men all over the Middle East. On the way out he grabbed a walking stick made of ivory, lashed around with bamboo. The handle was shaped like a snake's head. The snake's mouth was open, its huge fangs visible.

'Uday thought the walking stick suited the dishdasha,' Jaber told me later. 'It gave him dignity, like a sheikh in one of the Gulf States.'

The President's son had 150 walking sticks of varying quality and design to choose from. The art of restraint was unknown to him. If there was something he liked, one was never enough. In his uncle Watban's house he saw a water-pipe for smoking that took his fancy. A few weeks later a large shipment arrived from India.

'They were as tall as doors.'

It was the same with watches, jewels and rings, money, women and luxury cars. Uday could never get enough. In a garage near the Republican Palace more than a hundred BMW, Lexus, Mercedes, Ferrari and Rolls Royce cars were parked. Yet more were en route to Baghdad even as he was making his way over to Kamel Hanna with Jaber and the bodyguards.

The lawns and trees of al-Aras were an oasis in the increasingly dismal Iraqi landscape. The gaping wounds of war were evident everywhere. There were few beggars on the Baghdad streets before 1980; now every corner teemed with them. The treasury presses had been working overtime to finance the war and the result was galloping inflation, destroying peoples' standard of living. Before the war an Iraqi dinar was worth three American dollars. Now the rate of exchange was turned upside down: one thousand dinars was worth one dollar, but our salaries, in dinars, had remained static.

Civil servants were no longer able to support their families and they started to demand bribes to handle the applications and cases they were employed to manage. Before long every office, directorate and department in Iraq was permeated with corruption from top to bottom. Senior army officers had started the rot. During the war many of them accepted bribes to transfer soldiers from the most bloody theatres of war to others less dangerous. Some commandeered whole platoons to build their houses and places in the country. Respect for the Iraqi army, high before Saddam chose to attack Khomeini's Islamic regime to the east, was in free fall.

An appalling number of families had lost a father or brother and therefore no longer had a breadwinner to provide for the many mouths. Some turned to prostitution to make ends meet,

others to robbery and crime. Yet the most tragic scar left by the
senseless war was the multitudes of handicapped. About 150,000
young Iraqis were killed in the course of the war's eight years,
and, in addition, 750,000 were wounded. A horrifying number
were maimed for life, physically and psychologically.

Iraq was not at all prepared to care for these soldiers. A single
hospital, Ibn al-Kuf, built with Danish money, specialised in reha-
bilitating war victims with serious paralysis. Exhausted parents
and wives would arrive with their disabled sons and husbands at
night. Under the cover of darkness they would leave them in the
garden outside the rehabilitation centre where they were found by
the hospital staff the next morning. Usually not much could be
done for them. The Danish doctors and physiotherapists were
already overworked.

Even worse was the treatment available to the many thousands of soldiers who suffered psychological problems following
the horrors they had experienced on the battlefield. It quite
simply did not exist. In Iraq, as elsewhere in the Middle East,
there is little openness with regard to mental health problems.
Psychiatric patients are regarded with disdain and families try
hard to cover up what is considered shameful. Now, in every
town, village and neighbourhood, young men with serious problems roved around, lost. To me, as a doctor, it was an awful sight.

At Kamel Hanna's increasingly wild party on al-Aras few were
worrying about the troubled state of Iraq. When Uday turned up
with his ivory walking stick, however, there was suddenly dead
silence. The shooting, dancing and music stopped instantly.

Hanna was obviously the worse for drink and needed help to
stand up and greet Uday.

'You should be ashamed of yourself,' said Uday. 'I sent over a
bodyguard to ask you to calm down, but you've just ignored him.
Tah Hazak! [May all the world's ill fortunes strike you!] Adab Siz!
[You're an immoral worm!]'

'This is a private party,' Hanna answered. 'You're always
poking your nose into everything. Can't you at least leave us alone
tonight?'

Uday lifted the ivory walking stick. 'You're a dog. How dare you answer back like that?' Then he whacked Hanna over the head. The valet hit the ground.

'I'll tell my father about you,' Uday said, before leaving with Jaber and the two bodyguards. The party was over. All four of them thought it was the whisky that had caused Hanna to fall over, and that with help from his friends he would be up on his feet again after they left.

Saddam phoned his son early next morning. Uday was surprised; it was most unusual for the President to contact him thus. He started to tell his father about Kamel Hanna and the night's events, but was quickly interrupted.

'You have killed him,' Saddam said. His voice was icy. 'Give yourself up to the police and accept your punishment.'

On learning that Uday had beaten Kamel Hanna to death the President had completely lost control. 'I'll throttle him with my own hands,' he had screamed at his wife Sajida. She had been informed about what had happened and hurried home from the official residence where she had spent the night with the Egyptian President's wife. Saddam's raging reaction frightened her. In desperation she phoned her brother-in-law, Barzan, and told him what Saddam intended.

'Can you come over immediately and calm him down?'

When his half-brother arrived at the presidential palace Saddam was still incandescent with fury.

'I have no doubt that if Uday had been anywhere near him, he would have killed him on the spot,' Barzan told me later. 'I have never seen him so raging mad. He was beside himself.'

The President eventually calmed down and Barzan was able to reason with him. 'Listen, use your head. Killing your son won't bring Kamel Hanna back. You'll just lose more. It's better to take him to court and let them decide.'

'I'll take him to court,' Saddam said.

Jaber – who was still with his friend – noticed that Uday was devastated when he realised what he had done. Uday grabbed a bottle of tranquillisers and tossed them down his throat. When the pills started to take effect he collapsed and his bodyguards took him to Bin-Sina, the private hospital of the presidential family. Originally a private clinic it had been modernised and extended after the Baath Party came to power in 1968. The hospital had twenty beds, two operating theatres and was relatively well equipped, even by Western standards. Bin-Sina had a large staff of highly qualified doctors and nurses on call at any time for the President, his family and the regime's top echelon. Normally one surgeon and one internal specialist would be on duty to care for a steady flow of patients; those who could gain admission to the exclusive hospital included the wives, children, relatives and mistresses of the elite and they were not small in number.

Uday's stomach was pumped while there was still some life in him.

I was not on duty the day the President's son was admitted to Bin-Sina. My colleagues informed me some days later that he had attempted suicide but had recovered. His friend, Jaber, was later able to give me a blow-by-blow description of what happened before, during and after the attack on Kamel Hanna.

Uday was kept under observation overnight at Bin-Sina. He then returned to the official residence where he had settled. He dismissed his bodyguards and servants and barricaded the house with sandbags. When some of Saddam's bodyguards came to fetch him he shot at their car with a Kalashnikov. They retreated and informed the President that his son's mental state was still slightly precarious.

He was left alone for a few days. Then his mother and younger brother Qusay came to reason with him. They arrived alone without bodyguards and spent a considerable time persuading him to surrender.

Neither Uday nor Jaber was arrested immediately. Saddam wished to get to the bottom of the delicate affair before taking court action. The air was thick with rumours, eagerly seized upon by Uday's opponents in the continuous cat-and-dog fight between family members about who should fill the most important and prestigious positions below the President himself.

Hussein Kamel al-Majid, Saddam's son-in-law, was an energetic stirrer in these troubled waters.

Hussein Kamel was the nephew of Ali Hassan al-Majid, who was Saddam's cousin. Hussein occupied the important post of

Minister for Military and Industrial Development, responsible for Iraq's weapons-development programme. He was Saddam's favourite. Marriage to the President's daughter, Raghad, was clear evidence of that.

His brother Saddam Kamel al-Majid also enjoyed the President's confidence. To him befell Rana, Raghad's sister. He had risen to the post of most trusted bodyguard. He played the part of Saddam in *The Long Day*, a six-hour film about the President's life, which was shown on Iraqi TV and cinemas around the country night after night, year after year. The film's director was Terence Young, responsible for three James Bond films and he himself now also part of Baghdad history.

The marriages between Hussein and Saddam Kamel and the President's two daughters were not well received by Saddam's three half-brothers, Sabaawi, Barzan and Watban. The marriage between Raghad and Hussein Kamel in the autumn of 1983 caused particular bad feeling. The half-brothers had wanted Sabaawi's son, Yasser, for Raghad, to strengthen the blood ties between the two branches of the family. But Saddam said no, which was meant as a hint, a strong hint, to Barzan.

The middle half-brother had taken over as head of the dreaded Iraqi intelligence service, Mukhabarat, in 1980, and he took his duties very seriously. The organisation's operations and network of informers extended abroad as well as all over Iraq. Wholesale suppression of Iraqis who might be, or might be thought to be, in opposition to Saddam and the regime was introduced. Privately Barzan boasted to me that the intelligence service had agents and informers all over the world and that it had never been as efficient as during the years Saddam allowed him to run it.

'Not even an Iraqi sitting in a café in a remote part of Japan would feel safe if he spoke disparagingly of Saddam and our regime,' he said.

At primary schools, teachers would ask pupils whether their parents watched television during the President's broadcasts. If the answer was no the fathers risked being summoned by the secret police, which could have dire consequences.

As head of Mukhabarat Barzan was considered the second

most powerful man in Iraq. That stuck in the throat of Uday, Qusay, Hussein Kamel and his uncle Ali Hassan al-Majid. They viewed his operations with increasing envy and suspicion and became more and more frustrated at having fallen behind in the competition for the President's favour. Led by Hussein Kamel they started to question Barzan's motives and initiated a whispering campaign. The President must be made aware! The mighty half-brother might nurture ambitions of taking over power in Iraq.

Little by little Saddam became convinced that they were right and that the head of Mukhabarat posed a threat. When he ignored his half-brother's plea and wedded his daughter Raghad to Hussein Kamel, Barzan got the message. He was no longer in favour.

'I resigned on that very day. When I left I threw the keys down on the table in fury,' he told me. One of my paintings was hanging in his office, together with the compulsory one of Saddam. 'I was so angry I forgot to take the picture home with me. I still regret that.'

With Barzan kicked into touch Uday was next in line. But Hussein Kamel was still stirring energetically and threw himself into investigating what had really happened on the fateful night when Kamel Hanna was killed.

It was unfortunate for the President's elder son that Kamel Hanna died. The twenty-four-year-old was a rising star in Saddam's power structure. Four years earlier he had been appointed 'Youth Supervisor' and had established his own newspaper, *The Sporting Baathist*. This mouthpiece enabled him to have a go at ministers and other prominent persons of authority against whom he held a grudge, or who had got in his way. The attacks appeared on the front page, and scathing reports about their incompetence were repeated in further columns inside the paper.

Youths were rounded up in the streets and made to march beneath banners proclaiming 'Uday is our pride' and 'Uday is our hope'.

He also founded a new football club, al-Rashid. Iraq's best

football players quickly realised they had to request a transfer to the new club. The new club paid higher fees, the tracksuits were new, so were the football boots and there was even roast lamb for dinner now and again. But above all, Uday made sure none of them was sent to the front. All players were transferred to a special unit in the Republican Guard stationed in Baghdad.

The established clubs' fans fumed about this daylight robbery of their best players. Iraqis are football mad and many still remember the first match between Uday's new team and the capital's great favourite, Nadi al-Talabah, the Students' Club, at the People's Stadium in Baghdad one winter's evening at the beginning of 1985.

The football and athletics arena was built in 1966 with funds donated from the charitable trust set up by the Armenian oil baron Calouste Gulbenkian. Sixty thousand spectators were crammed into the People's Stadium when the whistle blew for kick-off. Fifty-nine thousand were fans of the Students' Club. The remaining thousand were paid to cheer for al-Rashid. The President's son had the commentator in his pocket. Following a small reward and a clear reminder of where his loyalties lay, the commentator used his loudspeaker enthusiastically to encourage the newcomers to crush the opposition.

Trouble broke out on the terraces and stones were thrown at the players who had betrayed the Students' Club and gone over to Uday. A large police force was called out to stop the stone-throwers and the riots which were brewing.

Worst affected was the referee. Every time he awarded a free kick against al-Rashid he glanced up at the owners' stand to gauge Uday's reaction.

The Students' Club were leading by one-nil for most of the match. But, hoping at least to save his life, the referee awarded al-Rashid a penalty kick in the very last minute of play. No one could see that the Students' Club players had committed any faults but they all understood that the poor referee had to do something.

The game ended in a draw.

Towards the end of 1985 Uday's Supervision of Youth was merged with Iraq's National Olympic Committee. Karim al-Mullah was the new boss, but only for a few months. Before long Uday donned the Olympic yellow jersey. All athletics associations, comprising millions of members, were absorbed within the Olympic rings. The Committee was a veritable springboard to more power and ever more important jobs for Uday. But now one moment of madness on al-Aras had spoilt it all.

Saddam searched frantically for an explanation and solution to the situation. Two days after Kamel Hanna's death Jaber and about fifty of Uday's other friends were asked to come to a joint interrogation at the Republican Palace. The President wanted to know if his son was keeping bad company and whether that was why he was experiencing such problems.

A printed questionnaire awaited the young men. The in-laws Hussein and Saddam Kamel made sure everyone completed them. General Arshed Yassin, the President's brother-in-law and private secretary, was also there, as was Qusay. Saddam himself sat at a glass table at the end of the hall, scrutinising everyone's face, one by one, obviously still hopping mad and cursing his valet's unkind fate.

'How did you meet Uday?' was the first question.

Most of them, like Jaber, had met him at primary school, secondary school or at university. Some had met him because they lived in the same neighbourhood and got talking. Many had met him at Baghdad's nightclubs. They all had one thing in common: they'd found it easy and rather exciting to befriend him; it was, however, more complicated to walk away from that friendship. They were his court and it was quite simply their duty to please him with their presence whenever it suited him, not them. Every afternoon he would instruct his bodyguards as to whom he wanted to spend the evening with. They were contacted and told where to meet; no one dared refuse.

'That would have been unthinkable. He could have thought up any number of dreaded punishments if any of us tried to avoid him.'

Abdul Wahab was someone who experienced the extremes of Uday's cruelty. He was at one time a close friend of Uday. It is not quite clear why he fell into disgrace but Jaber remembers that he was asked to come to a country property outside Baghdad where there was an empty swimming pool. The property was used to train guard dogs. Uday ordered Wahab down into the empty pool. On command from the trainer two Alsatians jumped in and started attacking him.

Wahab survived but had been severely savaged by the time Uday asked the trainer to blow the whistle and stop the punishment. Next day Uday turned up at the hospital to ask how he was.

Wahab smiled and said not too bad.

Uday would decide how much liquor they should drink, for example, and how quickly it should be gulped down. He mixed the drinks; some might get two thirds whisky and one third soda, others glasses filled with neat vodka. But it all had to go down and if anyone refused or tried to sneak away, the liquor would be forced into them.

It goes without saying that the friends dreaded the summons. According to Jaber, Uday became especially unpredictable during the vodka-drinking sessions in the evening. If either al-Rashid or the Iraqi national team lost important matches things could turn especially unpleasant. He had got hold of an electric rod of the type the security service torturers used to prod their victims during interrogations. He used to wave it around and poke people at random. To blow off steam he often fiddled with his shotgun which he then fired at his friends.

'To be sure, the shot had been removed from the cartridge, but the small plastic disc that separated the shot from the powder was still in the cartridge case. When he fired those plastic discs would hit us and they hurt and made horrible marks on the skin.'

Like his father and the rest of the family he was also exceedingly superstitious.

'If Iraq had won at football and we had been sitting on a sofa watching the match, he'd insist that we came back and sat in the same place on the same sofa next time the team played.'

From time to time Uday demanded that boxing matches were arranged with himself as umpire in the ring. Two of the friends present were told to don gloves and set to; the match was never over until one or the other was beaten to a pulp or unconscious or both and had to be taken to hospital.

'In the end we'd mimic a knock-out and feign unconsciousness.'

The questionnaire had without doubt been drawn up by Hussein Kamel. He had been casting around, asking repeatedly and inquisitively about Uday and his killing of Kamel Hanna. He had learnt a lot about his brother-in-law.

'How many times has he imprisoned you?' was one of the questions the fifty young men had to answer, shaking and fearing the worst as the President glared at them.

Saddam's personal bodyguards were stationed in a small military compound, al-Harithiya, near the HQ of the intelligence service in al-Nosour in the centre of Baghdad. Inside the compound Hussein Kamel had discovered six subterranean concrete cells which Uday had had constructed in secret and where he imprisoned friends with whom he was displeased. The cells were only one and a half metres high; their breadth and width about the same. A narrow crack in the concrete let in air and light. It was impossible to lie down or stand but you could sit down and stretch out your legs.

Jaber ended up in one of these cells following a late-night party where one of the more liberal female participants had, when drunk, poured a glass of spirits over him. He'd told her to pull herself together – and that was enough. She complained to Uday who got his bodyguards to remove him for a couple of days' punishment in al-Harithiya. He was still there when yet another of Uday's friends arrived: he'd dented a car Uday had lent him. Into the dungeon with him!

More details were investigated. Amongst other things Uday had fallen madly in love with an engineering student at Baghdad University. She was unusually beautiful and the President's son was meeting her clandestinely. The relationship between them had become intense and serious; her family, having caught a whiff of the liaison, were concerned. Now Saddam, too, was told about the blossoming love affair.

'Do you know anything about the love affair between the two?' was the question.

Of course they did. Uday had never denied his passionate preoccupation with her.

'How much alcohol does he drink?' 'How much and what sort of alcohol does he give you?' 'Does he use drugs?'

The friends sweated and answered as if this were a final university exam.

Hussein Kamel collected the completed questionnaires and gave them to Saddam, who was no longer able to contain himself. 'Uday is finished,' he shouted, banging his right hand down on the glass table-top so hard that it broke into a thousand pieces. Blood gushed everywhere.

The cut to the back of his hand was not deep, however. It needed only two stitches when he arrived at Bin-Sina following the questioning of his son's large and, in some cases, unwilling circle of friends at the Republican Palace.

Every one of the fifty was told no longer to associate with Uday. They signed a declaration to that effect, which was also collected. At the same time Saddam sent a bodyguard to the beautiful engineering student's father. He was told to put a stop to his daughter's secret meetings with the President's son. Saddam and Saddam alone would decide whom Uday should marry.

The next day Uday was stripped of all his official duties and appointments. The Fifth Army Corps operated a prison within the precincts of the Republican Palace and here cells were prepared for Uday and Jaber – or at least that was what Saddam was told. What Saddam did not realise was that the prison governor was related to Uday on his mother's side. Six soldiers were moved from their room in one of the barracks and Uday and Jaber moved in.

There they sat for fourteen days. Uday was depressed and testy all the time. Jaber tried to initiate conversations but never succeeded: Uday never spoke a word to his friend all the time they were in that room.

One day panic swept through the compound. Saddam was about to arrive on an unannounced visit. Uday and Jaber were each moved to a cell with all possible speed, but moved back after a couple of hours. False alarm!

In the meantime a special prison was being prepared for Uday.

The President owned a hilltop house in the Radwaniya neighbourhood of Baghdad. On the slope below the house were some old caves. One of them was transformed into a sort of cell and Uday was moved there.

One night Saddam slept outside his cell, another night Sajida slept inside the cell. They wanted to demonstrate that Uday was still their son. He was released after forty-six days, and his friend, who continued to serve his comfortable sentence with the Fifth Army Corps in the Republican Palace, was released two days later.

It was of course impossible to hide from the public that Uday had killed Kamel Hanna. Rumours spread like wildfire all over Iraq. Saddam therefore grabbed the bull by the horns and invited the valet's relatives and nearest family to the Republican Palace, complete with TV coverage of the reconciliation. It followed a well-established and traditional pattern in the family- and tribe-oriented Iraqi society.

'The problem which has arisen between our families has been solved amicably,' said the President. Thereafter Kamel Hanna's family begged him to show his oldest son mercy.

Two weeks after his release Uday was ordered by his father to Geneva where his uncle Barzan had been appointed Iraqi ambassador to the United Nations. The uncle was instructed to look after his nephew. A Boeing 727, belonging to Iraqi Airways, was ready to fly him from Baghdad to Switzerland.

Uday was appointed First Secretary to the Iraqi UN delegation, but contributed zero diplomatic effort on behalf of his uncle or his country. He never showed up for work and only survived forty days before disappearing to Paris to the great relief of the police authorities in Geneva. They were fed up with his excesses at the town's bars and nightclubs and seedier establishments. From Paris Uday travelled to Istanbul. He turned up at Baghdad airport after three months abroad, without actually having been given the green light to return.

One of his first acts on his return to Baghdad was to appoint one of Kamel Hanna's nephews to his staff.

Saddam never committed his son for trial. Two judges were given the task of investigating the case and pronouncing the sentence, but their work was never completed. The President's own investigations uncovered seedy sides to Kamel Hanna's character. The valet had used his position to appropriate and fit out one of the six luxurious guesthouses on al-Aras and had added an indoor swimming pool in addition to the outdoor one.

Uday told Jaber that it hurt Saddam to the quick to think that he had seduced Saddam's own housemaids, waitresses and housekeepers in this little love nest.

Saddam on a visit to Kuwait, October 1990. One month earlier he
had dismissed his Chief of Staff General Nizar al-Khazraji who had
warned him about the consequences of leaving Iraqi troops in the
sheikhdom for any length of time.

CHAPTER 7

Desert Storm

Iraq loses the Gulf War.
Saddam's little finger bothers him

I was having supper with my wife, three sons and daughter on 1 February 1991; the bombs were falling and the rockets raining down over Baghdad. As usual the electricity had gone off and there was one candle on the table. We were gathered in a room in the centre of the house. We would either survive the night, or, if our time was up, the family would be wiped out, all together.

It would be best like that, we thought, like so many other families who huddled together in terror.

The piercing metallic sound of the bombers overhead sounded to us like a deafening dentist's drill. Then the explosions followed, the windows shattered, our house shook and the sirens told us that ambulances were on their way to collect the dead and dying.

The massive air attacks had started fourteen days earlier as an overture to Operation Desert Storm, the world's answer to Iraq's invasion of Kuwait the previous August. The time had come to throw Saddam's soldiers out, but the first priority was to bomb to smithereens the dictator's military HQ, command centre and airports, government offices, communications centres, roads, bridges and power stations.

That evening my time spent with the family was rudely interrupted. At half past ten two of Saddam bodyguards banged on the door. They were with a chauffeur and appeared nervous and flustered; they asked me to come with them to Bin-Sina immediately.

We drove through Baghdad's blacked-out streets at a furious pace. Now and again the whole area lit up when a bomb or missile struck close by. I was sure the journey would end in catastrophe and thanked my Maker when we arrived safely.

The hospital was heaving with soldiers, inside and out. As I arrived a missile hit the offices of the President's security service near the Republican Palace by the Tigris. The large brick building was situated a mere couple of hundred yards from Bin-Sina. The explosion was so massive that many of the windows on that side of the hospital were blown in.

Saddam was lying in the operating theatre on the first floor. He wore a uniform and his face was not very pretty.

'I asked them to wait for you to come,' he said. The President was pale and bloody but calm and composed. Apparently his car had collided with another car at a crossroads. The left side of his face was especially affected. He was bleeding profusely from a cut in his forehead and a deep cut under his eye, right through to the cheekbone. The cut in his chin was even deeper.

He had also just about lost the tip of his little finger. It was attached only by a thin strip of skin and dangled loosely. The nail had been lost.

I cleaned the wounds, took X-rays of his head and hand and started to patch him together using local anaesthetic. I attached the tip of the little finger, sewed it on and propped it up. Then I secured it with a bandage.

'Can you avoid bandaging my face?' he asked.

I answered in the affirmative and said I could use tiny stitches under the top layer of skin and no one would be the wiser.

'You see, I am meeting Primakov tomorrow, and I don't want to look like a walking wounded on the world's TV screens.'

The diplomat Yevgeny Primakov was President Mikhail Gorbachev's foreign adviser. His mission in Baghdad was to negotiate an Iraqi withdrawal from Kuwait and a peace settlement that Saddam could agree to without losing face. He spoke Arabic and had got to know Saddam in the sixties, when he was Middle

Eastern correspondent for the Communist Party's mouthpiece *Pravda*. He was universally trusted in Baghdad, by King Hussein of Jordan and president Hafez al-Assad in Syria, who all listened to what he had to say.

The Iraqi President was not the only one to be hurt in the collision. His bodyguard and son-in-law, Saddam Kamel, was battered about too. I had cobbled him together once before when he had crashed under the influence, on a winter's night in 1986. His present injuries were just about the same. I could see his teeth through the deep cut in his lower lip.

'Can you take care of him too?' his father-in-law asked.

'Of course.'

I had started to prepare him for surgery when the President appeared at the door to the operating theatre. 'May I come in?'

'Of course,' I repeated.

He sat down and grabbed Saddam Kamel's hand. 'Make sure the scar won't show in the future.'

'I'll do my best.'

Throughout the forty-five-minute-long operation, the President kept his son-in-law's hand in his own. I have never seen him do that for anyone else.

More people were involved in the accident that evening. No sooner had I finished working on Saddam Kamel, when the President pulled me to one side and asked me to hasten over to the Kazimiya hospital.

'A female citizen is there. She too was hurt in the accident. Please do your utmost for her.'

One of the President's bodyguards was standing outside her room. That immediately told me that the female citizen was not just anybody. She was blonde, her eyes were blue and she was between forty and fifty. She had broken her left cheekbone and there was a deep cut in her forehead. I prepared her for surgery the next morning and told her about the President's solicitude. In her presence also I asked the bodyguard if he might help me get some petrol. The state of war had made it virtually impossible to find fuel anywhere in Baghdad.

'Get him fifty litres,' the female citizen said, looking at the bodyguard.

I then realised her relationship with Saddam was closer than I had initially thought. She was Samira Shahbandar, the president's second wife.

They had met by chance in the eighties. Iraqi Airways had bought a jumbo jet and the company's London representative came to Baghdad to be present at the handing-over ceremony and the subsequent festivities. He brought his wife with him. That was a mistake: Saddam caught sight of her.

Vague rumours circulated, but very few knew anything about the President's new paramour, not even his sons Uday and Qusay. But they smelt a rat. He had got hold of a new, large limousine; the window between him and the chauffeur and bodyguard in the front was opaque.

Zafer Muhammad Jaber, Uday's friend and secretary, had relatives who lived near the Chinese embassy in the Amariya district of Baghdad, far from the Republican Palace. Samira Shahbandar had moved into a house close to them.

Of course, over a period of time, neighbourhood gossip spread about the large Mercedes and bodyguards who were constantly picking her up or dropping her off. The neighbours also observed her arrival home from hospital.

One day Jaber was visiting his relatives. Uday was with him. They got talking about a neighbour who had arrived home with a bandaged face and accompanied by bodyguards. It didn't take long for the President's son to put two and two together. 'They were wounded in the same accident.'

According to Jaber he and Uday immediately made their way to one of Qusay's residences near the Republican Palace. 'I think our father's at it, just like we are,' Uday said.

'Don't talk about it,' Qusay answered. 'Don't even mention it.'

When the bombing started Baghdad turned into a ghost town. The roads were deserted. Only those with urgent business moved about. The risk of being hit by allied bombs or missiles wasn't the only problem; our own anti-aircraft defence was just as much of a threat. What goes up has a tendency to come down. A bullet shot in the air has enough power to kill on the way down.

Whenever American or British planes showed up anti-aircraft artillery burst forth, usually heavy machine guns. The range was laughably small, but the soldiers who manned them took pot-shots anyway. They shot at the planes until they disappeared over the horizon, never thinking that the projectile track by then was low enough to smash right into house and home. A majority of the wounded admitted to al-Wasiti hospital had been hit by Iraqi bullets.

We Iraqis now reaped the bitter fruits sown by Saddam, in agreement with Ali Hassan al-Majid, Qusay and Hussein Kamel. The President had decided that he wanted Kuwait. His cousin, younger son and son-in-law took command and sent the two elite units – the Republican Guard and the Special Republican Guard – over the border to the small sheikhdom, believing they could get away with it without the USA and the rest of the world retaliating.

Ali Hassan al-Majid was commander-in-chief of the invasion forces, Hussein Kamel his deputy. Neither the Minister of Defence Abdul Jabar Shanshal, nor the Chief of the General Staff Nizar Khazraji knew anything about the attacks before they were a fait accompli.

'We heard about the border crossing on the wireless in the morning,' General Khazraji told me about Iraq's invasion of Kuwait on 2 August 1990.

That was how the military structure in Iraq operated. The Republican Guard and the Special Republican Guard existed in a vacuum and neither the Defence Minister nor the Chief of the General Staff were kept up to date with the actions or movements of the elite forces. Any questions on their behalf would be met with suspicion and could be fatal.

During the summer of 1990 Iraq was sinking into an ever deeper economic quagmire. The eight-year-long war against Iran and the massive purchases of weapons, ammunition and other military hardware had thrown the regime into a spiral of debt out of which, unless the income from oil increased drastically, it would not be able to extract itself. Opening the taps further would anyway not help if OPEC was unable to prevent a downturn in the price of Saddam's most important and practically only revenue.

The last half of the eighties had been difficult for the organisation. Worldwide oil production exceeded demand. Many of the member countries cheated and produced more than had been agreed at the meeting of ministers in Geneva and Vienna. The price of oil had fallen to an all-time low. It rose only when Saudi Arabia and Iran jointly curbed production and introduced restrictions.

But now Kuwait threatened to spoil it all. The emirate pumped more than agreed, and at the same time demanded a new and larger quota from their colleagues when they convened to start a new round of tug of war in Geneva on 25 July 1990. The Emir, Sheikh Jaber al-Ahmed al-Sabah, was sailing close to the wind. At the summit of the Arab League in Baghdad the preceding month Saddam had issued a clear warning. If Kuwait continued their over-production he would consider it a declaration of war.

But no one thought the Iraqi President meant business when his thirty thousand elite soldiers were sent to the Kuwaiti border during the days leading up to the OPEC meeting in Geneva; when the emirate bowed under pressure and promised to mend its ways and henceforth stick to the agreed quotas, tension lessened perceptibly.

With the help of Saudi-Arabian intervention, negotiations about border adjustments, the price of oil and the large debt owed by Baghdad to Kuwait were initiated. We all thought reason had prevailed and heaved a sigh of relief.

But we jumped the gun. At two in the morning of the night of 2 August 1990, the Republican Guard and the Special Republican Guard rolled across the Kuwaiti border, supported by planes and helicopters. The invading force met with very little resistance.

The Republican Guard's helicopter squadron was led by Major General Hakem al-Tikriti. When I was medical officer in charge of the airbase at Habbaniya during my national service in the sixties he and I became good friends.

Before the attack the helicopter pilots were called in to Hussein Kamel for a briefing. He had no military experience worth mentioning, but was central to the planning of the operation. 'When you attack I want you to fly as low as possible, probably below fifteen metres, but on no account higher,' said Saddam's son-in-law.

Hakem al-Tikriti protested. 'It's impossible to fly at that height without whirling up sand and dust from the desert. Visibility will be reduced to zero. We'll have problems even from the cockpit.'

'Why are you trying to thwart the pilots' ambitions?' asked Hussein Kamel.

'I'm not,' the major general answered. 'I'm presenting facts. If they fly below fifteen metres I'll lose them.'

But Saddam's son-in-law had his way, Hakem al-Tikriti told me when we met after the Gulf War was over. 'In the first few hours of the invasion fifty-eight helicopters crashed. They collided or hit power lines in the bad visibility.'

In Baghdad the occupation, and the President's tactical and strategic stroke of genius in a national cause, were lauded by state-controlled radio, TV and newspapers. In Kuwait the late summer turned into a orgy of looting and pillaging of medieval dimensions. Ali Hassan al-Majid [alias Chemical Ali] and Sabaawi al-Tikriti, the President's oldest half-brother, who had been appointed governor of the new Iraqi province, were the worst perpetrators.

When the alarm sounded the Emir, his family and relatives, and the remainder of the sheikhdom's elite, were taken by surprise. At the crack of dawn and in great haste they fled over the border to Saudi Arabia. Ali Hassan and Sabaawi, and to some extent Hussein Kamel and Qusay too, could only roll their eyes heavenwards as they trawled the country with their bodyguards, from one palace to the other, and grabbed what they could of gold and diamonds, money, luxury cars and Italian antique furniture that the mega-rich Kuwaitis had left behind. Lorry- after lorry-load of stolen goods made its way back to Baghdad. Lower-ranking officers and enterprising Iraqi businessmen helped themselves to the leftovers the bigwigs hadn't bothered to take.

Saddam did in fact arrest and liquidate some of the worst and greediest offenders amongst the officers, but the biggest sharks, his close relatives, were let off scot-free.

Abdul Salam Muhammad Said was my Health Minister when the invasion and looting took place. He phoned me to tell me, after he was instructed by higher authority, that as Director of al-Wasiti I should get in on the act. 'There's a hospital in Kuwait with a spanking new and well-equipped burns unit. Get down there and see what might be useful to your hospital.'

I never went.

Two weeks later the Health Minister phoned again. 'Have you been?'

'No.'

'Why not?'

'I just couldn't make myself do it. Ask someone else.'

Not everyone was equally reluctant. Without hesitation, many of my colleagues followed the Health Minister's request and went to Kuwait. There they stripped the hospitals and health institutions of all the medicines, modern technical equipment, instruments and other medical supplies that they could. The professors and researchers from various technical universities and secondary schools followed suit. They too had been ordered from on high to go and help themselves from Kuwait's technical institutes and places of learning. Even the chairman of the Iraqi Medical Council, Dr Raji al-Tikriti, had joined the plundering sortie and emptied the emirate's stock of textbooks, medical periodicals, chairs, desks and computers. The loot gave my union boss little pleasure, however. He was bracketed together with a group of officers whom Saddam suspected of planning a coup d'état. Raji al-Tikriti was executed with them.

Inevitably, it was all going to end in disaster. The very day the invasion took place the UN's Security Council condemned the entry into Kuwait and demanded a complete withdrawal. Four days later the Council agreed to far-reaching economic sanctions against Iraq. The USA sent troops to Saudi Arabia to defend the kingdom in case Saddam's forces continued south from Kuwait.

A new war and much bloodletting appeared to be looming on the horizon.

On 18 September, a month and a half after Kuwait had been conquered, Saddam called his generals together to discuss the situation. It was now clear that the USA was prepared to use its enormous military power to throw him out of the sheikhdom if he did not immediately and unconditionally withdraw his soldiers. More than thirty countries were ready to supply planes, warships and troops to the UN-sponsored coalition, a campaign the Americans named Desert Storm.

Saddam's Chief of Staff, Nizar Khazraji, was the first to speak. He told the President that an immediate withdrawal of Iraqi soldiers was the best solution. 'We've taught the Emir a lesson and there's no need to stay any longer,' he said. He saw there was no chance of halting the build-up of allied forces in and around the Gulf. 'It's obvious. They're technologically speaking completely superior. Anyhow, our lines of supply are too long. If we stay our losses will be heavy.'

Saddam was furious. He glared at the general. 'Does this mean you have no stomach for fighting?'

'No, sir. I am a soldier and I follow orders. But you have asked for my opinion of the situation and I have given it.'

The President got up and left without a word.

At six o'clock the next morning, so Khazraji has told me, an officer arrived with a letter for him from Saddam. 'I am sorry to inform you that you are no longer needed as Chief of the General Staff. I thank you for your efforts. From now on you will do duty as an adviser, attached to my office,' he wrote.

Khazraji was not quite sure what the advisory function would entail. He phoned the head of the President's staff in the Republican Palace and asked what the new post involved.

'It involves your staying at home. If we need you we'll contact you.'

The Gulf War was over and the Kurds in the north and the Shia Muslims in the south had revolted before anyone phoned Nizar Khazraji.

*

The UN Security Council adopted a new resolution on 29
November. It was proposed by the USA and gave the allied forces
the green light to use all necessary means to 're-establish international peace and security' in the Gulf if the Iraqi soldiers had
not withdrawn from Kuwait by 15 January 1991. A diplomatic
initiative from Saddam, where he tried to link the question of
withdrawal with his wish to arrange a comprehensive international summit on the ongoing conflict between Jews and
Palestinians in the Holy Land, was in the meantime rejected out
of hand by America.

On 2 January I was asked to prepare al-Wasiti for casualties in
the event of Baghdad being bombed. A few simple changes
needed to be made. Experience and routine gained from the
Iran–Iraq war, only two and a half years past, were still fresh in
our minds. We had admitted and treated twenty thousand
wounded soldiers and officers during the eight years that war
lasted. We knew what to expect of death and disaster.

I was working on a new sculpture in my studio: a dove emerging
from a man's head. I felt it portrayed a desperate hope that war
might after all be averted. I was just putting the finishing touches
to it when Watban al-Tikriti, Saddam's youngest half-brother,
phoned me. His foot was hurting and he wanted me to come
over to his office in the Republican Palace and have a look at it.

'I'm sorry but I don't have time to come over to Bin-Sina,' he
said.

I finished the sculpture in a hurry and signed it 'Ala Bashir –
14.1.1991', then put it away in a safe place. I might not see my
studio for a long time. I had already closed my private clinic in the
Mansour district of Baghdad and sent the staff home.

Watban was in charge of the President's office for complaints;
a sort of civilian ombudsman to whom ordinary citizens could
submit their problems if they felt unjustly treated. Whether the
office had any practical significance is another matter. After all,
Watban was one of the regime's foxes set to mind the geese, and
this regime was growing increasingly more corrupt and ineffi-
cient.

This corruption was particularly widespread in the police

force. One morning one of my nurses came into my office in al-Wasiti. He was tearful and needed to talk.

'What's happened?' I asked.

He said that a police patrol had stopped him en route to the bus stop the night before and accused him of being a deserter.

'No,' said the nurse. 'Here is my ID card and military papers which show that I have served my time and am now a nurse at al-Wasiti.'

'They're false,' they insisted. 'You'll go to gaol until we've got to the bottom of this.'

Once you were thrown into one of Saddam's dungeons you could never be sure of getting out. You might be maltreated to the point of death or quite simply forgotten. The burden of proof was turned upside down. You had to prove that your papers were bona fide and that was impossible behind bars.

'But there is one way of solving the problem,' said the policemen. 'How much money have you got?'

'Just enough for my bus ticket.'

Thank God the nurse was wearing an expensive and warm leather jacket on this bitterly cold winter's night.

'We'll take your jacket.'

He had to walk home without a jacket or money for the bus, frozen stiff in his shirtsleeves.

There didn't seem to be anything wrong with Watban's foot, but that was not the reason he'd asked to see me. He needed to talk.

'Are we facing another war?' he asked.

'If only I knew,' I said. 'But I find it hard to believe that the President hasn't got something up his sleeve. If he doesn't stop it then everything in this country will just grind to a halt. I'm sure he'll find a way.'

'I hope you're right,' Watban said dejectedly. He appeared sad and pathetic.

The deadline for complete and unconditional withdrawal from Kuwait ran out on 15 January without Saddam giving in. A visit to Baghdad from the UN Secretary-General, Javier Pérez de Cuellar, one week earlier, had been fruitless. A few hours after midnight American and British planes unleashed bomb and missile attacks aimed at Iraqi military and civilian infrastructure.

Uday, his uncle Luai and his private secretary Jafer Muhammad Jaber travelled to Kuwait with Hussein Kamel on 13 January. This was the President's son's one and only visit to the occupied sheikhdom. When the bomb and missile attacks started four days later he was completely taken by surprise. According to Jaber, 'Uday couldn't believe that there was going to be war.'

During their visit they were accommodated by General Ayad Tayhe in the army's HQ. On 19 January Hussein Kamel approached Uday and told him that the President had decided to bomb Tel Aviv.

Jaber remembers Uday's terrified reaction. 'We'll go to hell. Israel is America's baby. We better get our arses back to Baghdad.'

On the return journey three days later Jafer Muhammad Jaber was seriously wounded when the armour-plated Mercedes he was driving was hit by an American missile. Uday, uncle Luai and Hussein Kamel, whose cars were at the back of the motorcade, reached the Iraqi capital unhurt.

Saddam's relatively simple Scud missiles caused a lot of hullabaloo but the military consequences were limited. In all thirty-nine were fired towards Israel and thirty-five towards Riyadh and other towns in Saudi Arabia. In Israel 2 people were killed and about 200 wounded. In Saudi Arabia 28 American soldiers were killed and 100 wounded when a military camp was hit. Compared to American and British bomb and missile attacks they were as a drop in the ocean.

During 45 days of air attacks and 100 hours of a final land war the allies flew more than 100,000 sorties. They dropped approximately 250,000 bombs and missiles, I have since read in an international military journal. In addition American warships in the Persian Gulf and Red Sea dispatched about 100 cruise missiles.

I have always been fond of Baghdad and it was heart-rending to see the town being destroyed by bombs and missiles. The raindrops were full of soot and buildings that escaped grew increasingly dirty.

The director's job at al-Wasiti, the duties at Bin-Sina and the constant summonses to treat the President following his car crash meant that I was rushing around Baghdad at all hours, every day, in an old beaten-up Scania lorry. It belonged to al-Wasiti and ran on diesel. We had enough of that. We had stocked up in time, initially to run the hospital's generators in emergencies. In time it was impossible to get hold of petrol.

Driving around the streets of Baghdad was very risky. One morning the lorry was struck by one of Saddam's anti-aircraft guns. Luckily the bullet hit the frame of the door; a centimetre to either side could have killed me. On 9 February I crossed the well-known suspension bridge over the Tigris in my lorry on the way home from al-Wasiti. Two hours later it collapsed following a direct hit. When I saw the sorry remains the next morning – the central part had fallen into the water and sunk – I too broke down. I couldn't hold back the tears.

Yevgeny Primakov fought unceasingly to broker a diplomatic solution to the international crisis caused by the invasion of Kuwait. After the air attacks had started he held a series of meetings with the Iraqi president.

No TV viewer would have noticed that anything was wrong with Saddam when he met the Soviet mediator the day after I had patched his face together. He was well made-up. No one asked the reason for the bandage on his little finger.

One afternoon I removed the small stitches with which I had sewn together the wounds. That incident cost the Bin-Sina director his job. His name was Samir al-Shaikhli, like Iraq's Interior Minister of the time, and as usual he had welcomed the President when he arrived at the hospital during the evening. For some reason a senior doctor entered the outpatients department while I was taking out the stitches. He stood in a corner and watched while I was working. He had not been called for and I saw how Saddam, who had been calm and relaxed, stiffened and looked disapproving. But he said nothing until I had finished.

As he left he looked at al-Shaikhli, who was waiting outside. 'You know very well that while I am being treated I do not like anyone in the room who has no reason to be there.'

'Sir, maybe one of your bodyguards asked our senior colleague to see to you,' al-Shaikhli said.

Saddam left outpatients with his private secretary and brother-in-law, Arshed Yassin, without answering. A few minutes later Yassin returned. He made a beeline for the unfortunate hospital director. 'You can choose between retiring and being transferred to normal medical work in the health ministry,' he snapped.

'Can I wait until tomorrow to decide? al-Shaikhli asked, bewildered.

Yassin rushed out to the President who was waiting in the car. He came storming back after a few moments. 'You're fired.'

I remained still while al-Shaikhli tried to collect himself. He was an honest and able administrator. To lose the top job in Saddam's own private hospital was an awful shock. Then I said, 'Samir, you should have said that it was up to the President to decide whether to pension you off or send you to the health ministry.'

'I forgot. I'm a complete idiot,' he said.

Once more I was reminded how absurdly easy it was to incur Saddam's disfavour.

When I think back the night of 13 February was the worst – and the one I remember best from the Gulf War. The air attacks arrived one by one like pearls on a string. Bombs and missiles rained down from evening to early morning lighting up the sky over Baghdad as if by gigantic fireworks. The bangs and whining metallic sounds from the lethal machines over our heads made the children cling to us grown-ups even harder. The dust and smoke from the explosions made it difficult to breathe.

At half past four in the morning we were woken by an almighty bang. The air pressure from the impact made the whole house shake. A few hours later I heard that an air-raid shelter only four kilometres away had been hit. I decided to go over and have a look.

Al-Amariya was, according to the neighbours, an air-raid shelter designated for the President's staff, but in the days before the outbreak of war the rules had been relaxed, allowing ordinary civilians to use it. The ceiling and walls of the bunker were two-metre-thick concrete, and anyone would feel safer there than at home.

Two 'smart' laser-guided bombs from the American stealth fighter planes sealed their fate. One bomb was directed through the air-raid shelter's ventilation shaft. When it exploded it tore a two- to three-metre-diameter hole in the concrete wall. The other bomb, which followed closely behind, exploded inside the actual bunker. Smoke poured out of the hole where the bombs pierced through the concrete.

The bunker was fenced in by a railing. By the gate, which police and soldiers had closed, hundreds of parents, aunts and uncles, brothers and sisters of the occupants of the shelter waited. Some screamed, others cried, most just stood, like petrified statues, and said nothing. The place was teeming with foreign journalists and TV crews accompanied by their information ministry minders. An official procession drove up and I was informed that it was the Russian peace-broker Primakov who had come to have a closer look.

In all 420 innocent civilian Iraqis – most of them women and children – were killed in the twinkling of an eye that morning in the bunker. Many were thrown against the walls with such unbelievable power that they were glued there before being totally incinerated by the searing inferno which followed the explosion. It is still possible to see the outline of a mother and small child on one of the walls. The imprint they left is not quite as black as the surrounding concrete.

I was still standing there horror-struck when the victims were carried out. They were so burnt it would be difficult to identify them. Trickles of blood were just visible. The combination of black and red reminded me of a piece of modern art.

'The ministry of information has done a magnificent job,' Saddam said two days later when I came to rebandage his little finger. 'TV pictures of America's criminal act have been shown all over the world.'

Initially I had been worried that Saddam would lose his finger to infection. But luckily both the finger and the facial wounds started to heal. His son-in-law Saddam Kamel and Samira

Shahbandar made progress too. However, the President never managed to keep the bandage dry when he was showering and while the allied air attacks continued undiminished around us in Baghdad and the land war and hour of truth drew ever nearer in Kuwait, I changed his bandages on a daily basis.

'I'm doing my best,' he apologised, 'but however hard I try, it gets wet. I can't really wash properly with my left hand.'

On 23 February, the bandage was wet, yet again. The President's bodyguards fetched me and drove me to a small house in the al-Jihad district, near the international airport. To my surprise the house was close to my own. It had a sitting room, a kitchen and three small bedrooms. One of the bedrooms was made into a tiny clinic and two of my colleagues were on duty round the clock. The President no longer dared use Bin-Sina. The hospital was dangerously close to his complex of offices and the Republican Palace, a major bomb target.

Saddam was in excellent spirits and smiled and laughed when he arrived at four o'clock. As always I washed and disinfected my hands before removing the wet bandage. While I was working the new Bin-Sina director, Hassan al-Tikriti, came to visit and stood watching by the door.

The President asked why he too did not wash and disinfect his hands.

'Sir, I am only visiting. I'm not taking part in Dr Ala's work,' the newly appointed hospital director said.

'Scrub them all the same,' the President said and Dr Hassan did as he was told.

The Saturday afternoon in the little house in al-Jihad was unreal. That morning I had listened to Voice of America on my short-wave radio. The latest push by Soviet arbitrators to prevent a land war had been turned down by America and its UN alliance partners. The American President, George Bush, gave Saddam a final ultimatum. The Iraqi forces in Kuwait must start withdrawing, on a broad front, by twelve o'clock Washington time; if not, General Norman Schwarzkopf and the more than fifty thousand allied soldiers mobilised in the Gulf area would commence Operation Desert Storm.

With a time difference of eight hours that meant eight o'clock in Baghdad. In other words it was less than four hours before the deadline expired and I was sitting with a calm and relaxed President who was more concerned with the new, dry bandage round his little finger.

'America refuses to give peace a chance,' said Saddam, 'and they're not going to war to liberate Kuwait. They have other motives, but we are ready to fight. God is with us.'

When I had finished with Saddam a couple of his bodyguards took me to Samira Shahbandar. She was now allowed to stay in Bin-Sina – everyone knew who she was. Her broken cheekbone was mending well, as was the cut on her forehead.

The next morning, 24 February, Operation Desert Storm had started and Saddam spoke to the people of Iraq on radio and TV. It was a long and rambling exposition of Iraq's proud civilisation and history and how important it was to stand together to conquer the evil imperial forces which threatened the nation. The speech culminated in an appeal to Iraqi soldiers in Kuwait and in the desert along the border with Saudi Arabia to fight to the end.

'This is the mother of all battles,' he said.

Like an impenetrable and depressing porridge, dust clouds and smoke from the explosions covered large parts of Baghdad again on 25 February. The allied air attacks caused more death and destruction. But after forty days of persistent efforts it was obvious that the pilots and the men who programmed the missiles had run out of targets. They reset their computers and bombed for a second time buildings, centres of communication, power stations and bridges which had already been shot to smithereens.

The majority of wounded brought in to al-Wasiti were civilians, many of them women and children, innocent victims as always in war.

During the afternoon Saddam's bodyguards turned up, as usual, for my daily visit. We set off for the little house in al-Jihad, where the President, once again, came to have the bandage on his little finger changed.

He immediately set to with a lengthy elucidation of Iraq's illustrious history, international solidarity and fighting spirit and I know not what. It was a repetition of his forty-five-minute-long radio and TV talk the day before.

I asked how he managed to go on for so long about a single subject. I myself could only manage five minutes, I remarked, and then nearly bit my tongue off when I realised what I had said.

Saddam looked at me, puzzled, and was quiet for a time.

'It's because I read so many books in prison,' he said finally. He was forever referring to the arrest and prison stay he had been subjected to under President Abdul Salam Aref in the sixties. 'Honestly, I should have remained in prison a bit longer. I had masses of unread books in my cell.'

Now the President augmented his speech with a comprehensive disquisition on the important part reading played in a person's development. He spent a lot of time on belles-lettres and poetry but preferred political biographies and history.

'Based on everything I have read in those types of books I have come to the conclusion that America is the worst of the Western countries. Americans have no history, no past which they can be proud of and lean on. They've made great technological progress but lack the historic and cultural basis that is the cornerstone of civilised countries. Anyhow, as a nation they're too mixed. They come from all over the world and you can't trust them,' said Saddam while I was removing the wet bandage and replacing it with a dry one. 'During the war with Iran our intelligence chaps got information from the CIA about enemy troop movements. But I told them: Don't trust America.'

He rated the British only slightly higher.

'They're good organisers and more clever than the Americans and that's because of their long history. But they have no friends. They only think of themselves'.

'What about the French?' I asked.

'They're much better than the British. They're honest and have a solid cultural and humanistic grounding. But they too are being poisoned by American influences. Thank God they still have far-sighted leaders who resist. They've always had good leaders. General Charles de Gaulle may be the greatest statesman the world has ever seen. He was a war hero, a patriot and a proper nationalist: a genuine product of French civilisation. His decision to pull French troops out of Algeria compels deep respect.'

That wasn't the first time Saddam praised the great French president and his role in history. He returned to him many times during our conversations. He had no time, however, for Adolf Hitler: 'He looked down on us Arabs.' And Josef Stalin, who allegedly is the Iraqi President's model, according to the many books written about him, was conspicuously never mentioned. Saddam hated Communists. 'They are Godless.'

In the evening of 25 February it was announced that the President had ordered Iraqi forces to withdraw from Kuwait. But they were already fleeing. The massive, highly technological allied offensive rolled over them in the desert with merciless power, speed and weight. It was uncompromising slaughter.

Operation Desert Storm was nearly over when Saddam came once again with his little finger to the temporary mini-clinic in al-Jihad just after seven on 27 February. Every Iraqi tank, armoured personnel carrier, jeep and lorry in the theatre of war had been shot to pieces – from the air and the ground by the coalition forces. They lay in an endless line of burnt-out wrecks along the motorway of death from Kuwait to Basra.

The numbers were never confirmed but at least thirty thousand of Saddam's soldiers lost their lives in the hundred hours the allied offensive raged. Many more were wounded and more than fifty thousand were taken captive by the Allied forces.

There was chaos in Baghdad too. A power vacuum had developed. Top civil servants abandoned their desks. Members of the Baath Party, who controlled every neighbourhood, were suddenly nowhere to be seen. Policemen stayed at home. The regime was on its last legs, so the rumours whispered. Either the generals would intervene and the army take over or we would see American soldiers in Baghdad. The signs of break-up were obvious. All over the capital, even in the centre of town, pictures and murals of Saddam were being defaced with black paint.

I had expected Saddam to show some signs of stress amidst the military catastrophe and the chaos. But he was calm and smiled as always when he greeted me. He had a small portable radio in his pocket and had heard the latest news from Voice of America before entering the house. Now he put the radio down, unbuckled his pistol belt and gave it to me. He had lost weight. His hip bones were clearly visible under his shirt. One of the bodyguards handed him a prayer rug and he turned towards Mecca. When he had finished praying he flopped down on the sofa beside me.

'I am so tired,' he said. He was too tired to get up. Please could I change the bandage there and then, on the sofa.

'Have the strain and stress these last days affected your sleeping?' I was bold enough to ask.

'No, I never suffer from insomnia, Dr Ala, never. Sometimes, when I have to make important decisions, I have a bit of trouble going to sleep. But as soon as I have made up my mind I'm asleep within five minutes.'

I had to kneel down to change the bandage: the sofa was very low.

'But understand one thing,' Saddam went on. 'The decision to invade Kuwait was not mine, it was God's.'

The remnants of the beaten Iraqi army walked home. The hundreds of thousands of soldiers were ragged, unshaven; their heads were bent, not daring to look people in the eye.

They ran the gauntlet through Basra, Amara, Nasiriya, Kut and all the villages and hamlets along the way. They were robbed, hectored and derided. Their weapons and personal possessions were taken from them; the majority arrived home bare-footed.

The degradation was total.

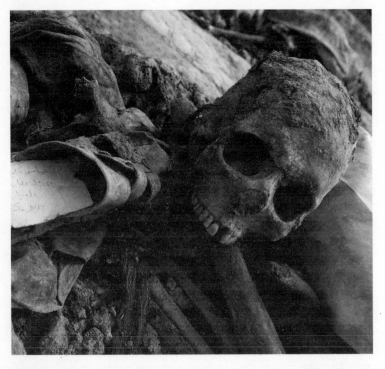

Mass grave in Abu Hajil outside Hilla in Central Iraq. Allied forces failed to come to the aid of Shia and Kurdish rebels in March and April 1991, when the rebellion following the Gulf War was cruelly put down by Saddam's elite forces. (Benjamin Lowy/Corbis)

CHAPTER 8

The Uprising

Shias and Kurds rebel and are put down.
A lorry driver escapes death.

Baghdad International Airport lies about twenty-five kilometres south-west of the city. Close to it was a large military base, of which part was a penal colony with a dedicated prison for soldiers who had committed acts of insubordination. When needed, the cells were also used to house criminals and political prisoners.

A lorry driver was an inmate of the prison during the time the Shia Muslims in the south and the Kurds in the north rose in rebellion following Saddam's crushing military defeat in Kuwait. He had been imprisoned a year earlier after trying to deliver some goods to the airport with his heavy goods vehicle. The cargo was piled up on the back of the lorry and, unfortunately, he miscalculated the clearance when he passed underneath a bridge over the motorway. Cargo and bridge made contact and both the latter and the lorry were destroyed. Unfortunately the bridge was not just any bridge. It led exclusively to Saddam's large palace complex in Radwaniya. Not many minutes passed before the lorry driver was enjoying the hospitality of Saddam's penal colony.

Then he was forgotten.

The remnants of Saddam's battered and humiliated warrior force making its way home to barracks and military camps left behind a clear signal to anyone who saw the soldiers drag themselves by: the regime was on shaky ground.

By 1 March the insurrection was at its height in Basra and spreading like wildfire. In the course of a few days Najaf, Karbala, Nasiriya, Amara, Kut and Hilla and many other towns in Southern Iraq were in the hands of the rebels.

Initially Islamic opposition groups, wearing green headbands, were in charge. But in no time the activists had encouraged the masses of Shia Muslims to join them. Glimpsing the possibility of avenging the oppression and poverty that had been visited upon them, as if on command they threw themselves into an orgy of plunder directed against Saddam's men. It became a witch-hunt. If any of the President's supporters were caught they were either shot on the spot or chopped to mincemeat by the mob in what came to be known as the nights – and days – of the long knives.

Two of my cousins, Hashem Karim and Kasim Karim Bashir, were among the leaders of the uprising in Tuwayrij, a medium-sized town between Karbala and Hilla. 'It was quite simply not possible for us to prevent the lynching once it had started,' they told me later.

It was blind rage. The mob stormed and plundered every-thing that got in its way: police stations, military camps, public offices and buildings, hospitals and the homes and houses of Baath Party employees and bigwigs. The collective outburst of fury blew like a blood-curdling storm through town after town, district after district, street after street.

At al-Wasiti hospital we just had time to draw breath. There was barely a pause between caring for victims of the forty-day-long rain of bombs and missiles over Baghdad before the prey from the insurgent areas in Southern Iraq started to arrive.

One young soldier springs immediately to mind. He had been on duty at the Khalid Bridge in Basra. His comrade was attacked by the furious swarm, shot and killed. He himself was wounded in the leg and paraded in front of a Shia Muslim priest who acted as a sort of magistrate. The priest decided to throw him into prison. It had been taken over by the rebels, the prisoners freed – and was now rapidly filling up again. En route to prison the soldier tried to escape, was shot at again and put behind bars.

'I couldn't understand why I had been attacked – after all, I was only a conscript – or why I was thrown into prison. I hadn't even resisted when the mob arrived.'

The next morning he and eight other soldiers were driven to Amara, two hundred kilometres north of Basra.

'There I was paraded in front of a mullah who sentenced me and the other eight to death. Why, we had no clue.'

Outside town a firing squad awaited them and they were sprayed by machine guns.

'My hands were tied behind me and I fell to the ground. One of the rebels then used a pistol to our heads, to be on the safe side. A bullet grazed my forehead and I fainted. When I woke up I was in the military hospital.'

As a war surgeon I have seen and experienced most things, but that this soldier survived what he had been through is one of nature's miracles. His whole body was riddled; he had been hit by more than twenty-five bullets.

The rebellion gave vent to intense hatred, hatred which had built up over the years. Since the collapse of the Ottoman Empire and the formation of Iraq the Shias in Southern Iraq had been ruled by the Sunni Muslim elite in Baghdad and consequently they lagged behind economically. Matters had not improved after the Baath Party came to power in 1968. Under Saddam the Southern Iraqi Shias had sunk ever lower, economically and socially, while being held in an iron grip by the regime. Many of their religious leaders had either been killed or forced to flee to Iran. Unemployment and poverty were accelerating, both in the towns and the countryside. More and more families lived from hand to mouth, and sometimes not even that. Disease and epidemics spread and infant mortality reached new and frightening proportions. The war against Iran had made matters worse. The bulk of the soldiers were recruited from amongst the Shias in Southern Iraq. There was hardly a family who had not lost a father or one or several sons on the battlefields in the eight-year-long war.

Yet even worse – they were deeply faithful Muslims – were the restraints put on their religious worship by the regime. Even the annual pilgrimage to Karbala, their holy town, on foot, to honour the Imam Hussein, was curtailed. Either the authorities made it too difficult for the millions of believers to get away, or they forbade the entire migration and the acts of penance in the holy town.

Hussein, Imam Ali's son and the Prophet Muhammad's grand-child, fell in battle against the Caliph Yazid's troops on the plains outside the holy town in AD 680. The Imam Hussein is buried in Karbala and his heroic fight against the superior forces of the Caliph marks the most important event in Shia Muslims' mythol-ogy and history. To them Imam Hussein is the martyr par excellence. His uprightness and courage are the ultimate example for all.

I was always aware of the oppression suffered by Shia Muslims. My first job in Iraq, having completed my further education in Great Britain in 1972, was as chief surgeon at the department of plastic surgery in Basra.

One day I was on duty in the outpatients department when two policemen arrived with a prisoner. I was asked to examine his hand, which had been badly burnt. The wound on the back of his hand was in the shape of a triangle and skin, flesh, tendon and muscle were burnt through to the bone.

'They used a domestic iron,' the patient revealed as he recounted his treatment at the hands of the secret police. He was a well-known lawyer and champion of the Shia cause.

On another occasion a captain in the secret police visited me in the hospital in Basra. He was unhappy and depressed. 'We've been told to go out in the streets and stop people from cooking food for the poor in remembrance of Hussein,' he told me.

Every year, forty days after the anniversary of the imam's death, better-off Shias cooked food for their less well-off fellow believers. Big pots of meat, rice and gravy were fired up on the pavements on this religious festival.

'If they've already started cooking we're supposed to kick the pots over and make sure the food is spoilt. The poor things are hardly threatening the authorities. They wouldn't hurt a fly,' said the captain.

It didn't take long after the military collapse in Kuwait for

Saddam and his cronies to realise that the allied forces were not
going to come and get them. The American President George
Bush was satisfied with the results and the advance was halted
after the small sheikhdom had been liberated. A coup d'état in
the shape of disgruntled generals did not seem to be on the cards
either, and as if by magic, the ministers, civil servants, police
chiefs and Baath Party activists turned up at their offices again.

Saddam was in charge once more and immediately targeted
the Shias in the south. Large parts of the Republican Guard had
been withdrawn from the war zones in plenty of time before
Operation Desert Storm started and these troops now put down
the rebels who were neither properly organised nor properly
armed. It was a horribly one-sided contest.

The White House dithered for a few days but relatively quickly
the unequivocal signal from Washington was clear. The USA was
not about to come to their aid. Nor did the ayatollahs in Tehran
feel inclined to embroil themselves in a civil war.

Before the rebellion broke out my friend Nizar Khazraji was dispatched to Southern Iraq to take charge of the military
command in Nasiriya. He had now, after a period spent as the
President's adviser, been resurrected to his former role as a general.

'It is possible that American airborne troops will occupy the
city,' Saddam had told him. 'You must go and organise its
defences.' Khazraji left with a staff of thirty officers and other
ranks, amongst them one of his sons. No sooner had they arrived
when the rebellion spread to Nasiriya.

'We were settling ourselves into a house in town when we were
suddenly surrounded and shot at from all sides. I lost several of
my friends. I myself was shot in the stomach, and the last thing I
remember was lying with my head in my son's lap. Everything
had gone black. I could just make out the gleam from a bright star
in the gloom before I lost consciousness.'

The general woke in Nasiriya hospital. A surgeon had sewn up
his stomach as best he could. The beds around him were full of
rebels. One of them had a long beard and was wearing a green
headband.

'He said that I was very important and they needed to keep me alive.'

Two days later the government troops took the hospital and found Khazraji. His son too was alive and was freed. The general was flown to Baghdad in a helicopter and taken to Bin-Sina. Saddam arrived immediately to find out what had happened.

'It's unbelievable how they hate us down there,' Khazraji said. 'Even young women attacked us with Kalashnikovs. We must have done something awful.'

I watched Saddam turn white. He did not like what he heard. It had been a long time since anyone had told him that his regime was not universally popular and that he was not as all-embracingly loved as he imagined.

'Dr Ala will look after you well,' was all he said to his former Chief of Staff before making for the door.

Khazraji was in a bad way. The wound in the stomach had been badly patched up; intestines and guts oozed out. I used a piece of artificial fibre – Dacron – and all my war-surgery experience to sew him up and save his life. He was up and about a few months later but Saddam was no longer interested in his services. He was sidelined yet again.

The civil war was raging violently when, on 7 March, two Saddam bodyguards came to fetch me. The President wanted his little finger checked.

They drove me first to a small house near the stricken suspension bridge over the Tigris. There two more bodyguards took over and drove me to the President's palace complex in Radwaniya. The broken bridge over the motorway had been repaired after the ill-fated lorry driver's collision the year before.

In the reception hall in one of the palaces I waited for a while with the President's youngest son, Qusay, and Abed Hamoud. Saddam's bodyguard had become his private secretary after General Arshed Yassin, the President's brother-in-law, was alleged to be involved in the illegal export and sale of invaluable Iraqi antiquities on the international black market. When Saddam appeared he was wearing a large and heavy military overcoat. He embraced his son; it was obvious that they had not met for some time.

Then he turned to me. 'How are you, big doctor?'

'Well,' I said and gave his little finger the once-over. It was in perfect order.

'What are the Iraqis saying about present events?'

'I apologise, sir, I have spoken to too few, and can't give you a satisfactory answer.'

'Tell me what they said, those you have spoken to.' The President would not give in.

Saddam never said so in as many words, but I am sure the Shia uprising had come as a great shock to him. The reports he received from Baath Party activists, the secret police and the intelligence services all told a different story: that the Iraqi people were happy and satisfied with life.

'They feel bitter about the fate of the Iraqi army. But when I ask about other things, I'm not sure they give me honest answers.'

Before the rendezvous with Saddam, I myself, all the chief surgeons and chief nurses at al-Wasiti had met to report on the status of the various hospital departments. Were we able to offer the wounded the services they were entitled to? Of course everything was perfectly all right, there were no shortages of anything, and the staffing was just fine.

'But,' I went on, 'when I walked around to check up on the situation I soon discovered that eighty per cent of what they had told me was in fact not true.'

The President smiled. 'Probably more,' he said.

'Dishonesty is a problem in the entire administration,' I said. 'If I had taken the testimony of my colleagues to be gospel truth and forwarded it to the Health Minister, he too would have had the wool pulled over his eyes and based his planning on false premises. As I have said before, sir, we must attach more importance to what people do than to what they say.'

To that, the President said nothing.

Saddam gave the task of crushing the Shia rebellion to his cousin, Ali Hassan al-Majid. He had led the forces which invaded and occupied Kuwait, but above all it was his zealous efforts as a mass murderer in Northern Iraq which, in the President's eyes, made him an obvious candidate for the new assignment in the south.

In March 1987, towards the end of the war with Iran, the forty-six-year-old had been given carte blanche to defeat the freedom fighters in the Kurdish areas, fighting under their leaders Masoud Barzani and Jalal Talabani, by whatever means necessary. The numbers are not certain, but Human Rights Watch has estimated that within two and a half years Ali Hassan had captured and liquidated between 50,000 and 100,000 Kurdish men between fifteen and fifty years of age. The Kurdish autonomous authorities maintain that more than 180,000 men, women and children were killed. About 2000 villages had been burnt and razed to the ground, many hundreds of thousands of Kurds were expelled from their homes and what existed of power lines, schools, wells and mosques were demolished.

During the operation, code-named 'Anfal' or booty, he did not baulk at using poison gas. On 16 March 1988, Iraqi planes bombed the Kurdish village of Halabja with a mixture of nerve and mustard gas. Between 3200 and 5000 villagers died, according to some reports.

From that day on Ali Hassan al-Majid would go down in history as Chemical Ali.

A majority of Saddam's relatives and closest colleagues wanted a hand in the suppression of the rebellious southern Iraqis. They too wanted to show the President that they possessed the necessary brutality and barbarity to teach the Shias a lesson they would not soon forget. Ali Hassan would have to share some of the glory.

The sons-in-law Hussein and Saddam Kamel, son Qusay, secretary Abed Hamoud, Vice-President Taha Yassin Ramadhan and Izzat Ibrahim al-Douri, second-in-command of the mighty Revolutionary Command Council, reported for duty with much delight when it became clear that neither America nor any other country was going to poke its nose into the civil war.

Only Uday held back. Zafer Muhammad Jaber told me that Qusay tried to persuade his brother: 'You must lead a detachment, you too.'

'No,' said Uday, 'I don't have the stomach for shooting Shias.'

*

Saddam appeared calm and collected in the Radwaniya Palace on this March morning at the height of the civil war. When I had finished with his little finger he asked me whether I was busy. If not, would I take a turn with him in the park outside; he wanted to discuss something with me.

The rain had stopped and the sun was peeping through the clouds. A brick wall had been built in front of the main door.

'The cruise missiles have already been programmed and this will confuse them,' the President said.

We dodged the puddles on the path; Qusay and Abed Hamoud padded along thirty metres behind us.

'Something has been bothering me these last few days,' Saddam continued. 'The Marsh Arabs. They are not real Arabs.'

About half a million Marsh Arabs lived in the reed-covered marshes north of Basra, at the point where the Euphrates and Tigris join: an area of outstanding natural history. Towards the end of the eighties it became clear that this section of the population had a gloomy future indeed. Plans were in place to drain the marshes. Work had already started and would inexorably force the majority of the Marsh Arabs, who had lived and supported themselves in the marshes for hundreds of years, to move from their villages and reed huts.

The project was scientifically founded. The cultivation of cereals and vegetables under the burning Middle Eastern sun requires irrigation, and the subsequent evaporation of the water causes the nutritious salts in the ground to break up and migrate towards the surface. The run-off then carries the salt to the rivers, and, under normal circumstances, out to sea. But in Iraq the marshes act like a vast sponge. The saline water from the agricultural areas in Central Iraq is prevented from reaching the Persian Gulf. By 1948 British scientists were already recommending the diversion of the large, life-giving river courses around the marshes; if this was not done the salinity of the Euphrates and Tigris would rise and reach catastrophic levels.

Obviously Saddam's motives were political; he gave the green light to the extensive drainage project which would dry up the fifteen- to twenty-thousand-square kilometre area of natural beauty. He had no objection in killing two birds with one stone and giving the Marsh Arabs a decisive kick below the belt at the same time. They had been a thorn in his flesh for many years.

'They arrived with their huge buffaloes from India because the Abbasid Arabs needed manpower. That was twelve hundred and fifty years ago and they haven't developed since. They are not like other Arabs. They have no moral standards,' said Saddam.

During the Iran–Iraq war many deserters hid in the marshland's tall and often impenetrable reed-forest. Many were helped by the local population. That had not escaped the President's attention. Nor had the fact that the Marsh Arabs were now taking part in the uprising.

'They have stoked the fires. They feel no loyalty to our country!'

He did not articulate it in so many words but I perceived that he wanted an explanation for the uprising which was raging in the south: someone to blame, in fact.

'You can't trust the Marsh Arabs. They lie and steal and have no pride. They don't live like civilised people. And as for their women – they have no principles. They're quite immoral – no, indecent.'

We stopped by a small stream in the park. The sun caught the back of the President. We were standing only half a metre apart. Suddenly I was fixated by the sight of his ears and could no longer concentrate on what he said. His earlobes were transparent in the sunshine, as though made of grey wax, bloodless. Nor could I resist examining his eyelids. They were heavy and flabby and fell over his lashes.

Having exhausted the 'unreliable and treacherous Marsh Arabs', on our way back to the palace the President started on a lengthy discourse about how lucky we Iraqis were to be Arabs and Muslims to boot.

'We are a great nation because we are Arabs and we are even greater because our nation is based on Islam,' he said.

Then he wanted to know why I had named my oldest son, Sumer.

'Because I associate it with the cradle of civilisation, the Sumerians,' I answered. I still find it incredible how our ancestors learned to write, cultivate the land and build cities more than 5000 or 6000 years ago.

When the Shia uprising was crushed after a few weeks no one knew the exact number of killed and maimed or imprisoned. But as expected, it was an easy match for Ali Hassan al-Majid, Qusay, Abed Hamoud, Izzat Ibrahim al-Douri, Taha Yassin Ramadhan, Hussein and Saddam Kamel and other Saddam cronies.

America and the world community gave them carte blanche, and cannons, tanks, and helicopter gunships were used during the systematic slaughter. Saddam's revenge was as merciless as the Shia witch-hunt had been when the civil war broke out.

I was told by a relative of mine who is a sheikh of the local al-Jabouri tribe what had gone on. Saleh al-Jabouri lives in Eskanderiya, about sixty kilometres south of Baghdad. The little town was called after Alexander the Great whose soldiers bivouacked there when his army was on the march more than 2330 years ago, en route to conquer the Persian Empire.

Al-Jabouri was standing in front of his house when a military lorry passed by on its way to a desolate area north of the city. The back of the lorry held about twenty-five young men and women. They were being guarded by soldiers from the Republican Guard.

After two hours the lorry returned. 'It was empty,' al-Jabouri told me.

Four days later a neighbour in Eskanderya heard wild dogs barking in the area where the lorry had been observed. He went to investigate and discovered the bodies. They were not even properly buried. The dogs had had a feast.

The victims were from Karbala, where, near Imam Hussein's magnificent sepulchre in the centre of town, the Republican Guard had been especially thorough. The various bazaars attached to the holy site had been levelled to the ground. Many innocent women and children were killed. The crack troops showed neither human nor cultural consideration when the gunships attacked and the tanks rolled in. In Karbala and Najaf, the other holy town in Southern Iraq, they left in their wake religious, cultural and historical wounds which would take a long time to heal.

Imam Ali, the Prophet Muhammad's cousin and son-in-law, is, as mentioned earlier, buried in Najaf. The sepulchre, which was built in the ninth century, has a gilded cupola, and is, after Mecca and Medina, one of the Shia Muslims' greatest shrines. Pilgrims have come here for more than a thousand years. In addition, the last and greatest wish for millions and millions of believers is to be laid to rest in Najaf. The closer they lie to the Imam the greater the chance that his intercessory prayers will hasten their path to God and Paradise. The town's graveyard, 'the Valley of Peace', is the biggest in the world. It stretches into the desert as far as the eye can see.

When the Republican Guard repelled the rebels in Najaf many fled into the Valley of Peace. To prevent their escape large areas of the cemetery were fired upon with heavy artillery.

My father, who died of a heart attack in 1966, lies in the Valley of Peace. Over the grave we built a small house which protects us from the sun and heat whenever we come to visit. Thousands upon thousands of similar constructions, both large and small, are built over the graves. It's easy to get lost in the multitude of narrow alleyways and passages, and just as easy to hide away.

When the fighting was over I travelled to Najaf to inspect my father's grave. That visit was one of the most heartbreaking experiences of my life. Not even the dead had escaped Saddam's revenge. Cannon fire had levelled large parts of the valley to the desert floor. Nothing was left of graves, plaques or buildings. Thousands of relatives searched in vain, desperate to find some sign of their loved ones, and in Shia fashion beat their chests and cried out their sorrow and desperation.

I found my father's grave in the middle of all the misery. It was only partly ruined. What the Republican Guard's tanks and artillery had failed to smash, others of my countrymen had done their best to finish off. Everything of value in the little house over the grave had disappeared: door, windows, even window sills were stolen. The steel girders in the ceiling had gone; the grave-robbers had made off with the frame and glass which had surrounded my father's photograph.

I had an appointment with the President and his little finger at ten in the morning on 14 March, but it was nine in the evening before the guards came to fetch me. We drove towards the palace complex but took off down a side road before we got there. We came instead to a field with some trees and a small hillock. We stopped in front of it and I caught sight of a door which led into a tiny concrete bunker, no larger than three by three metres. Saddam was sitting behind a desk.

'Salaam aleikum, peace be with you, Dr Ala,' the President said. He was wearing large black-framed glasses and writing energetically on a piece of paper with a fountain pen. A map of the Middle East was hanging on the wall behind him. Kuwait was just a small white spot, unnamed. After a quarter of an hour the President put his glasses and pen down. 'I'm ready,' he said.

I checked the little finger; it was slightly red round the scar where it had been reattached, but otherwise there were no problems.

'I suppose I've been writing for too long.'

I assured him that all was in perfect order.

The next evening the speech that he had been writing in the bunker was broadcast on radio and TV. He praised the army and the Republican Guard for having re-established peace and calm in Southern Iraq. 'Criminal elements' had exploited the difficult situation that had developed after the withdrawal from Kuwait, to promote their own 'treasonable interests'. But, God be praised, the 'bandits' had now got their just deserts. The nation had emerged strengthened and 'victorious' from the problems caused by the traitors.

Saddam never mentioned the problems that still existed in the mountainous north. While Ali Hassan al-Majid and the Republican Guard were busy beating the Shias in the south, Kurdish guerrillas had captured one town after the other: Arbil, Sulaimaniya, Duhok and Zakho were taken. On 20 March the oil town Kirkuk fell into their hands too. The dream of an independent Kurdistan was about to become a reality. Masoud Barzani and Jalal Talabani and their peshmerga soldiers were now in control of nearly all Kurdish areas in Northern Iraq.

However, no sooner were the Shias in the south smashed than Ali Hassan al-Majid and the Republican Guard once again set to in the north. Here, too, Saddam's cousin was given a free rein to use helicopter gunships, tanks and heavy artillery, and here too interference from the USA and the world was conspicuous by its absence.

In record time the Kurdish towns were recaptured. On 3 April it was made known that the authorities were in full control of all and every Iraqi province. Tens of thousands of Barzani's and Talabani's guerrilla soldiers were killed in battle against the vastly superior government forces. A large part of the population, fearing a repetition of Chemical Ali's genocide, fled up into the mountains towards Iran and Turkey.

The world community only woke up to the atrocities when TV coverage of two million despairing and helpless Kurds, fighting their way to the borders through mud and frost and snow with their children and elderly parents, started to flood over the screens. A humanitarian catastrophe was forecast. Many hundreds of refugees died every day of the hardships encountered in the cold and inhospitable mountain wilds.

But the big crisis soon passed. Emergency aid provisions got under way and little by little safe areas for the refugees were established under American, British and French control. Saddam himself met the Kurdish leader Jalal Talabani and a representative of Masoud Barzani. The President promised extensive autonomy and safe passage back home to anyone who had fled to the mountains. By the end of the year ninety per cent of the refugees had returned from Iran and the border areas to Turkey.

The Iraqi government forces withdrew from the three northern regions. The KDP – the Kurdistan Democratic Party – under Barzani, and the PUK – Kurdistan Patriotic Union – under Talabani, would now, largely, rule themselves.

It was soon evident that this was easier said than done.

In the south the Republican Guard continued their hunt for Shia Muslim rebels throughout the summer. Many hid in the marshes and we had frequent reports of hard skirmishes in these areas. The Marsh Arabs, too, took part in the battles. They read the writing on the wall and knew that in a few years their way of life would disappear. Saddam's drainage project would soon make them refugees in their own country.

My two cousins, Hashem Karim and Kasim Karim Bashir, evaded both the Republican Guard and the secret police. They escaped the big mopping-up operations with their lives intact. When the hunt for them and other rebel leaders started in Tuwayrij, they fled to Baghdad. I helped them with money and they went into hiding until it was safe enough to return home.

In the military penal colony near the airport, however, the firing squads were busy far into autumn. The camp was being used as a collection point for Shias on death row and that, of all things, was the salvation of the unfortunate lorry driver who had demolished the bridge the year before.

Saddam's son-in-law, Saddam Kamel al-Majid, took active part in the executions: there was a steady stream of them. One of his bodyguards told me that when a new group of Shias was taken to the place of execution one of them had waved his arms around frantically and screamed to Saddam Kamel that this had nothing to do with him and he was innocent.

It was the lorry driver. The night before his cell had been stuffed with rebels awaiting execution and when their time was up, in the mêlée, he had been included. His escape from oblivion was sudden and unkind.

'The boss chose to believe him and let him go. He was in a good mood that morning,' the bodyguard said, and laughed.

'The Victim': commemorating the bombing of the air-raid shelter al-Amariya in February 1991. From my 1992 exhibition of terracotta sculptures at the Saddam Art Centre in Baghdad. (Author's collection)

CHAPTER 9

Hunger

The Iraqi population descends into
extreme poverty.
Saddam's nearest enrich themselves.

After the Gulf War, when the uprisings in the north and south of
the country had been put down, satellite television began to grow
in popularity. I was one of those who acquired a receiver and a
dish. Strictly speaking it was not absolutely legal, but the regime
closed its eyes to the news broadcasts and evening entertainment
with which we supplemented Iraqi state television and Uday's
al-Shabab channel.

Gradually, however, a forest of dishes appeared on Baghdad's
rooftops and Saddam decided that enough was enough. He told
his half-brother, Sabaawi al-Tikriti, new head of the secret police,
to get to grips with the problem. Sabaawi passed the job on to his
trusted collaborator, Ibrahim Allawi.

Allawi was from Falluja and one of the regime's most corrupt
and bloodthirsty butchers. He had risen to become a general and
head of the secret police in Baghdad. It was his people who
arrived at our house one afternoon to stop the extended viewing.

'It has come to our attention that you have a satellite receiver,'
said the police officer. He was a captain but was wearing civilian
clothes, like the rest of the gang with him.

'That's no secret,' I said. 'Just look up at the roof.' We had
made no attempts to hide the satellite dish.

'It's illegal,' he said.

'How would I know? Nothing has been said in the papers or on TV as far as I can see.'

'It's illegal.' They marched in and grabbed the receiver. 'We'll come and get the aerial tomorrow.'

I sent my second oldest son, Tahsin, up on to the roof. We knew the score. Saddam's half-brother and Ibrahim Allawi were raking in money by capitalising on the satellite ban. Anyone willing to grease the necessary palms could keep the equipment. Anyone who refused had to accept the loss, and it would then be sold to viewers more willing to fork out. But as I was on good terms with the President the captain was loath to suggest a *pragmatic* solution to the problem.

Tahsin unscrewed the dish and sent it crashing to the ground. General Allawi's envoys went berserk when they arrived next morning to find it smashed to smithereens, and immediately rumours started to circulate around Baghdad. One morning, when visiting Sajida, Saddam's first wife, in a professional capacity, she raised the subject.

'I hear the secret police came to your house to confiscate the satellite equipment. Excellent that you smashed it in front of their eyes.'

'That's not quite what happened. But you are right; the dish was broken before they could get their hands on it.'

'Whatever. You did a great job.'

I never replaced the equipment. I might have got away with it, but I was reluctant to make myself at all vulnerable to the pack of wolves round the President. It was always looking for some weapon to use against me when the increasing merry-go-round of jealousy demanded I be cut down to size.

Ali al-Sabti had to pay a price. He was Saddam's ambassador in Tripoli and when he returned from Libya in the middle of the nineties he bought satellite equipment. He was a quick-talking cynic, and always had something both comical and cruel to say about everyone and everything around him. He was appointed in the foreign office with special responsibility for Iran but his style and mocking remarks were not well received by His Excellency Muhammad Said al-Sahhaf, the Information Minister who later became world-famous as 'Comical Ali'.

One day the secret police 'discovered' Ali al-Sabti's dish and receiver. He went to gaol. He was let out after three months and the President asked to see him. 'I punished you because people need to see that I also imprison those closest to me when necessary,' said Saddam. 'Everyone must realise that I keep my word where rules and regulations are concerned.' Then he patted the freed prisoner on the back and sent him as ambassador to Bahrain.

Muin Kassem was another of my cousins. He was an entrepreneur and had had several projects under way in Amara in Southern Iraq before the Shia uprising. During the war and the troubles he lived in Baghdad. He returned to Amara when the situation had calmed down and discovered that one of his lorries had disappeared from the building site where his firm was working. He was taken aback. He had made an arrangement with the influential tribe controlling the town that they would look after his lorry.

He asked the sheikh, the tribal chieftain, what was going on.

'People arrived from the secret police and said General Allawi wanted it,' he said.

Muin asked me for help and together we drove over to an office in the al-Jadiriya district of Baghdad. From these premises Ibrahim Allawi ruled his private business emporium, in close interaction with his official police duties as head of the secret police in Baghdad.

He was a large man, enormously fat. His hair was close-cropped and his head as round as a football. His arms, legs and fingers were like swollen sausages. The stomach, protruding over his belt, was vast. He operated a string of firms and had now set himself up as an entrepreneur, a lucrative undertaking as roads, bridges and power stations were being rebuilt after the destruction of the Gulf War. His men in the secret police had scoured Iraq for much-needed lorries and plant machinery. They arrived, grabbed and left.

My cousin had spotted his lorry at one of Allawi's sites. 'Can I have it back?'

'I've paid for it. I bought from a man in Ramadi.'

'Could you tell us who he is and where we might find him?'

'Unfortunately', the general had thrown away the scrap of paper with the information.

'Well,' I said. 'I think we'll go to the President's complaints office and see what they can do.'

Allawi changed his mind. 'As it's you, Dr Ala, I'll compensate your cousin.'

He took me into an adjoining room. It was the size of a bedroom and full of boxes and cartons stuffed with Iraqi dinars. From floor to ceiling. Even taking into account the watered-down value caused by inflation, the general's hoard was worth enormous sums of money.

Muin Kassem got 750,000 dinars – the equivalent of 250 dollars – for his lorry. It was worth 10,000 dollars on the open market.

'We'll write to the President,' I said.

'No,' my cousin answered. 'It's not worth risking your life for a lorry.'

On General Allawi's back there was a sore which refused to heal. He wanted me to look at it and undressed. I was disinclined to add this fat-mountain to my list of clients and answered in vague and evasive terms when he asked what could be done. Frankly I was surprised that such an overweight person was in public employment. Saddam had introduced clear rules. Public employees and military officers were obliged to keep below a certain ideal weight, set according to height and age. If they went over the strict weight limit they received an official warning and were told to slim. They had to produce results within six months. If unsuccessful they were summarily dismissed.

'I'm sorry,' I said to the general, 'but how have you escaped the compulsory weight control?'

'Sabaawi put in a good word for me,' he said.

Apparently Allawi had been fired but when Saddam's half-brother was appointed chief of the secret police he had interceded on his behalf. The general had had to appear in front of the President who wanted to know why he was so fat.

'I beat my big belly and said: "Sir, what is in here is the blood of your enemies."'

Ibrahim Allawi gloated with pride when he told me the story. Few had personally tortured and killed more Iraqis, ex officio, than he had. The number must have reached many thousands during his tour of duty.

Early in 1992 Saddam introduced a ceiling on the price of rice, wheat, sugar and other basic foodstuffs. Inflation was about to take off and the President resorted to this well-known but often ineffective economic initiative in a desperate measure to get it under control. But many merchants ignored the decree; if they stuck to the maximum sales price set by the government they simply could not make a profit. The President therefore called in Sabaawi and told him to put in place measures to warn and intimidate.

General Allawi and his henchmen got busy.

My oldest son, Sumer, was a student at Baghdad's technical university. One of his fellow students, Muhammad Rahim, came from an impoverished family, but was bright as a button. Relatives and friends had clubbed together enough dinars to enable him to fulfil his dreams to study engineering. To help make ends meet he worked an evening shift in a small grocer's shop owned by the father of one of his friends.

The first evening Muhammad was alone in the shop one of Allawi's secret agents came in. He asked the price of a kilo of rice and was given a figure. It was above the publicly fixed top price. Muhammad was apprehended and despite protesting his innocence, insisting that he had not known it was illegal, he was beaten up and chained to the outside of the shop with a placard around his neck, which said that he was a scoundrel who had 'cheated the public'.

The next day he was hanged.

My son, Sumer, visited his parents to express his sympathy. They were so poor there was not a stick of furniture in the house.

In Baghdad alone more than forty grocers were executed as a result of the price controls. There was no chance of a court case, for poor students or anyone else behind the counter. Many of those who were hanged were either obliging relatives or friends keeping shop while the owners were away on some errand.

*

The UN sanctions, which were introduced following Saddam's invasion of Kuwait and which were still in place after the Gulf War, reinforced the downward spiral we Iraqis had already found ourselves in at the end of the war against Iran. The sanctions were the most severe the world community had imposed against any country in the twentieth century. They struck the central nerve of Iraq's economy: the export of oil.

Without the oil revenue it was no longer possible for the regime to maintain Iraqi living standards at any kind of acceptable level. The result was more ill health and more poverty amongst the masses. An increasing number of desperate and helpless parents sent their children to bed hungry. Auction houses, where carpets, jewellery, valuables, TV sets and furniture came under the hammer, proliferated like miserable toadstools all over Iraq.

As early as 1991 the UN Security Council allowed Saddam to sell a limited amount of oil in exchange for food and medicine for the impoverished population. But the President said no. He wanted to get rid of the sanctions regime in its entirety rather than indulge in half-measures to make life a bit easier. It took the President about five years to bend to the realities of the country's needs and accept the UN conditions for the oil-for-food programme. In the meantime twenty million Iraqis suffered hardships as great as the ones they had suffered in the wars against Iran and Kuwait and the civil wars in the south and north.

Conditions were deteriorating. Saddam's price freeze had no permanent effect, if any at all. Food and other vital commodities rose steadily in price, while salaries remained static.

Samir Ali Muhammad al-Chafy is one of my close friends. He made 2800 dinars a month as culture editor and art critic of the weekly *Alif-Ba*, published by the ministry of information. The rate of exchange from the money changers on the street corners was 3000 dinars to one US dollar.

To secure food for himself, his wife and three small daughters, the culture editor first sold his car. It was followed by his wife's gold and jewellery, their TV set and furniture. Even the baby's cot went to the auctioneer. In the end there were four mattresses left in the flat. They managed to hold on to a small paraffin burner on which they could cook and which heated the house, a small pot and four plates.

'The plates were too big. The daily portions of evil-smelling macaroni, which was all we could afford, looked tiny on the big plates.' Samir al-Chafy remembers.

They could no longer eat bread. The stuff they could afford was black and stinking and all too reminiscent of old-fashioned bark-bread.

'I was sure that anything that could be ground up was mixed into the flour which came from the state-owned mills.'

Every morning he walked six kilometres from his flat in the Mansour district to his office in the information ministry near the Republican Palace in the centre of Baghdad. He walked home too. There was no money for the bus or a taxi or to buy a bicycle.

'We could not even afford an egg. Fruit was unheard of. But worst of all for me was the feeling that I was inadequate as a father, having to put the children to bed without giving them enough food.'

Yet the powerful elite suffered not at all. Smuggling and black marketeering during times of shortage always provided undreamt-of possibilities for profit, and the President's older son snatched at every chance in the wild business euphoria which developed in the shadow of UN sanctions. The unfortunate episode which led to Kamel Hanna, his father's valet, being killed in August 1988 was no longer discussed in the family circle. Gradually Uday came in from the cold; he was soon rolling in money.

Al-Amir Co. was the name of one of the companies which was established by Uday and his second cousin Hussein Kamel towards the end of 1991 to import goods and equipment hit by sanctions. The name was chosen carefully. The word 'amir' – prince – has a special significance for Shia Muslims. It is synonymous with Ali, the Prophet Muhammad's cousin, buried in their holy town Najaf, between Baghdad and Basra. The target of the cousins' business plans was the Iranians, who are Shia Muslims

Hussein Kamel was Minister for Military and Industrial

Development, including Iraq's weapons-development pro-gramme. The new company, which rapidly established new contacts and contracts on the Iranian side of the border, allowed him to circumvent sanctions and keep the wheels running in the enterprises and programmes which belonged to his ministry. In addition he and Uday creamed off the profits and ploughed the money into what rapidly became a property empire spanning all Iraq.

UN sanctions or not, the mullahs in Tehran had no objections to providing the necessary loopholes in the border fences to their arch-enemy in the west, as long as they were rewarded accord-ingly. Al-Amir Co. got hold of and imported most of what trade and industry and the elite of solvent consumers wanted and were screaming for. Cars from Germany, combine harvesters from Russia, rice from Thailand and cognac from France: all these Uday and Hussein Kamel delivered via their Iranian friends at sky-high black-market prices. Out of Iraq, through the same well-greased channels and loopholes, flowed oil, cement, urea and dates.

'As long as it lasted this was gilt-edged business for Uday,' Zafer Muhammad Jaber told me. 'He salted away many hundreds of millions of dollars from these dealings with the Iranians.'

Samir al-Chafy and his family were suffering, but were still amongst the more fortunate. At least he had a job during this dif-ficult period up to 1996, when Saddam and the UN Security Council, after a protracted tug of war, at last agreed that Iraq could sell a significant amount of oil for food and medicine to benefit the increasingly poor, starving and sick population.

The oil-for-food programme checked the hunger for the majority when it was implemented during the spring of 1997; monthly rations of rice, flour, sugar, tea, cooking oil and soap were distributed all over the country. But prior to that the sanc-tions, combined with the corrupt regime and the economic misrule, had brought inconceivable suffering, especially upon those who had no one to provide for them.

A widow lived close to Samir al-Chafy together with her five daughters. They were between five and sixteen years old. The father of the house, a colonel, died in 1989. The widow's pension from the army was simply not enough for them to live on.

'It was awful to see how they struggled. They had nothing left; they were starving. But we ourselves had nothing to give them.'

One day the two oldest daughters took the family's reserves of paraffin into the bathroom. There they poured it over themselves and set fire to it. They were still holding each other when they were found.

'The mother took the three youngest to Mosul. I don't know what happened to them, they never returned.'

Muzaffar al-Ali was one of the many who started up a shop selling second-hand goods. He was a retired brigadier whom I knew from the time when I was a young doctor and doing my national service in the air force.

A young man came into the shop one evening wanting to sell a video-recorder. 'Can you come and see it? I live just round the corner.'

When al-Ali came to his house he saw that all the doors and windows had gone. The door and window frames had been sold too. The home was stripped bare of fixtures and furniture. A young woman was sitting on a carpet close to a small paraffin oven. By her side were two tin bowls. The video-recorder sat in the corner, but it was not of the type used in Iraq: it was obviously booty from the war with Kuwait.

'I'm sorry,' said al-Ali. 'But I won't be able to sell it.'

The young man looked at him, desperate. 'No, OK. But if you want you can sleep with my wife.' He pointed to her.

The brigadier left.

'It made me sick to my stomach. I nearly fainted. I had no idea what things had come to,' said al-Ali when he told me about the visit to the young family.

During the war with Iran refugees had already begun to stream out of Iraq. Young men not wanting to be sent to the front got hold of false passports and escaped to Turkey or Syria through the Kurdish areas in the north. In 1991 permission was granted for people to leave legally, but doctors, engineers, professors and researchers, and officers in the armed forces were excluded. Tens of thousands took advantage of this and moved to Jordan where King Hussein permitted entry without a visa – if they could afford it. It was expensive to leave the misery that was Iraq. A passport cost four hundred thousand dinars; the monthly average salary was between two and three thousand.

But not even money could solve everyone's problems. Hayat Shahrara was a professor of Russian at Baghdad University. She was Lebanese, the author of many books and married to Muhammad Smaisim, a prominent orthopaedic surgeon at al-Wasiti hospital. In 1989 he had a stroke and died. In due course Professor Shahrara's pitiful university salary proved inadequate to provide for herself and her two daughters. In order to maintain any sort of dignified life the only solution would be to return to the Lebanon with her daughters.

When she turned up at the passport office in Baghdad an exit permit was refused. The Muslim-inspired regulation in force requires that a woman leaving the country must do so in the company of either her husband or brother or other male relative. Following her husband's death, Professor Shahrara had no male relative in Iraq.

In an attempt to help her I asked for a meeting with Watban al-Tikriti. He had been promoted from the position of head of the President's office for complaints to Minister of the Interior. But the meeting led nowhere.

'The law is crystal-clear,' he said, 'and I am obliged to follow it.'

I then assisted Professor Shahrara in writing a letter to Saddam, which in the normal way was handed to his complaints office in the Republican Palace. That led nowhere either. The official in charge kept the letter: it went no further than him. Hayat Shahrara was forced to stay in Baghdad because there was no one available to accompany her and her children out of the country.

A few months later I learnt that she had taken the two daughters into the bathroom with her. She stopped up the air-valve, the door and the windows and opened the propane gas container from the kitchen. One daughter survived. When her mother and sister collapsed on the floor she thought better of it and decided to live.

Watban's promotion to Minister of the Interior was at the expense of Samir al-Shaikhli. In addition to his membership of many years' standing of the Baath Party central committee, al-Shaikhli was Saddam's Interior Minister from 1987 to September 1991. Unfortunately he trod on Ali Hassan al-Majid's – Chemical Ali's – toes and what happened to him shows how difficult it became for members of the social elite to stay afloat in the foul waters in which they were swimming.

With the exception of the secret police and the various intelligence and security services, law and order in Iraq was controlled by the interior ministry and al-Shaikhli. One of the cases that landed on his desk before the Gulf War erupted concerned a villa in one of Baghdad's more fashionable districts, where a group of high-class prostitutes plied their trade in great style and to the considerable inconvenience to the neighbours.

The district's Chief of Police wanted to close down the elegant and obviously popular establishment. Al-Shaikhli agreed and signed the recommendation. He was unfortunately unaware, before one of Chemical Ali's bodyguards forced himself into his office and angrily demanded that the resolution be reversed, that the intensive activity in the villa had tacit blessing from a far higher political level than the one in which the Interior Minister himself operated.

However, al-Shaikhli chose to take a stand, the local Chief of Police was given the go-ahead to act and, not unexpectedly, events took their course.

In September 1991 the Baath Party's central committee's first meeting after the end of the Gulf War took place. Iraqi television was on the spot and recorded the session, which was later broadcast in peak viewing time. The meeting kicked off with the usual eulogy to Saddam about his unique and self-sacrificing leadership and government of the country during the difficult times the nation had experienced and triumphed over. Chemical Ali then spoke out against al-Shaikhli. His attack quivered with resentment.

Not only had the Interior Minister wickedly failed the Iraqi people before, during and after hostilities, he had also brought the

Baath Party into disrespect and no longer deserved to be a member of the central committee. He had been irresponsible and feckless and disloyal towards the President and the people.

Saddam nodded.

A few months later I met al-Shaikhli in the street and asked why he hadn't stood up for himself. I had watched him sitting quietly, staring at the floor, during his dismissal.

'It had already been decided, and I have no doubt that my order to close the brothel was the reason for me no longer being a minister or a member of the Baath Party central committee and also because of my objection to the invasion of Kuwait,' he said.

When he left the premises that September evening no chauffeur-driven Mercedes was waiting for him. The car with the bodyguards had also disappeared. He took a taxi home, but the ministerial residence was already closed up and his wife and children thrown on to the street.

Interior Minister al-Shaikhli's humiliating dismissal in public on Iraqi TV when he fell out with Chemical Ali over the brothel was not all he suffered. Uday too interfered.

Al-Shaikhli owned a little farm on the banks of the Tigris near al-Jadiriya, close to Baghdad University, a beautiful location. Now that his political career was over he decided to withdraw to his estate. The problem however was that his property bordered the President's son's villa, and Uday did not want him as neighbour. He had asked to have the farm transferred to his name, gratis, of course.

Al-Shaikhli refused, so Uday's bodyguards began a campaign of intimidation. One morning sheep and goats were found killed. Windows and doors in a small house on the farm were smashed. Whenever he visited his life was in danger. Uday's bodyguards enjoyed shooting warning shots around his legs until he eventually gave up and went home.

By the time the Americans moved into Baghdad in spring 2003 Uday had started to dispose of large parts of al-Shaikhli's idyllic Tigris property – while the former Interior Minister spent his retired life in a modest house in town.

Chemical Ali no doubt patronised several ladies of ill repute in the Iraqi capital. One winter's evening in the eighties, during the war against Iran, a twenty-year-old woman arrived at the emergency reception at al-Wasiti, which in those days largely functioned as a military hospital. She had been trying to light a gas stove when it exploded. She was badly burnt; her entire body was affected. Her sister, a stunning beauty, also about twenty, accompanied her in the ambulance. Both ladies were known to belong to the elite of Baghdad's prostitutes.

While we worked hard to save the life of one, the other wandered about the intensive care ward getting in our way. She completely disregarded our instructions about hospital guidelines, then and later when she came to visit her sister. She came and went as it suited her.

The staff eventually intervened and restricted the young lady's freedom of movement in intensive care. Less than one hour later Chemical Ali was on the phone with a clear and unambiguous request that I, the director, must sharpen up and take better care of the two sisters. The sister not confined to bed had obviously complained that their treatment was not worthy of such good and close friends of a government minister.

I told Chemical Ali that there was no need to upbraid us. We had treated the burnt woman with everything at our disposal and the sister had been awarded the same respect and courtesy as any other relative in the same tragic situation. With regard to the victim there was unfortunately little hope of saving her. The burns were too extensive: they were second degree and covered ninety per cent of her body.

She died three days later.

After the Gulf War corruption and high-handedness gathered pace. No one felt safe, least of all the ministers and the prominent members of the Revolutionary Command Council; nor did army officers and employees of the security forces escape purges and the executions that often followed. Honour, money, cars and numerous privileges followed in the wake of high office, but the drawback for those individuals who had clawed their way up was the amount of time spent at the top – it got shorter and shorter. Increasingly trivial matters would cause

Saddam and the mighty and unpredictable relatives around him to lash out.

The President and his inner circle, Ali Hassan al-Majid, Abed Hamoud, Izzat Ibrahim al-Douri, Taha Yassin Ramadhan and his sons Qusay and Uday, could at any moment bare their teeth. The most laughable and trifling disagreements – as in the case of Interior Minister al-Shaikhli – might condemn you to oblivion. It was like swimming amongst sharks.

Uday's life was a continuously upwardly mobile experience. By 1995 Al-Amir Co.'s activities were so extensive and successful that even Saddam got to hear about it. Uday and Hussein Kamel were called in to the President's office in the Republican Palace and asked what it was they actually did.

'We are working in the interest of the nation,' they answered.

Saddam thanked them and told them to close down operations immediately.

But from a business point of view Uday had many more strings to his bow. The contraband routes, in addition to Iran, covered Jordan, Syria and Turkey too, and he had acquired Pepsi Cola's only bottling plant in Iraq. It was bought cheaply in 1992 when Saddam had put a stop to the production of fizzy drinks owing to the country's lack of sugar.

Uday foresaw that the prohibition would not last for ever and he moved the factory to a small farm he owned just outside Baghdad. He built a new production plant which was ready to fill bottles and cans when the Pepsi ban was lifted after a couple of years.

Initially the Pepsi tasted ghastly. The carbonic acid and other ingredients he imported from Jordan had been stored for too long and should have been dumped, but he used the raw materials anyway, and the Iraqis drank what was produced. There was nothing else.

It was principally Uday's brother who made sure Uday could start afresh in the endless battle for power. Qusay was on good terms with Abed Hamoud, Saddam's private secretary, and he kept a wary eye on his unstable brother. If Uday wanted something from his father he first went to Qusay who in turn asked Hamoud to approach the President.

Hamoud, who was fortyish and a distant relative, had gradually advanced from Saddam's bodyguard to become a focal point in the machine of power around the President. He was secretary of the National Security Council, of which the President himself, of course, was chairman. All civilian and military intelligence gathered by the secret police was forwarded to the council and the secretary sifted the information which the chairman ultimately received. Hamoud regulated to a large extent the agendas and controlled access to Saddam. Consciously or unconsciously he vetoed unpleasant news: Abed Hamoud took great pride in never upsetting his boss.

In his private life the secretary was just as crude and brutal as the rest of the thugs who ruled Iraq. He had two wives, the second of whom was known to the President. She was married to a Kurd who quickly learnt what life was really like when Abed Hamoud came on the scene. The wife asked for a divorce, which he of course granted her, but in addition she demanded their house in Baghdad, a demand which, according to Iraqi law, cannot be approved without the husband's consent. The husband refused, but given Hamoud's position and power, the Kurd found it prudent to beat it back to his farm in Suleimaniya. He was a pleasant, homely man. I knew him personally.

The President's older son was forced to move out of the official guesthouse by the Tigris after the fateful night he killed Saddam's valet. But with the aid of his brother and the intervention of Abed Hamoud, when the Gulf War was over, the President allowed him to move back. He even managed to wangle consent to modernise and enlarge the well-equipped building.

He liked the new guesthouse, al-Abed. It lay close to the Republican Palace's helicopter pad, perfect for going hunting. Uday was a keen hunter. He enjoyed shooting birds, not only from the ground but from above too.

I was once asked to participate. Qusay suggested it when he dropped into Bin-Sina to congratulate one of his relatives who had just given birth. We started talking about hunting and he asked if I would like to join them.

'No,' I said. I did have a sporting rifle, given to me when I served as a doctor in the air force in the sixties. I had used it once. 'I shot some birds but didn't enjoy it.'

'Why not?' asked Qusay.

'It's unfair to shoot small birds that have no means of defence other than to fly away. And when they do they expose themselves to our bullets.'

Qusay looked at me. 'Does that mean that you think we're criminals?'

'Not at all, but it doesn't make me happy to shoot little birds.'

'What an odd man you are,' said Qusay.

A few months later he came to the hospital with his father and brought the question up again, jokingly. 'Dr Ala doesn't like hunting. He thinks it's criminal.'

Saddam laughed. 'Dr Ala is a thoughtful man. He sees life from many different angles.'

Not long after the Gulf War the Iraqi Olympic Committee was back in Uday's hands. All athletics clubs and youth organisations, comprising millions of members, already fell under this heading. Now the President's son extended the committee to include a cultural dimension. Art organisations, journalists', authors' and actors' unions were incorporated, as were associations of decorated war veterans.

Once again Uday was a very important man. However, football was his first love. Under his inspired leadership the Iraqi national team would undoubtedly reach dizzy new heights. The mainstay of this ethos was to make sure the players knew that if they didn't succeed punishment awaited them. And if they lost matches, that punishment would be harsh and merciless.

A hard blow under the foot with a bar was the norm.

One of the team had a habit of stumbling at decisive moments. Uday threatened him with ten strokes under his foot for every stumble over and above a maximum of three.

Another, milder, form of punishment was to close-crop their hair. Or a visit to the army's disciplinary camp in Radwaniya might feature. Here they experienced rock-hard punishment exercises and a prison sentence, including a diet of bread and water.

Following an unsuccessful match in 1994 the entire national team was sent there to contemplate their fate.

It was no joke being part of his support team either. Uday's private secretary, Zafer Muhammad Jaber, has told me what it was like when the team was in Doha in Qatar in the spring of 1993 playing World Cup qualifiers against Korea, Iran and Saudi Arabia. Jaber was the team manager and before the match against Saudi Arabia Uday had instructed him to remain seated when the national anthem of the kingdom was being played.

'It was extremely embarrassing. Prince Faisal bin Fahd bin Abdul Aziz was team manager of the Saudi Arabian national team and a good friend of mine. I had to feign a sudden stomach upset and rush off to the loo just as the kingdom's anthem came over the public address system.'

The match was a draw but Iraq lost the matches against Iran and Korea and failed to qualify for the World Cup in the United States the following year. The players feared the worst when they returned to Iraq, but for once the President's son was magnanimous and forwent any punishment.

The Olympic Committee soon became a state within the state and extended its long arm into a number of other departments. In the end no one could be employed in the departments of culture, information, education or research without having been vetted by Uday's Olympic cronies first. Everyone knew where the real power lay. Before anyone applied for jobs or promoted a cause in the various departments, the first port of call was usually the Olympic Committee – accompanied by the usual bribe.

Uday played a decisive role in the corruption of all government affairs. He destroyed any trust in Saddam and his regime that still lingered. He was talked about all over Iraq. The President was aware of Uday's debaucheries but rarely interfered. He was frightened to rock the boat and cause Uday's mental condition to deteriorate even further.

What we witnessed was often surreal and tragicomic. Uday's Olympic Committee was housed a stone's throw away from the interior ministry where Watban was minister. Entry to and exit

from the two offices converged at a crossroads where two policemen directed the traffic. Uday and Watban had right of way
when they approached with their motorcades. All other traffic
was halted until they had passed. But one morning the two processions arrived at the crossroads simultaneously. The constables
had to make an instant decision. Should they let the head of the
police, the Interior Minister, through first, and stop Uday, or vice
versa, and hold Watban instead?

Zafer Muhammad Jaber was in Uday's car that morning.
'They held Watban and I have never seen such a huge smile on
Uday's face.'

His uncle, however, was furious and directed his bodyguards to
beat up the two constables, whereupon they were bundled in the
boot of his black Mercedes and taken to the nearest prison. There
they were beaten up for a second time and thrown into a dark
dungeon.

According to Jaber he and Uday were having lunch when they
were informed of what had occurred. 'The rest of the day was
spent trying to contact the President so we could set the two
policemen free. We managed in the end but only after Abed
Hamoud had phoned Watban with explicit instructions from the
President that the two policemen be released.'

Someone who also experienced the primitive day-to-day
capriciousness of Saddam's administration was my close and
good friend Khaudir Abdul Azziz al-Douri. He was a member of
the Revolutionary Command Council and regional chief of the
Baath Party in Northern Iraq. He was greatly respected as an
honest and decent man by the Kurds, and by both Sunni and
Shia Muslims. His ability to work well and steadily was widely
known. Al-Douri still believed in the party's fundamental ideas of
socialism and just distribution of social benefits and he soon
became a fly in the ointment of the power elite surrounding
him.

One spring day in 1993 I drove past his house which he had
kept in the Yarmouk district of Baghdad after having been
appointed regional boss in Kirkuk. His large official car, a black
Mercedes, was parked in the garage, and I stopped to say hello.
He was pale and nervous.

'You look tired. Are you OK?'

'I'm OK, but let's go into the garden.' Al-Douri took it for granted that the house was bugged.

Out in the open he told me what had happened when the car was being parked in the garage after the drive from Kirkuk. 'The whole gearbox fell out. The chauffeur is still in shock. We would have been killed if it had happened en route. Normally we're doing a hundred and fifty kilometres an hour on the motorway.'

I looked at him. A string of top people in the Baath Party had died in recent months as a result of car accidents whilst en route to or from their respective areas around Iraq. Rumours were rife. Quite simply there were too many to be a coincidence. 'I've warned you already. The northerners praise your integrity and you know that won't win you any friends among the hierarchy.'

'But what can I do? Am I to start killing and beating people just to please the bigwigs?'

Three months later the central committee met. Before the meeting al-Douri was placed across the table from the Command Council's vice-chairman, Izzat Ibrahim al-Douri. Saddam arrived; everyone got up and then sat down again. The President looked straight at the regional boss from Kirkuk.

'Listen, Khaudir. You've become a rich man lately. You've come by several large properties. Where do you get the money from?'

The question shocked al-Douri. 'Well, sir, all I have I owe to your generosity.'

'But how did you manage to get hold of the house in Yarmouk? I hear it's large and has several storeys?'

'I bought it more than thirty years ago and now I'm extending it.'

Saddam changed the subject. 'You have also placed a young friend from your village, Azziz al-Douri, in a top job in the Kirkuk Baath Party.'

'Well, sir, the fact that he was transferred from Baghdad to Kirkuk lies outside my jurisdiction. Izzat Ibrahim sent him, and asked me to make sure he got a top job.'

The President turned his gaze to Izzat Ibrahim. The deputy chairman looked down and shook his head. 'That's not true. That's not true. Not at all.'

Saddam got angry. 'Izzat Ibrahim and Khaudir al-Douri: sort it out between yourselves. But I want to know the result.'

After the meeting al-Douri left for Kirkuk. The next morning a secretary from the central committee arrived with a letter from Saddam. He was being recalled to Baghdad, told to go home and stay there. He was kicked off the Command Council and lost all his privileges. The black Mercedes and all his bodyguards were taken too.

'But what I told the President was true.'

According to al-Douri, what had happened was typical of Izzat Ibrahim al-Douri. Saddam's loyal right-hand man would lie and cheat and resort to whatever was necessary to get rid of an unwanted colleague.

Al-Douri, a good-looking, tall man – he was nearly two metres tall – was not one of the President's favourites. Saddam hated being photographed beside him during meetings in the Command Council. 'Whenever a picture is taken of the two of us together, I feel unwell. You're so much taller than me,' Saddam said to him once.

'It sounds stupid, but what the President said reflects his mentality,' al-Douri said when we were discussing it.

Most of his friends disappeared when he was dismissed from the Revolutionary Command Council and the job in Kirkuk and was placed under house arrest. They were frightened of visiting him. Only myself and a few others kept in contact with him. When the American forces marched in to Baghdad in April 2003 he had been under house arrest for ten years. But the liberation didn't do much for him. Matters only got worse. He was amongst the first from the old regime whom the new rulers arrested and imprisoned. None of us who knows him can understand why.

During our conversations Saddam rarely talked about his family and the problems they caused him. He was careful too when we discussed the power elite around him. But there is no doubt that he was quickly aware of the misrule that developed. During the spring of 1992 we were discussing his special bodyguards. Most of them were relatives – some close, some distant – and many of them were arrogant thugs. They caused problems wherever they went.

'If your dog is young and small, you can hit and kick and punish it in various ways,' Saddam said. 'But when it is big and strong you have to think twice before punishing it. It might bite you. So imagine what it is like to be surrounded by one hundred dogs.'

They were all doing their own thing, enriching themselves from the fat of the land.

One of my brothers-in-law, Saad al-Ani, was for many years deputy secretary at the directorate for water supply and irrigation. One summer's day he went with his colleagues to an irrigation project in the small town of Suawiara, which lies in an agricultural area about forty kilometres south of Baghdad. The fields were planted with spinach, the area was very large and the crop first class.

My brother-in-law and his staff were talking to the farmer's wife when three helicopters landed. Saddam alighted from one of them. 'This is most impressive. The management of this farm seems to be excellent. The spinach is superb,' he said.

With Abed Hamoud and the bodyguards in tow he wandered around for a bit and then walked over to the farmer's wife and praised her yet again for the wonderful produce. He bent down and picked up some leaves. He lifted the bunch of spinach triumphantly over his head. 'Is it OK if I take this with me?'

'But it's yours,' she said.

'What do you mean it's mine?'

'Barzan al-Tikriti owns these fields.'

My brother-in-law saw Saddam's face darken.

'There's a lot around here I know nothing about,' he said.

He flew into a passion, threw the spinach on the ground and stormed off.

Khairallah Tulfah, Saddam's uncle and father-in-law, was one of those who laughed all the way to the bank during the increasingly flourishing corruption. He became mayor of Baghdad when the Baath Party took power in 1968 and used his position to get his hands on large parcels of real estate both legally and illegally. His long, greedy fingers reached all over town and he was soon one of Iraq's richest men.

No opportunity to profit, small or large, escaped his attention or interest. When impoverished farmers came to town to sell sheep or vegetables in the open markets and on the fields round about, the mayor levied a tax. Not for the town coffers, but for himself.

That was one transgression too far and when Saddam dismissed him as mayor of Baghdad in 1972 Khairallah Tulfah took to lobbying on a grand scale. Anyone with problems which the administration failed to solve went to the President's uncle and greased his palm. Tulfah then showed up at the respective department and made sure the result was as agreed by the payer.

He was a huge man with strong facial features and he swore and cursed constantly while strewing around dirty jokes. He bawled at everyone who got in his way. Even the nephew got his just deserts if he dared give his ministers orders which contradicted those of his father-in-law, but then he was protected by the very highest patronage. When Saddam grew up in poverty in Tikrit his uncle looked after him and became a sort of foster-father to him. Now Saddam could not find it in himself to stop the old man, and his far-reaching business ventures became ever more obnoxious.

Towards the end of his life Khairallah Tulfah had one leg amputated. He suffered badly from diabetes and the leg, which had become infected, developed gangrene. Before the operation Saddam came to visit him at Bin-Sina. As the President left I heard him tell one of his bodyguards that it was a good thing that 'Haji Khairallah' – the father-in-law had once taken part in the pilgrimage to Mecca and could therefore add 'haji' to his name – had calmed down a bit. 'Now he's here he can't rush around pestering all the ministries with his errands,' the President said.

Saddam never, however, managed to put a lid on the old man's corruption. Khairallah Tulfah's behaviour was a major topic of conversation in Baghdad but he remained under the protection of the President until his death in 1993.

On occasions the President hit out when family members or other close relatives behaved too atrociously. But not often. Once was when Luai Khairallah, Saddam's wife Sajida's brother, attended Baghdad University in the eighties. The brother-in-law failed one of the subjects, went to the professor, beat him up and broke his arm. The President heard about it and thought it a bit over the top. He dispatched a couple of his bodyguards to Luai and ordered them to break his arm in the same place. Naturally they complied with the order.

Saddam also reacted a few years ago when his half-brother Sabaawi picked a quarrel with a neighbour about a piece of land outside Tikrit. A policeman tried to separate them before they came to blows and Sabaawi got his bodyguard to break his arm. The conscientious policeman complained to Saddam and the President agreed that he had only tried to enforce law and order. Sabaawi went to gaol for four days on account of the broken arm, but otherwise the family got away with murder – sometimes literally.

Omar al-Tikriti was one of Sabaawi's sons and he was a chip off the old block. One day he phoned me to tell me that he had driven a youth to al-Wasiti. He wanted me to take care of him. I went to the hospital to find the young man had been shot in the face. The bullet had entered under the left cheekbone and exited under the right. It was a miracle that he had not been killed.

His father told me that the boy had been driving his car and had not realised that Omar was in the car behind him and wanted to overtake. Omar sounded his horn repeatedly. When his son eventually drove to the side and let Omar pass he was forced into the ditch and had to stop. Omar was furious and shot at him.

I suggested to the father that he write a letter to the President's complaints office.

'I don't dare,' said the father.

Omar had long been known for his trigger-happy habits. He and my son, Tahsin, were at university together in Baghdad. He told me that Sabaawi's son, in 1992, had shot and killed the

president of the Students' Union in a break between two lec-
tures. They had come to blows over a trivial matter. Tahsin and
many other students saw it happen. The case was amicably settled between the two families, with payment of compensation,
as so often happens in Iraq, whereupon Omar, who had been a
committee member, took over as President of the Students'
Union.

Non-family members were not treated quite as leniently. In the
end Saddam gave the obese devil and butcher Ibrahim Allawi his
just deserts. He was arrested in 1997 and put on trial for his
extensive black-marketeering affairs while chief of the secret
police in Baghdad. During the court case it was revealed that he
had stolen and taken extensive bribes in close collaboration with
Sabaawi. Not least they had been extremely active during the
orgy of plunder after the invasion of Kuwait in the autumn of
1990, the general admitted during the trial. Sabaawi was sub-
poenaed as a witness and denied nothing.

Allawi was sentenced to death but the sentence was never carried out. The general was left to rot in the infamous Abu Ghraib
prison until Saddam pardoned him and all criminal and political
prisoners at the beginning of March 2003, one month before the
fall of Baghdad.

He had, apparently, lost a lot of weight.

Better days. Saddam and his closest family in 1988/89. Clockwise from left: son-in-law Saddam Kamel al-Majid, daughter Rana, son Qusay, daughter-in-law Sahar, daughter Raghad, son-in-law Hussein Kamel al-Majid, son Uday, daughter Hala, the President and Sajida Khairallah, his wife. (Reuters/Corbis)

CHAPTER 10

A Family Affair

Saddam's sons-in-law flee to Jordan.
Uday shoots his uncle.

The night of 8 August 1995 was to go down in Iraqi history. It was the day Saddam's family seriously started to disintegrate, led by his son Uday, his youngest half-brother Watban and his two oldest sons-in-laws – Hussein and Saddam Kamel, who were married to his daughters Raghad and Rana.

It had not taken Saddam long to establish 8 August, the day in 1988 when the bloody and senseless war against Iran ended, as Iraq's national holiday. He called it 'the Day of all Days'. All over the country the 'victory' was celebrated with large demonstrations and processions. The President's clear-sighted leadership and effort throughout the eight arduous war years were the subject of endless praise and homage from a united and grateful people.

The festivities and celebrations usually started on the evening of 7 August, and, to judge by the general mood, August 1995 would set new records. Watban was in no mood to celebrate, however. Like so many others he had fallen into Saddam's bad books and had recently been dismissed as Minister of the Interior. Now he was drowning his sorrows in his new capacity as the President's 'adviser' and was celebrating the Day of all Days with one of his friends who owned a small farm in the al-Dora neighbourhood in southern Baghdad. It was a mixed-sex party with about 150 people present. Singers, musicians and dancers had been booked for the occasion, whole lambs were being grilled and alcohol flowed freely. In addition, the capital's leading pimps had put their shoulders to the wheel on the supply side. It certainly wouldn't be their fault if the party was a flop.

Uday too was celebrating. His party was at the yacht club Nadi al-Zawareq, by the Tigris, close to Baghdad's centre. While his uncle Barzan was still in Saddam's good books as head of the mighty Mukhabarat in the middle of the eighties, he had built the club as a leisure centre for the feared intelligence service's senior officers and their collaborators. When he fell into disgrace the place was taken over by the President. He opened it up to the Baath Party hierarchy, senior officers, ministers and their families. Food and drink, including alcohol, was served free of charge and Nadi al-Zawareq had long been a very popular party and rendezvous venue for the elite of the regime.

But in 1992 Saddam turned the taps off. Beer, wine and spirits were now taboo. The privileged guests had to pay for their own meals. They started to drift away and when the activities by the river bank shrivelled up Uday saw his chance to get his hands on the club secretly. He got a handful of his bodyguards to move in and take control and he appointed a new chef and waiting staff.

With its large hall, guest rooms, restaurant and bar shaped like a boat's deck, surrounded by trees and with a beautiful uninterrupted view of the Tigris, the place was tailor-made for Uday's debaucheries. He used it constantly and threw most of his parties here.

On the eve of the Day of all Days in 1995 the boat club was chock-a-block with young women. According to Zafer Muhammad Jaber, more than five hundred of them were crammed in. Not counting the bodyguards, there were only about six to seven men there. Uday could never get enough of what he liked.

Much can be said about prostitutes, but some are definitely prettier than others. At the al-Dora farm this fact was obviously going to lead to a disaster when the party celebrating the approaching national day neared its more intimate phase. It was

Watban's stunningly beautiful first choice of the night who triggered off the unrest. The former Interior Minister was not alone
in having cast his gaze on her.

Luai Khairallah too was smitten and, amidst the hotchpotch of
uncles and cousins, in-laws and other relatives clinging to the
power hierarchy below the President, he was not a nobody. Luai
was the brother of Sajida, Saddam's wife, and thus Saddam's
brother-in-law. And not only that, his sister Ilham was married to
none other than Watban. It was thus two in-laws who came to
blows over the queen of the night and the consequences were to
prove fateful.

Initially Luai got one of his friends to ask Watban to give up
the object of his desire. That did not meet with much success.
Saddam's half-brother asked one of the guards to intervene and
beat up his brother-in-law's envoy, who was bleeding profusely by
the time he returned to Luai empty-handed. The two friends,
who by this time were pissed out of their minds, decided to call
for reinforcements.

They both thought of Uday and went straight off to Nadi al-
Zawareq to ask for assistance. When Uncle Luai and his battered
friend approached him, Uday was most enthusiastic. He too was
high on booze, and had just got hold of a new, automatic pump-
action 'Jackhammer' type gun, the sort used by Sylvester Stallone
and Arnold Schwarzenegger in their films. The President's son
thus felt adequately armed and ready to intervene in the showdown between his two uncles.

The party was still going strong but Watban and most of his
bodyguards had left the farm when Uday arrived to take care of
matters together with Luai, his go-between friend, Jaber and eight
of his bodyguards. Only a few friends and guards had stayed
behind. Since they had taken part in the fracas during which
Luai's friend was injured, they were the first to be shot. Thereafter
Uday sprayed the rest of the party with his new pump-action gun.
Three of the guests were killed, many wounded.

Then Watban returned. On his way home he had spotted
Uday's motorcade and wanted to find out what he was up to.
That was a mistake. When he stepped out of his large, black

Mercedes with his bodyguards, Uday opened fire. The uncle was hit in both legs and in his right thigh. His bodyguards did not defend him; after all, this was the President's son shooting.

Blood spurted everywhere and Watban was unconscious when Uday stuffed his uncle into the car and drove him to Bin-Sina. 'I thought he was going to shoot me. I shot in self-defence,' he told his friend Jaber.

It was six-thirty in the morning of 8 August when I was called and asked to come to Bin-Sina. The place was surrounded by security police and bodyguards. Uday's brother Qusay and Saddam's private secretary Abed Hamoud were in with the director. They were both pale, nervous and looked tired.

Watban was already on the operating table. He had been given a blood transfusion and was on a drip, conscious. But he was suffering great pain and was, to put it mildly, disgusted at having been mown down by his nephew. His left leg was in a bad way. The top third of his tibia had been shot away and the muscles and main nerve had suffered a great deal of damage. His right leg too had been hit but less seriously. It was decided that Bin-Sina's orthopaedic surgeon and I would carry out the first crucial operation.

Having done what we could we were standing outside the operating theatre a few hours later when Saddam arrived. 'I am sorry to have to constantly bother you with our problems,' he said. In spite of appearing tense he was calm and controlled. But the President was not smiling, as he usually did. He asked how Watban was getting on.

'All things considered, not bad. He won't die. The bullet wounds in his left leg are serious.'

Saddam went in to see his half-brother alone. He came out a few moments later and left Bin-Sina with Qusay and Abed Hamoud. They were obviously in a hurry.

Abed Hamoud had a nephew, Rafed, who was one of the presidential bodyguards. He, too, had been at Hassan al-Khasab's farm to celebrate the Day of all Days with Watban. He had not survived unhurt either. One of Uday's bullets had grazed the skin immediately below his left eye and, on its way past, taken off his ear. Miraculously he had not been killed. He had been brought to Bin-Sina and while we prepared him for surgery he told me that Watban had been making fun of Uday. Uday's upper jaw protruded abnormally over his lower jaw and from birth he had suffered from a speech defect. At the party the uncle had mimicked him and ridiculed his speech deficiency to the wild jubilation of anyone wanting to listen.

This had enraged Luai, Uday's uncle and Watban's brother-in-law. Uday was no less enraged when he got to hear of it. Many who gathered around Watban while he was mocking the President's son were not even close family.

'Uday was fuming when he arrived and started picking people off at random,' Abed Hamoud's nephew told me. Then he dropped a bombshell: 'But worse things went on last night. Hussein and Saddam Kamel have run off to Jordan with their wives and children. Their brother, Hakim Kamel has gone too.'

The penny dropped. This explained why Saddam was not smiling and why he had appeared so stressed when he came to visit his wounded half-brother earlier that morning.

The sons-in-law Hussein and Saddam Kamel were the President's favourites. Not only had he rewarded them with his two daughters, Raghad and Rana, they had both been given prominent and influential positions.

Hussein Kamel was Minister for Military and Industrial Development with special responsibility for Iraq's weapons programme. To Saddam Kamel was entrusted the very important position of head of the President's personal bodyguards. He had been on duty when he escaped with his brother and their wives and children.

It is difficult to imagine what Saddam must have felt when he was betrayed by two of his inner circle: family who were possibly closer to him than anyone.

Uday, his uncle Luai and Jaber went to ground after Watban had been shot. They hid with Abed Hassan al-Majid, whom they trusted and whom they counted on not to betray them. Abed was Luai's uncle and the brother of Ali Hassan al-Majid – Chemical Ali.

Saddam was now frantically looking for them. Qusay had been given clear instructions to find his brother immediately, and during the afternoon he managed to contact Jaber with a request to phone him.

Jaber asked Uday if that was OK.

'You can tell him you'll meet him but you mustn't say where I am. My father will have to calm down first.'

The nationwide celebration of the Day of all Days was progressing apace in the streets and parks of Baghdad when Jaber drove to the Republican Palace to meet Qusay.

'You must tell me where he is. We must hold a family council as soon as possible.'

Jaber refused and was threatened with imprisonment.

In the meantime Abed Hassan al-Majid had been informed of Hussein and Saddam Kamel's flight to Jordan with their families. They were his nephews and he immediately grasped the seriousness of the situation. Abed Hassan then contacted Qusay and told him where his brother and uncle were hiding.

Soon after Qusay phoned his brother. 'Come immediately. There are more important things to discuss than what happened to Watban,' he said.

Jaber was packed off with a handwritten message to the newspapers and radio and TV channels stating that Watban had met with an accident during the celebrations of the Day of all Days. No details were given.

'We wish him a speedy recovery,' said the message.

Saddam led the family council which took place in Kaser al-Deyata palace at eleven that evening. The President was cool, calm and composed during the discussions. It was decided to send Uday, Jaber, Chemical Ali and Maneh Abed al-Rashid, who was head of the Iraqi intelligence service, to Jordan to persuade Hussein and Saddam Kamel to change their minds.

They set off through the desert in cars at four in the morning of 8 August. They were in Amman by lunchtime. Using King Hussein as an intermediary, they desperately tried to engage Saddam's two sons-in-law in conversation, but both refused. During the afternoon it became clear that the expedition was not getting them anywhere and after a quick lunch with the Iraqi ambassador in Amman, the delegation decided to return to Baghdad.

'During the entire return journey I was pressurised to take the blame for Watban's accident. It would make everything so much easier for the President, I was told. But I refused to be the scapegoat,' Zafer Muhammad Jaber told me later.

Saddam's three half-brothers demanded that Uday be made to pay for his behaviour. But the President dithered. Neither the family nor the regime would benefit from washing their dirty linen in public. Nor had Watban's role in the disastrous affair been especially defensible. A newly dismissed intoxicated Interior Minister squabbling with his brother-in-law over a prostitute was nothing to be proud of should it become generally known. Both parties were to blame.

Sabaawi, Barzan and Watban swallowed their half-brother's decision with difficulty. Whenever I met them they complained that the President had let Uday off lightly. Saddam went no further than to demand that Uday visit his uncle at Bin-Sina and give him an unconditional apology. He was to take his pistol, give it to Watban and ask him to shoot Uday in exactly the same place as Uday's pump-action gun had smashed his uncle's leg in order to settle the account the Bedouin way.

The three brothers already hated their nephew like the plague and the shooting incident did nothing to improve matters. But not much love was lost between the three either. They engaged in wholesale backbiting and never hesitated to trip each other up. Relations deteriorated further when Sabaawi backed Saddam in his decision not to punish Uday. The oldest of the half-brothers had by then been appointed head of the Iraqi secret police and was keen not to quarrel with the President for fear of losing his position.

Discussions over who was best qualified to treat Watban were many and protracted. His leg needed comprehensive orthopaedic and neurological surgery. Saddam made it known that unlimited money was available. However expensive, his half-brother would receive the very best medical help obtainable.

The President himself toyed with the idea of asking the world-famous Cuban surgeon Alvaris Cambris to come to the rescue. The relations between the two and between Saddam and the Cuban president Fidel Castro were excellent. But in the end the choice fell on France. A team of doctors from Paris came to Bin-Sina and carried out the many and complicated operations needed to get Watban on his feet.

It was important to Saddam that his half-brother got the help he needed in Iraq. He was loath to send family members abroad for medical treatment. I therefore smelt a rat – and feared being pulled into one of the endless intrigues which constantly whirled about in the power-sphere around the President – when Sabaawi pulled me aside one day in the autumn and asked to have a heart-to-heart talk with me.

He put his arm around me. 'Dr Ala, has my brother Barzan spoken to you about the possibility of sending Watban to Switzerland for further medical treatment?'

Barzan was still at that time Iraq's UN ambassador in Geneva.

'Not at all. He has never phoned me nor suggested anything like that.'

Sabaawi said no more but I feared the worst from the head of the secret police. I had become increasingly unpopular in the wolf's lair around Saddam. I was respected by the President: suspicion and envy were the result. It would enrage Saddam to send Watban to a Swiss hospital and now Sabaawi might accuse both me and his brother in Geneva of having made such a suggestion. That was how his like got rid of people they detested.

A few days later Saddam came to visit Watban in Bin-Sina and to say goodbye to the French surgeons who had performed yet another round of operations on Watban's leg. They were about to set off for Paris via Amman and a drive through the desert. Sabaawi was with him.

'I want to thank you for your splendid efforts and for your courage in the face of America's continued propaganda against Iraq,' the President said.

When the French doctors left he asked me to stay behind in Watban's room with Sabaawi.

'I have followed Dr Ala's achievements both as an artist and surgeon for a long time. Iraq has every reason to be proud of him.' He looked straight at Sabaawi. 'I have got to know him both privately and through official channels and I am convinced that he is honourable in every way. I will never forget what he did for me after the traffic accident in 1991.'

The praise continued and it was starting to get embarrassing.

'Thank you for all your kind words, Mr President,' I said. 'But if you will excuse me, I would like to go as I have a patient waiting.'

I was aware of what was going on. 'Don't touch him,' was Saddam's message to the two half-brothers. Next morning Sabaawi was released from his position as head of the secret police.

Uday's collection mania reached dizzy heights this eventful autumn. While the majority of Iraqis sank ever deeper into poverty, ill health and wretchedness, the President's son continued to import cars to add to his collection. The number of vehicles was approaching one thousand. Around one hundred of the most expensive and impressive were parked in a garage in the strictly guarded Republican Palace: Rolls Royces, Bentleys, Lexuses, Audis, BMWs, Mercedes, Porsches, Ferraris, Lamborghinis – you name it, Uday had it. In addition the garage housed an exquisite collection of antique cars. They were Uday's prize possessions.

One morning black smoke rose over the Republican Palace. The garage was burning and nothing was being done to stop it.

Saddam had been to visit his half-brother at Bin-Sina. The awful reality of Watban's situation suddenly dawned upon him. Watban was trapped in hospital and would be for a long time. In a dark mood Saddam went to Uday's garage, asked the bodyguards to fetch petrol cans and matches, and while he calmly smoked one of his large Havana cigars, he watched the cars burn to cinders, enjoying sweet revenge.

Saddam had left by the time Uday and Zafer Muhammad Jaber came rushing up, in time to catch a last glimpse of the burnt-out luxury cars. Qusay too had been warned about his father's retaliation and arrived before them.

'Why didn't you stop him!' Uday shouted, stifling sobs. He was beside himself with anger. 'Have you forgotten that I got you out of prison?'

Uday always brought this up when he was less than pleased with his younger brother. In 1984 Qusay had been unfortunate enough to floor a Saudi Arabian diplomat during a drunken party at the Mansour Melia Hotel in Baghdad. It was never clear what the quarrel was about but the diplomat complained to the Iraqi foreign ministry. Saddam got to hear about it and imprisoned his son.

Qusay went to the prison where Uday and Jaber had been incarcerated when Saddam's valet, Kamel Hanna, was killed. But after only a few days Uday came to his rescue. He turned up at the prison director's office with a couple of friends and demanded he be let go. When the prison director refused Uday shot at his feet with a Kalashnikov and forced him to free Qusay. The two brothers then went to earth until Saddam had calmed down. After a while the affair was forgotten.

'You should have done something and stopped him!' Uday continued to accuse his brother.

'I was too late. The garage was already in flames,' Qusay answered. 'At least I persuaded him to leave your other cars alone.'

Many of them were in a large warehouse close to the Republican Palace. Uday could not get there fast enough. He barricaded himself by the front door with sandbags and got hold of a heavy machine gun, but fortunately he did not have to use it. Saddam had had enough of chastening his son.

'If he had turned up I am sure Uday would have shot him on the spot,' was Jaber's assessment of his friend's state of mind.

The autumn and winter in Amman were hard for Saddam's sons-in-law. Initially it was exciting. Western intelligence agencies led by America's CIA threw themselves like ravenous wolves on all and anything they could glean from the brothers, as did Rolf Ekeus, head of the UN weapons inspection team. But after Hussein Kamel had told them everything he knew about Iraq's weapons development programme and his brother Saddam had no more to tell of the inner workings of the regime, the monotonous grind of everyday life in the Jordanian capital quickly took over.

The transition from a life of luxury lived at the summit of power to an anonymous existence in exile in Amman was tougher than they had envisaged. Rumours circulated that Hussein Kamel was homesick, that he was unwell. Ministers I spoke to hinted that an envoy from the mighty and influential Kherbeet family in Ramadi had visited Amman as the President's go-between and that he had offered the sons-in-law safe conduct home. Saddam promised not to punish them.

Three hundred kilometres from Amman and five hundred kilometres from Baghdad, in the barren and inhospitable Arab desert, runs the border between Iraq and Jordan. The border post on the Iraqi side is called Trabil. It is said – and seems plausible – that the name comes from the English word 'trouble'. Many thousand British soldiers fell in battles against the Turks in this area towards the end of the First World War, when the remains of the Ottoman Empire were falling apart.

Hisham al-Durari was the station chief when Hussein, Saddam and Hakim Kamel and their wives and children came to Trabil on 20 February 1996. I don't know what made them decide to return to Iraq, but I have heard that Hussein Kamel could no longer bear Amman and that he, as the oldest brother, had put pressure on the others to get them to return with him to Baghdad.

According to al-Durari Saddam Kamel was in a bad way when he came to Trabil: 'He seemed to be sleepwalking. He was unshaven and wore pyjamas.'

He was also carrying a pistol which al-Durari relieved him of, following direct instructions from the President. The station chief then gave the orders for Raghad and Rana and their children to join the President's sons and drive to Baghdad with them. Uday and Qusay were already at Trabil with their bodyguards to receive the party from Amman.

'Why?' Hussein Kamel asked.

'It's best like that,' said al-Durari.

After the President's sons, daughters and grandchildren had

left, the sons-in-law were driven to Baghdad in their own heavily guarded car.

Two days later an announcement appeared in the newspapers and on television that Raghad and Rana had decided to divorce their husbands. The announcement came as Muslims were celebrating the end of Ramadan, the annual holy month of fasting. Saddam and his family were gathered for Eid al-Fitr in one of the presidential palaces in Tikrit. The two prodigal sons-in-law were not invited to this feast.

'I promised not to punish them for having fled to Jordan and betraying me,' Saddam said when the roast lamb and rice had been consumed and the bowls of fruit and dates had appeared on the table. He looked out over the abundant gathering and caught the eye of Ali Hassan al-Majid, their uncle. 'But this is a family matter.'

Ali Hassan nodded. He was no one's fool.

Hussein, Saddam and Hakim had chosen to stay with their sister when they returned. She lived with three small children in Saydia, a southern suburb of Baghdad, near the road to Babylon. Their father, Kamel al-Majid, had joined them and had got hold of weapons. They all knew what was in store. The rumours from the family feast had preceded the horde of heavily armed relatives who moved off towards the south to resurrect family honour.

The offensive force reached its goal at five in the morning and surrounded the house in Saydia. But Chemical Ali was loath to kill his brother. He called to Kamel al-Majid and asked him to come out with his daughter and her child. Kamel refused.

The traditional Arabic scarf, the keffiyeh, was on his head. It was kept in place by the agal, the black piece of rope wound twice round the forehead. When Ali Hassan repeated that no one had any intention of killing anyone in the house but the three nephews who had disgraced the family by their flight to Jordan, Kamel took off the agal and threw it out to his brother in the street.

In the Arab world there is no mistaking this signal. The matter is settled. Nothing can be achieved by continuing the discussion.

The person to whom the rings are thrown must bear the consequences of the disagreement.

Kamel al-Majid and his three sons defended themselves bravely; the attacking party suffered losses. Thahir Suleiman al-Majid, a cousin of Hussein Kamel, was the first to be shot and killed. He was known to the Iraqis for having stolen cement and building materials from the Ministry of Industry just after the Gulf War. He was exposed in the newspapers and on TV, and had been put in gaol for a couple of years. Now his corrupt life ended in a fight to restore his family's honour. Next to fall was Ahmed Rafour, one of Saddam's guards. He was also a distant relative of the four who defended themselves so bravely in the besieged house.

We were kept busy at Bin-Sina with wounded family members who were brought in and could inform me in detail of how the showdown was proceeding.

After three hours Ali Hassan decided to use an RPG – a rocket-propelled grenade – against his brother and the nephews to get things moving in the stalemate that was developing. When the rocket hit its target and exploded, Saddam, Hakim and their father were all killed as was the sister and her three children. They were between three and six years old and had sought refuge in one of the bathrooms. They were badly burnt when brought to the morgue at Saddam's centre for heart surgery in Baghdad.

Hussein Kamel survived and continued the fight.

The sun was setting and the bloody family drama had lasted over twelve hours when Hussein Kamel's brother-in-law, Jamal Mustafa, entered the house with a younger cousin. Mustafa was married to the President's youngest daughter Hala, and was one of his bodyguards.

Hussein Kamel was ensconced behind the stairs between the ground and first floors. The smoking machine gun in his hands had killed two and wounded two more of his relatives.

'Saddam is an evil man. You must get rid of him! He is an American agent and not to be trusted,' he called out to his brother-in-law.

Jamal Mustafa's answer was to open fire. Hussein Kamel was badly wounded but his brother-in-law and his cousin were also hit during the exchange of fire and collapsed. The President's former favourite and son-in-law had been hit in the stomach and knew the end was approaching. With a mighty effort he got up and staggered out on to the street.

'I am Hussein Kamel,' he cried. He wanted to die standing up.

A machine-gun volley from one of his relatives sent him crashing to the ground.

Ali Hassan al-Majid went over and stood on his face. In the Arab world this is a sign of total humiliation. Then he aimed his gun at the nephew's head. He emptied the magazine.

'That's what happens to traitors!' he shouted.

Neither Uday nor Qusay took part in the fight. It was not through lack of ability or enthusiasm, but their father had promised the sons-in-law that he would not punish them and the President's words were binding for his sons too. However, they did not miss one juicy detail. They sat in the car with an uninterrupted view and watched it all from beginning to end.

Jamal Mustafa and his cousin survived the close-quarters fighting. I operated on Mustafa at Bin-Sina. He had been hit in the stomach and shoulders but the wounds were not serious. Saddam arrived to visit his son-in-law at ten in the evening. The President didn't appear too happy but was relaxed, standing by the sickbed.

'I can't think how he could have left Iraq, and I certainly don't understand how he could have thought of returning,' I heard him say. He was talking about Hussein Kamel.

Two months later I visited Hussein Kamel's widow, Raghad, to carry out a minor operation. She was dressed in black and appeared sad.

The nurse with me wished her a speedy recovery.

'It would have been better if you had wished that I had never returned,' said Saddam's daughter, and added: 'I wish I could build a mosque to the memory of my husband.'

A further two months later I returned to complete Raghad's treatment. She was still wearing black but could only indulge her sorrow at home. When she visited Saddam and the rest of the family with her sister Rana, they were expected to wear light and colourful clothes. There was to be no mourning. Hussein and Saddam Kamel were traitors and had been punished.

To cut away tissue I used a small electric knife, which stops any bleeding by cauterising the incision. This is a perfectly normal medical procedure but the patient has to be grounded by means of a small plate which is attached to the back or thigh before the cauterisation starts. The patient would otherwise be electrocuted.

Raghad got an electric shock. She jerked slightly when I used the electric pen. The nurse had slipped up and attached the plate incorrectly. Fortunately the shock was mild.

'Thank God,' I said. 'I would have got into trouble if anything had happened to you.'

Raghad looked at me. 'On the contrary. You are quite safe. They would have cheered.'

By 'they' she meant her father.

Hussein Kamel left behind a substantial fortune when he was killed. While still in office his bribes and secret commissions had reached considerable heights. After his death Saddam summoned his lawyer to explain how much it amounted to.

'I had to tell him,' she told me one day when she came to my clinic for a minor operation.

Kamel had put his money into more than two hundred houses, commercial properties and other real estate in and around Baghdad. All deeds had been issued in different names, but the lawyer knew the reality behind the camouflaged transactions.

Normally, any property or money belonging to 'traitors' who had been executed would be confiscated by the government.

'But in this case the President decided that all of the properties should go to Raghad and her children,' the lawyer told me.

Thanks to the French doctors' efforts and skill Watban was on his feet after about a year. But he still limped and had difficulty moving around. Not unexpectedly, Uday's close friend Zafer Muhammad Jaber was made jointly responsible and the scapegoat for Watban's cruel fate. He was tried in a court of law and sentenced to death but after six months in prison he was pardoned by Saddam Hussein and freed. Uday wished to have him back as confidant and secretary but Jaber had had enough and said no.

Another of Ali Hassan al-Majid's nephews escaped to Jordan in 2002, adding another stain to the family's honour. This time Ala Suleiman al-Majid was enticed by a new and better life outside Iraqi borders. Ala Suleiman was Thahir al-Majid's brother; he was shot and killed by Kamel Hussein in the family showdown in Saydia.

Ala's brothers persuaded him to return to Baghdad after a few months. He too was shot – by his brother Salam – for having escaped abroad and disgraced the family.

Salam was one of Saddam's closest bodyguards and when Baghdad fell in April 2003 he and his father and brothers appeared on Iraqi TV claiming that it was the President, whom they hated and abhorred, who had forced them to shoot Suleiman al-Majid.

'If you hated Saddam so much yet were always in possession of a weapon when you were near him, why did you not shoot him instead?' Salam was asked.

He didn't know how to answer and the whole Middle East laughed at him, his father and brothers for their hypocritical TV appearance.

Rendering the President's dream – a painting of which
I am not proud! (Author's collection)

CHAPTER 11

The Snake

Saddam has a dream and wants it painted. He is re-elected President.

On 13 July 1996 one of the President's bodyguards phoned and asked me to come to Bin-Sina; thence I was driven to the Republican Palace, where Saddam was expecting me. His leg was hurting. A toe on his right foot was painful when he walked and the cause was immediately obvious. Saddam was a vain man. His suits fitted perfectly and his shoes were small and dainty.

'Your shoes are too narrow, sir,' I said. 'You'll have to increase them by a size or two.'

'I can't walk if my shoes are too wide or too big,' he answered. 'I feel like I'm going to fall over.'

'You'll have to; otherwise you'll develop a corn.'

Saddam didn't answer.

I had finished my job and was packing up my bag when the President patted my arm. 'What's happened to the painting we were talking about?'

'I'm still working on it. It's not all that easy to compose.'

'It's taking its time,' Saddam said and smiled, making me realise this was serious. Time had run out.

'I'll have it finished in a couple of weeks,' I said.

In March 1991, when chaos and civil war reigned in both North and South Iraq, Saddam commissioned me to immortalise an extraordinary dream he had had. He recounted how he'd been walking through a dark forest with his bodyguards when a huge, green snake slithered towards him. 'I drew my sword and cut its head off. Blood was everywhere; my trousers were covered with it by the time my bodyguards finished it off.' The President became quite animated when he told me about the dream and insisted: 'I'd like you to use this as an inspiration for one of your paintings.'

This was the first and last time he commissioned a work from me. Initially I stalled when he asked how the painting was getting on and when would it be finished. My standard reply was: 'I'm working on the shape and composition. It takes time.' But now we were five years on and I realised Saddam was getting impatient. I would have to bite the bullet and get on with it.

It wasn't as though there was a dearth of portraits of Saddam. Ministers and party bosses had surpassed themselves, and each other, raising statues and hanging paintings of Saddam all over Iraq. They appeared in every conceivable size, showing Saddam in every possible pose. The President didn't ask for it, but he didn't forbid it either. His silence was interpreted as an endorsement of a country-wide embellishment; albeit occasionally rather primitive in its execution – some of the stuff adorning the country lacked even the most basic artistic merit. An entire industry had developed, which made good money reproducing the President's likeness and elevated figure.

The approach of his birthday on 28 April always triggered a flood; then there seemed no limit to what artwork could do to show the overflowing and real love the nation felt for its brilliant son, saviour and lodestar. Many of the paintings and sculptures unveiled at various events on the President's big day – and which resulted in immediate gifts of money straight from his office – were so ingenious that they took your breath away. But Saddam was relaxed about it.

'People must be allowed to express their feelings for me as they see fit,' he said when we were once talking about this special attention he received every year. 'It doesn't matter that they're not professional artists, as long as they do their best. It's the thought that matters, not necessarily the result.'

At home in his palaces and houses, on the whole realistic landscapes and horse paintings dominated the walls, together with

portraits of himself. They were not his choice – the embellishment had been left to a few art connoisseurs on his staff – but
they were not about to take any chances. They knew what he preferred.

On the other hand, 'Saddam's Centre for Art' had been
allowed to develop into Iraq's national gallery and our most
important art forum. The Centre was full of classical, impres-
sionist, expressionist, surrealist and abstract art, just to mention a
few categories. The President never questioned any purchases.
'The artists must be left alone to create what they want, as long as
they don't stand in our way,' he used to say.

That's what Layla al-Attar, the centre's director, thought too.
She was herself a recognised artist and I thoroughly enjoyed
working with her on my exhibitions. It still hurts to think of her
sudden death; yet another casual and completely innocent victim
of the power games being played out around us.

On 26 June 1993 I was making final arrangements for a new
exhibition which was to open the next day in her gallery. The
paintings were in situ, the lighting was perfect and a catalogue
had been printed which was surgically free of the usual homage
to the President and the regime's beneficence to and blessings
upon all Iraqi artists. The culture and information department
normally demanded that all catalogues printed such a glorifica-
tion of Saddam, together with a picture of him. But I refused to
mix art and politics thus. My special relationship with the
President allowed me to get away with it. Many of my fellow
artists found it much harder to avoid the political demands from
the ministry. They were to a certain degree economically depend-
ent on their relationship with the party bigwigs. If they got
difficult and refused to be a pawn in the regime's propaganda,
they might as well give up.

I was better off. Economically I was making ends meet on my
salary from al-Wasiti and what I earned from my private clinic.
Those who gave in were finished as free artists. They could no
longer work in peace because of the innumerable bureaucrats
chasing them, ensuring their work endorsed the spirit of the
regime. Undersecretaries, civil servants, architects, yes, even

Saddam's bodyguards interfered with the shape or size of statues and monuments. They had the nerve to suggest 'improvements' and didn't give up until they got their way, to the artists' great despair.

But corruption was, nevertheless, the worst aspect of it all. It spread like wildfire, even within the art community, as Saddam proclaimed a series of architectural and decorative competitions. Iraq might be squeezed like a lemon by UN sanctions and lack of oil revenue but the President insisted that the construction of palaces and mosques and all types of monumental buildings should go ahead in an ever more grandiose style. He admired Paris and other European capitals. Important secular and sacred buildings, together with other grand schemes, would put Baghdad firmly on the world architectural and cultural map and Saddam himself would be remembered by posterity. The majority of the architectural and decorative competitions were judged by official committees. The committee members were all, without exception, open to bribery. The artist who paid most won the competition.

Layla al-Attar, thank God, kept to the straight and narrow in her job as director and chief buyer of Saddam's Centre for Art. She was generous and companionable and put the artists' interest before her own, and before the omnipresent bureaucrat's fear of not behaving politically correctly at all times.

Before leaving the gallery on the eve of my new exhibition I dropped into her office to let her know that I was very pleased with the work and the preparations that were being made. She thanked me and suggested we go and have a look at the paintings together. I hesitated, as normally she always waited until the preview.

'It has occurred to me that I need to see them now and not wait until later,' she said.

We made the rounds and she was full of praise for what she saw.

The next morning American warships in the Persian Gulf fired twenty-three Tomahawk missiles. Destination: Baghdad, and more specifically the office complex belonging to the Iraqi intelligence service.

Two months earlier George H. W. Bush, whom Bill Clinton succeeded as American president in January 1993, visited Kuwait to, amongst other things, relive the memories from the time when Saddam was thrown out of the sheikhdom during the Gulf War. During Bush's visit the authorities discovered and disarmed an explosives-packed car in the centre of Kuwait City. The charge was timed to coincide with Bush's presence in the vicinity and was strong enough to have destroyed large parts of the city centre.

Specialists from the CIA, who examined the bomb, pointed a finger at Baghdad and Saddam's Mukhabarat. A number of Iraqis were apprehended and duly executed by the authorities in Kuwait. The court case was, to put it mildly, summary.

The twenty-three Tomahawk missiles which arrived on the morning of 27 June were Clinton's revenge for what he thought was Saddam's attempt to kill the retired American president.

Layla al-Attar lived with her husband and daughter near the Mukhabarat office complex in the al-Harithiya district of Baghdad. The offices were bombed in February 1991 too, during the Gulf War. A stray bomb completely demolished the al-Attar house. Luckily the family were visiting a friend who lived in the Rasidia district north of Baghdad, and so were saved. They had to move to her sister's house, about two hundred metres further down the road from their demolished home.

This time the Tomahawk missiles also missed their mark. One of them hit the sister's house and destroyed that too. Al-Attar, her husband and a maid were killed; the daughter was badly wounded.

I postponed the exhibition for a month. During the preview it was the Foreign Minister, Muhammad Said al-Sahhaf, later to be world-famous as 'Comical Ali', who lent lustre to the occasion.

'This is a very special exhibition which says a lot,' he said.

For once I agreed with him.

Not long after Layla al-Attar's death I found myself out in the open desert west of Baghdad. Hundreds of naked men were standing behind tables and I was looking on from behind. They were busy washing corpses with soap and water.

There were a few women amongst all the men. They howled

and screamed and dug up dead children from the sand; children who had not been long dead. I was drawn towards the women and started to dig myself. I wanted to find my father.

As I dug deeper and deeper I started to wonder what sort of state I would find my father in: a skeleton or just a heap of bones?

When I had dug down far enough I was able to make out his facial features, but otherwise he was just a skeleton, bound up in a bit of skin. Someone helped me to haul him out and lay him on the table; then I too started washing him in soap and water.

I was petrified. My heart felt as though it would jump out of my chest. I screamed and woke up dripping wet when my wife roused me from the nightmare. It occurred to me that this was the first emotional reaction I had suffered, after having witnessed so much death and destruction.

It took me no time to paint Saddam's snake-dream once I'd realised there was no avoiding it. It was of respectable dimensions, 170 by 160 centimetres, and it arrived in his office, accompanied by cordial greeting, only one month after his unequivocal reminder.

What I had not bargained for was the return message from his mighty private secretary, Abed Hamoud. The figurative snake-dream would be unveiled and presented to Saddam on his re-election anniversary as a symbol of the country's renewed trust in their President.

I didn't think that was necessarily a great honour.

The re-election, which took place on 15 October 1995, would be valid for another seven years. The deputy chairman of the Revolutionary Command Council, Izzat Ibrahim al-Douri, took charge of the preparations and made sure the outcome was fixed.

Of Iraq's 8.4 million electors 99.96 per cent wanted Saddam to continue as President. Attendance at the ballot box was not quite so dramatic, but 99.47 per cent was nevertheless acceptable.

Unfortunately, to avoid unpleasantness, even I had to give Saddam my vote. Local Baath Party activists sat in the polling stations and oversaw the voting with eagle eyes. The ballot papers with yes or no squares had to be filled out in front of them. And if when the polling stations closed some of those qualified to vote had, for one reason or another, not turned up, the activists would vote for them. Such practices lead to exceptional results.

I remained behind to drink tea and talk to the President after the snake-dream had been unveiled and all the bigwigs had left. He had always praised my art, but there was no doubt that he valued this painting above all as, compared to my other works, it was purely figurative.

'You are a great artist,' he said. 'Without people like you, and good politicians, we cannot build the country.'

While I was sitting there, Abed Hamoud entered with a note which he gave to the President. Saddam skimmed it quickly and a few moments later a Kurdish tribal chief from Dahouk was waved in. Saddam showed him great respect. 'What do you want?' Saddam asked.

The sheikh explained that his oldest son had just completed his law studies and should now be given a seat on the important executive council for Kurdish questions.

'The council has already been appointed and there are no spare places. But I can help with another exciting job, if you're interested,' the President answered.

'No, the executive council or nothing,' said the sheikh and left. Abed Hamoud came in.

'Give him a car as a consolation prize,' said the President.

In the wake of the revolts following the 1991 Gulf War three Iraqi administrative areas were established as so-called buffer zones under international protection. There had been constant turbulence in these Kurdish regions; this mountainous part of the country had now broken away from Baghdad and was left to its own devices under a sort of autonomy, led by the Kurds Masoud Barzani and Jalal Talabani.

The Iraqi government forces had withdrawn but Saddam had also cut off all economic help. Supplies of food, fuel and heating oil stopped. Doctors, nurses, teachers and civil servants employed in local and regional administration were unpaid.

There were between 3.2 and 3.5 million Kurds in the affected areas. The UN High Commission for Refugees and the World

Food Programme managed to feed about 750,000 of them during their first winter of independence. The remainder froze and starved and struggled as best they could.

The situation was not ameliorated when Barzani and Talabani failed to agree to a uniform, democratic management of the new, independent areas following their breakaway from Iraq. Elections for a legislative assembly took place in May 1992 and received international praise and congratulations, but both Kurdish leaders stayed away from the new regional government which was formed during the summer. Barzani and his KDP, the Kurdistan Democratic Party, chose to maintain their power and influence in the northern part of the country, while Talabani and the PUK, the Patriotic Union of Kurdistan, continued their dominance in the south. The new Kurdistan was divided in two, Barazani and KDP in Arbil, Talabani and PUK in Sulaimaniya.

And then they went to war.

'That was my decision,' said Saddam.

We were still drinking tea in his office after the unveiling ceremony. The president started to pontificate about the situation in the north when the sheikh from Dahouk had left.

'Many of my generals and a greater part of the Baath Party leadership did not want us to withdraw from the three northern areas. But I insisted. It was important for the Kurds to see for themselves how evil Barzani and Talabani are. I knew they would understand sooner or late.' And he smiled.

The conflict between KDP and PUK guerrilla soldiers cost the lives of many thousands of people. It developed into a full-blown war when Barzani and Talabani fell out over the border lines between the two self-proclaimed administrative units. But in reality the disagreement ran deeper. Tribal and family feuds have characterised life in the Kurdish areas from historic times, as in Iraq as a whole. But now, above all, the differences centred on smuggling and the division of profits. A lot of money was involved.

UN sanctions affected all trade with Baghdad and the regime, and gave rise to ever-increasing and lucrative smuggling between Iraq and Turkey – to Barzani's great delight. Tankers with oil and lorries with urea and cement were obliged to cross KDP road-blocks before crossing into Turkey. The driver could not pass without paying a transit tax to Barzani. Equally taxes were paid to the Kurdish leader when goods and commodities passed the other way, from Turkey.

Talabani too demanded tax at his roadblocks when oil, cement and fertiliser for Iran passed PUK areas to the south-east. But the traffic of contraband to the Islamic Republic was less extensive than that which passed over the Turkish border. Talabani's income could therefore not measure up to Barzani's. He demanded that the two should meet to discuss a fairer division of the loot, but the KDP leader refused.

In December 1994 – after considerable success on the battle-fields – Talabani's guerrilla soldiers forced KDP forces out of Arbil. But only eighteen months later Barzani hit back – and this time with help from Saddam.

The world opened its eyes wide.

On 31 August 1996, more than thirty thousand Iraqi crack troops, supported by tanks and heavy artillery, advanced over the border to the autonomous Kurdish areas and captured Arbil. The massive advance, in cooperation with Barzani's peshmerga soldiers, was led by the president's son Qusay. It did not halt until the PUK's guerrilla soldiers were also thrown out of their centre of operations in and around Sulaimaniya. It was Saddam's great-est military manoeuvre since the invasion of Kuwait and defeat in the Gulf War. Talabani, his soldiers and tens of thousands of refugees fled over the border to Iran.

Confusion and frustration reigned, particularly in Washington when America realised that Masoud Barzani had allied himself in secret to Saddam in order to regain lost power and influence. They found it especially irksome that the Iraqi National Congress (INC) took a battering when Saddam and the KDP overran the autonomous Kurdish regions.

The INC had been established with American money and was led by the well-known exiled Iraqi Ahmed Chalabi. In the Arab world Chalabi was best known for his involvement with the bank-ruptcy of the Petra Bank in Amman at the end of the eighties. Chalabi had left Jordan by the time the case came before the

court. He was convicted in absentia and sentenced to twenty
years' hard labour.

'The biggest economic crook in the history of the Middle
East', were the words used during the court case. Chalabi himself
protests his innocence and denies all charges brought against
him.

However, it is a long way from the ruined investors in Jordan to
the real power-brokers in the American capital. Here Chalabi
had managed to ingratiate himself and persuade the decision-
makers that the organisation he was in the process of establishing
would be an important tool in the toppling of Saddam and his
regime. In cooperation with the CIA, the INC quickly established groups of 'freedom fighters' in many towns in the
autonomous Kurdish areas. Now they were drawn into the under-
tow of the Saddam/Barzani offensive. In Arbil alone about a
hundred of Chalabi's adherents were executed. Other INC resistance groups packed their bags and fled.

Saddam had good reason to smile this autumn day when the
snake-dream was his at last. Not only had he rid himself of
Chalabi's freedom fighters in Northern Iraq, but the Republican
Guard crack troops, which had now been withdrawn from the
autonomous areas, had shown the Kurds that there was still life in
him. The international protection awarded to their self-government proved to be limited, especially when they spent their time
fighting bitterly amongst each other.

The PUK guerrillas and the refugees had now, in the autumn
of 1996, started to return to Iraq, battles against the KDP had
resumed and it would take another couple of years for the
American brokers to persuade Barzani and Talabani to make
peace.

'I gave them freedom to choose,' said Saddam. 'Only then
could they decide what they really wanted.'

I asked whether he would like to hear a story by the British paediatrician John Roper which he used to read to his sons, Thomas
and Matthew, at bedtime. Dr Roper had been a colleague of my
wife from the Royal Devon and Exeter General Hospital at the
end of the sixties and our two families had remained good friends.

'Tell me,' said the President.

'Once upon a time a wolf lived in a big forest. He spent time roaming around and hunting and there was plenty of small game for him to eat. The wolf had a friend, a dog. They often met on the outskirts of the forest to have a talk and enjoy each other's company. Then a lean year arrived. There was no longer anything for the wolf to hunt and eat in the forest. He got thinner and thinner and was about to die of hunger. One day he decided to go and see his friend the dog and ask for help. The dog was frisky and well fed and offered to help the wolf. "Just come with me to town and I'll help you find a master. You just need to do as I do. Look after his house, and he will give you food and water and a little house to sleep in."

'The wolf thought this sounded like a good idea. He went to town with the dog. But when they got nearer the master's house the wolf suddenly spotted the collar with the nameplate on it. "What's that?" he asked.

'"Well," said the dog, "the collar tells the world that I have a master and the nameplate who that master is. In the daytime I am tied up but when night falls the master feeds me and lets me loose so I can guard his house."

'The wolf stopped and looked down. "Dear friend," he said after he had thought for a moment, "I cannot sell my freedom just because I haven't got any food. I can't bear the thought of being tied up all day and having a collar like that round my neck. It's better to live hungry than to be bound to a master in town."

'The wolf turned and went home.'

Saddam looked at me for a long time and said nothing. It was obvious he did not appreciate the story.

'The snake-dream painting will be given place of honour in my museum,' he said and got up. The audience was over.

He was referring to the 'Leader's Museum', where all the gifts from home and abroad were exhibited. They were housed in a magnificent new building in Baghdad. Architecturally it was reminiscent of a modern cathedral.

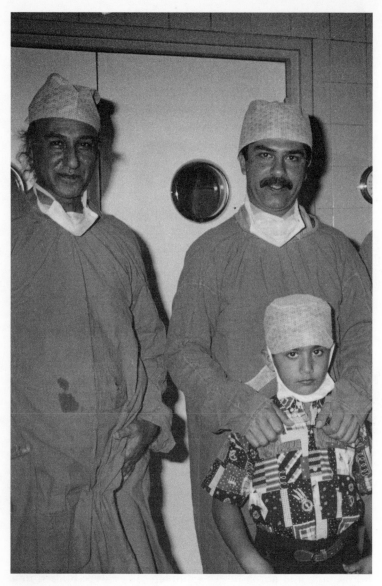

Qusay and his son Mustafa visit Bin-Sina. Following the fall of the regime thirteen-year-old Mustafa was killed together with his father and uncle Uday in Mosul in Northern Iraq when American soldiers attacked the house in which they had hidden. Mustafa fought tenaciously in the exchange of fire that took place. (Author's collection)

CHAPTER 12

The Pursuit of Women

Uday is shot. Is it God's punishment?

Al-Ruwad was known for its delicious ice-cream and the many pretty girls who frequented the place. It lay on the corner of two commercial thoroughfares: Abu Jafaar al-Mansour and al-Mansour, and good-looking young men from the capital's better-off homes buzzed around the ice-cream parlour like bees round a honeypot in the afternoons and evenings.

Uday's face was well known in the neighbourhood. As a rule the son of the President cruised around in one of his innumerable Mercedes, while he pondered whom he could lay his hands on for the evening's entertainment. When his eyes alighted upon an exciting prospect he would dispatch a friend or a bodyguard carrying a visiting card and a phone number. If she was interested, she could phone.

Quite a few were. Perhaps they were motivated by desire for financial reward; by the hope that Uday might fix them up with a job; or by having the opportunity to ask about a brother or father lost in the dark and deadly maze of security police operations. Or perhaps it was just pure and simple curiosity, a spirit of adventure and the dream of experiencing a life of luxury behind the tall, guarded walls of the palaces.

Few knew what awaited them. Uday exercised little if any restraint. Several times I treated female party-goers who came to my clinic having been knifed, disfigured by burning cigarettes or otherwise ill-treated during the night's frolicking in bed. Uday showed them no respect whatsoever. If he rewarded them it was never with more than a five- or ten-dollar make-up set or something similar; he looked after his billions like a veritable Scrooge. But he needed women every evening and had six staff to take care of the procurement. He wasn't particularly fussy whom he slept with. Zafer Muhammad Jaber remembers a party when a beautiful young woman complained: 'I thought he was interested in me, but he's gone off with my mother.'

Some of Uday's female colleagues in the Iraqi Olympic Committee were especially zealous in rounding up women. They had perfected the art of trawling universities and secondary schools in Baghdad, providing invitations to apparently innocent Olympic Committee garden parties at various venues around the Iraqi capital. Transport was provided to parks and places of entertainment where sumptuous banquets, music and drink were provided. Many of the girls turned up chaperoned by brothers or aunts or mothers. It was all very proper, even after Uday had made an entrance in order to vet those present with a view to inviting them to the next, more intimate, gathering.

Having decided whom to invite, he left the dirty work of persuading the chosen one to show up to his female colleagues. Some of them smelt a rat and foresaw the consequences; others agreed. After all, *this* party was sedate and innocent enough.

The system eventually fell apart, however; the whole of Baghdad was talking, and Uday got rid of the collaborators whose job it had been to gather in and persuade the girls.

One of them turned up at my clinic explaining that she had had the bad luck to burn herself on the family's paraffin stove. At least, that was her story. But having examined her I noticed two identical round burns, each of them approximately ten centimetres in diameter, on her buttocks. In the centre of each I could read the word 'Shame'.

This was Uday's way of rewarding her loyal Olympian efforts: by branding her bottom like any old cow.

On Thursday 12 December 1996, Uday was at it again, trawling the area around al-Ruwad. This was no longer without its risks. A lot of people knew about his frequent visits to Mansour, and it was no secret that he was not always accompanied by a bodyguard when out reconnoitring before the evening's debauchery.

Several attempts had been made on his life over the years, the last one in 1993 when two bombs were placed in rubbish bins outside his office in the Olympic Committee premises. They went off before he got there.

This particular evening he was accompanied by his friend Ali al-Sahr. They circled Mansour, driving slowly, in a Porsche Carrera. Uday had just slowed down outside al-Ruwad and let al-Sahr out on to the pavement by the ice-cream parlour, furnished with a telephone number to entice yet another potential party-goer, when two masked men rushed out from an alleyway nearby firing Kalashnikovs. The bullets riddled both the Porsche and the President's son.

In order to cause chaos and panic around the busy street crossing – it was late in the afternoon and rush hour – the two fired a few extra shots into the air before escaping down a narrow passageway to the road that runs parallel to al-Mansour. There they disappeared into a waiting car. The perpetrators were never caught but most likely they were Shia Muslim opponents of the regime.

Uday's Porsche continued thirty or forty metres down the road before coming to a halt. Al-Sahr ran after it and dragged him out. He then lifted him into a taxi and drove him to Bin-Sina. Uday was unconscious and bleeding like a stuck pig; his left leg dangled loosely from his body.

I was not on duty in Bin-Sina on the day Uday was attacked and shot. I was at home painting in my studio when I was summoned at seven p.m. and asked to report to the hospital without delay. When I arrived forty-five minutes later the place was swarming with his bodyguards and agents from the special security service.

Inside the operating theatre three surgeons were already working. Uday's blood pressure had been close to zero when al-Sahr brought him in. My colleagues had put him on a drip while preparing the blood transfusion, which was now in progress. One of the bullets had penetrated the left side of his ribcage, about ten centimetres below the armpit. The bullet had just missed his heart, continued through one lung before cutting through the stomach on its way out. The top part of his calf bone was shattered. Several bullets had also hit his right thigh and calf but bone and muscle there had not been affected.

We worked for six hours before we had patched him together tolerably well and the heavy haemorrhaging had stopped. He could not have been closer to death than he was on that December night.

We were scrubbing off outside the operating theatre when Saddam arrived together with Abed Hamoud and a couple of bodyguards. He was to all appearances neither nervous nor worried but conspicuously calm and level-headed.

'We are worrying you with our problems again,' he said after having greeted us. Then he fell silent. 'But the most important thing is Iraq and Iraq's safety.' He asked how Uday was getting on and we answered that, considering the circumstances, it could have been worse.

Saddam then moved towards the operating theatre. I signalled to Abed Hamoud that maybe it would not be a good idea for the President to enter the room – the scene inside was not a pleasant one – but Hamoud was too frightened to stop him.

Uday was still under the anaesthetic and lay naked on the operating table. His chest, stomach and legs were wrapped in bandages. The floor was covered in blood, blood-soaked bandages and towels. Saddam looked at him and walked over to the table. 'My son, men must allow for such setbacks as these.' He took Uday's right hand and held it in his own. 'But we are right and they are wrong.' Then he kissed Uday's brow. Qusay, who had arrived in the meantime, followed suit.

On the way out of the operating theatre Qusay took his father's right hand and held it to his mouth, embraced him and kissed him on both cheeks.

'What happened to your brother?' asked Saddam.

Qusay, who was head of the special security service whose task it was to guard the family's welfare, explained that Uday had been fasting and had driven to Mansour with Ali al-Sahr after sunset. He was hungry and wanted to buy some sandwiches. It was still some time before Ramadan, the Muslim holy month of fasting, but Uday insisted that quite independent of the religious calendar he never ate or drank from sun up to sun down on Mondays and Thursdays. Today of course was Thursday.

'While al-Sahr went to pick up sandwiches the assassins struck.'

Saddam appeared sceptical and demanded to talk to al-Sahr. He was fetched and put up against the wall.

'I know that you were after girls.' The President glared at him; there was no mention of a thank you for his quick thinking in getting Uday to hospital in time. Al-Sahr was petrified and unable to say a word.

Qusay's attempts to explain away his brother's trip to al-Ruwad as a mission to buy sandwiches were not entirely preposterous. To a certain extent Uday followed Islam and the Koran. Since the death of his uncle Adnan Khairallah in a helicopter accident in Northern Iraq in 1989 he had actually started to pray. Uday had been close to his uncle, Saddam's Defence Minister, who had perished in somewhat obscure circumstances. Khairallah had enjoyed great popularity amongst the armed forces and the officer corps. It had become clear, however, that he no longer figured amongst the President's favourites.

Uday's display of religious fervour did not always run smoothly, however. The five daily and compulsory acts of obeisance to Mecca were a particular problem. Forget Morning Prayer; he was either still awake and too drunk after the night's debaucheries or he was sleeping it off. Midday Prayer suffered for the same reasons. He thus compressed his devotion to the Prophet into one good spell sometime during the evening.

The question of alcohol use was more difficult to deal with; one cannot easily reconcile alcohol and Islam. But Uday employed his own sheikh, Abdul Ghaffar al-Abbassi, who was in charge of religious programmes on Uday's TV channel al-Shabab. One day Uday asked him, via Zafer Muhammad Jaber, whether it was OK to have a glass of brandy after evening prayers.

'Who's asking?' said the sheikh.

'Uday,' said Jaber.

'In his case, yes,' said the sheikh.

Saddam had left before Uday's mother Sajida arrived at Bin-Sina. She was agitated and had clearly left home in a hurry: her hair was unkempt and uncombed. I followed her to Uday's room.

'He'll kill my sons,' she screamed.

It was easy to see what she meant. Saddam's popularity was at an all-time low. Iraqis were fed up but frightened to speak out. Now they were avenging themselves on the President by trying to kill his son.

Not since the economic and social downturn at the beginning of the eighties had Iraqis found themselves in such straitened circumstances. The last sixteen years – two wars, internal strife, and UN sanctions – had drained the people of all their energy. Several hundred thousand of society's weakest, our small children, had succumbed. Poverty, hunger and sickness, crime and prostitution proliferated while the international community, headed by America and Great Britain, were more interested in the UN inspectors and the weapons of mass destruction which they never found.

The next morning it was clear that movement in Uday's left arm, hand and leg was reduced. His left eye had started to quiver. A CT-scan was reported to show some brain damage due to the lack of blood pressure we had registered when he was brought into Bin-Sina after the shots in Mansour.

The diagnosis was extremely sensitive. What Uday least of all needed was brain damage added to his already increasing mental instability. Bin-Sina's neurologists and neurosurgeons refused point-blank to confirm the scan report, and if they had they certainly would never have put it down on paper. It was safer to keep the bad news away from Uday and his family.

Doctors in this unusual hospital walked constantly on thin ice. Our patients were more powerful and influential than anyone else in Iraq. Misdiagnoses or treatments that failed could have a negative effect on the patients concerned, but, to put it bluntly, our destinies were at stake too.

It was more difficult to cure Uday than we had initially anticipated. On 20 December he complained of severe chest pains.
The intern on duty, Riad Saleh, and I examined him and came to
the conclusion that he might be suffering from pulmonary
embolism, or, in lay terms, blocked blood vessels in the lungs.
During major operations it is not unusual for so-called thrombi to
form in the veins. They can be difficult to detect before it is too
late. If they work loose they can be carried to the lungs where
they block the blood supply, with death as a likely result. Uday's
chest pains indicated that tiny venous thrombi had detached
themselves and it was only a matter of time before the entire
mass loosened.

Nine doctors in all treated Uday and during the day on New
Year's Eve we were all called to Saddam's al-Sujoud palace. The
palace lies on the banks of the Tigris, near the HQ of the Baath
Party and the large monument to the Unknown Soldier. The
President wanted to know how his son was doing. We explained
that we were concerned about the risk of pulmonary embolism,
and that we were treating him with blood-thinning medicine.

Saddam looked at us all and observed that when the battle
rages, 'we do not normally care about our dead and dying'. But
when it is all over, 'we must give our wounded soldiers the best
care and concern we can afford. The same goes for Uday,' he
added.

The meeting ended.

A week later Uday dismissed all but me from his room during
the doctors' round. 'Tell me, Dr Ala, as you were the one who
treated both me and my uncle Watban, where was he wounded?
Was it the right leg or the left leg?'

'Left.'

'Can you tell me exactly where?'

'Exactly where you have been injured.'

'Oh no,' Uday exclaimed. 'I am being punished by God.' He
was silent for a moment but then wanted to know where I thought
he might get the best treatment, in Baghdad or abroad.

While I was weighing up the various advantages and disad-
vantages Saddam entered the room with his half-brother,
Watban. Watban had been discharged from Bin-Sina but had

great problems walking. By a supreme act of irony Uday had now suffered the same fate as his uncle whose leg he had shot to bits during that drinking spree by the banks of the Tigris on 8 August – the same momentous day when Saddam's sons-in-law escaped to Jordan with their wives and children. Uday had apologised to his uncle and begged forgiveness for the ill-fated episode once the family drama had settled down somewhat. But I sensed that Watban had difficulty suppressing his malicious pleasure beneath a serious mask as he asked his nephew how things were going. He still loathed Uday like the plague.

'Dr Ala, tell me how things stand. Be honest, what are my prospects of complete recovery?'

Saddam and Watban sat down and I told them that Uday's condition was still pretty serious, and in particular the condition of his left leg gave rise to concern. The doctors and nurses at Bin-Sina had done a marvellous job by saving both his life and his leg, but Uday would never again be able to walk normally.

'Why?' asked Saddam.

'Because many of the muscles are damaged, some of them irreparably.'

Uday interrupted the conversation and demanded a hundred per cent cure.

'We aren't able to do that, only God can.'

Uday started to cry.

'You must accept this. Dr Ala is telling the truth,' Saddam said. Then the President asked us if we had all the equipment needed to treat Uday.

I answered that we lacked the facility to chart the flow of blood through his body. We did not have the latest ultrasound equipment and I was still uncertain about the thrombi that lurked somewhere in his veins and which could detach at any moment and kill him. Uday had once again experienced severe chest pains and we had poured painkillers and anticoagulants into him.

Saddam suggested that it might be an idea to treat Uday outside Iraq, for instance in Paris. He had great faith in French doctors. 'They have always been good friends and have helped us when we needed it. We have good relations with France and the

French,' he said. 'If you know of a good French doctor, could you contact him?'

I said I would.

I phoned one of France's leading orthopaedic surgeons, Professor Dominique Le Veit, a good friend of mine. I explained the situation and our problems at Bin-Sina and asked whether he might arrange for Uday to be treated in Paris. Professor Le Veit said he would investigate, but the response was quick and negative. Initial reactions from the government were such that he did not think Uday would be welcomed in France.

On 10 January the case was discussed in the French foreign ministry, which rejected our request. But the fax from Quai d'Orsay went on to say that there was no reason why a French team of doctors should not travel to Iraq with the necessary equipment to help Saddam's son.

We accepted gratefully, and on 16 January a team of doctors arrived in Baghdad from Paris. Uday was examined using state-of-the-art French Doppler ultrasound equipment and a thrombus was detected in the large vein of his left groin. The thrombus was five centimetres long and barely attached to the wall of the vein. Incredibly, Uday was as close to death now as he was when Ali al-Sahr brought him to Bin-Sina on 12 December. The French doctors suggested removing the thrombus by means of an advanced technique tested and tried internationally, but Uday refused. We subsequently increased the dose of blood-thinning medicine and told him to lie as still as possible. Slowly the thrombus dissolved. By the beginning of March it was no longer there.

Professor Le Veit arrived in Baghdad on 2 February to operate on Uday's left leg. It should have been possible to use a bone graft from his pelvis to reconstruct the damaged bone in his tibia, but the leg was still swollen and Le Veit decided to postpone the operation a few months until the swelling subsided.

Uday was furious. He wanted the operation immediately and refused even to discuss it with the French professor. It was decided that my colleague, Dr Hassan al-Khodeiri, would travel to Europe to enquire as to who might perform the operation. He would also look into innovations in the orthopaedic field that might benefit Uday. I myself had no faith in the proposed journey but was outvoted by my colleagues when we discussed the proposal.

Dr al-Khodeiri returned to Iraq on 2 March, having visited Germany, Sweden and France. As predicted, he had not stumbled upon any revolutionary orthopaedic techniques and when Saddam came to Bin-Sina to enquire about the journey he was humble and not very persuasive.

The President wanted to know what we all thought. One of my colleagues said that Dr al-Khodeiri had unearthed nothing new, we were familiar with everything he told us and we should stick with the French team and Professor Le Veit whom we knew and trusted.

Saddam agreed. 'I can see no reason for exchanging the French doctors. They've done a good job, they're our friends and they reacted immediately when we asked them. This is my decision and no one must suggest anything else. That would just confuse Uday.'

'What about treating Uday in Switzerland? They're neutral, after all,' ventured Hassan al-Khodeiri bravely. Saddam became angry.

'To hell with Switzerland! What a stupid idea. We believe in God. Everything that's happened is caused by Him, and we'll just have to accept it.' And with that he left.

Dr al-Khodeiri immediately went to Uday's room to inform him of the discussion and his father's decision. Uday continued to refuse to be operated on by Professor Le Veit. The next morning he got his own way and a German orthopaedic surgeon from Stuttgart carried out the necessary operations on his leg during the spring.

Saddam never much liked imposing his will on Uday and Qusay.

Subsequently I learned why Uday had special reasons for wanting the doctor from Stuttgart. In addition to his skill as an orthopaedic surgeon he had business links to a German firm that was owed a substantial sum of money; there was talk of twenty million dollars. Uday and his brother Qusay had persuaded the Germans to settle for ten million. This the Germans could accept, but not that Uday and his brother keep five of the ten million as commission for their accommodating attitude.

By mistake an angry fax from Stuttgart was sent to the Olympic Committee. It was not inconceivable that someone there might have read it. Uday and Qusay were terrified that someone might leak it and Saddam start to ask questions why they were hell-bent on having a German rather than Professor Le Veit perform the operation. The brothers decided to lay all the blame on Hassan al-Khodeiri who was accused of engaging in monkey business on a large scale. Dr al-Khodeiri saw which way the wind was blowing and disappeared in a flash to Saudi Arabia where he has lived ever since.

We did everything we could to get the skin graft on Uday's left thigh to heal; I had removed a large piece in order to cover the hole on his wounded left leg. Normally new skin grows without problems when removed like that but Uday's rehabilitation was hampered by a succession of infections. We couldn't understand what caused them: we were scrupulously careful with the use of antibiotics and changing bandages that protected the infected area.

One day, however, I was pulled aside by a nurse. She told me that, on his initiative, Uday's friends had resumed their reconnoitring near al-Ruwad. There was a booze-up in the hospital every evening, culminating in female visitors to Uday's room. The large, ungainly bandage on the inside of his thigh hampered subsequent activities in the sickbed, so he took it off and pushed it to the side. The reason for the infections became obvious.

On 29 May 1997 his father came to see him at Bin-Sina. Qusay was with him. On their way out they stopped at the hospital director's office to greet the doctors on duty. Saddam asked about Uday's progress, and we told him that his son would be discharged soon, probably within a few days. Saddam looked relieved. He turned to Qusay. 'You and your brother have to be aware of the possibility of incidents like this. Be prepared for the worst. You are both in a position where you will meet difficult times. They will come,' he said.

At the beginning of June Uday was discharged from Bin-Sina after a stay of nearly six months. He was barely able to walk. By and large mobility had returned to his left arm and hand and his left eye no longer squinted, but when he wrote, what he put down was incoherent. It was also more difficult to understand his speech. Uday had never been talkative. His upper jaw was larger than his lower jaw and his speech was always unclear: now it was worse than ever.

It was more difficult to gauge the extent of any damage to the brain; he was already insane. But towards the end of his stay in hospital and after he had been discharged he appeared significantly more short-tempered and aggressive towards those around him than before the attempted assassination in Mansour.

For various reasons Uday was reassured by a few Iraqi doctors that he would be able to walk normally as he was. To that goal thousands of dollars were spent. Doctors and physiotherapists from the UK, Germany, France, the United States, Russia and from China were all consulted – with no noticeable improvement in Uday's condition at all.

His friend and saviour, Ali al-Sahr, tried to escape to Jordan with his wife and children in the autumn of 2002. He was stopped at the border post Trabil and returned to Baghdad. Uday got wind of the attempted escape and called him over to the Olympic Committee. 'You'll try again, and like other friends who've cleared off, no doubt you'll blab,' he said. 'I'll have to make sure that won't happen.'

A few days later Uday sent a gang of his paramilitary Fedayeen militia to Ali al-Sahr's home. There, in front of his wife, children and neighbours, they cut off his tongue.

The President meets Iraqi mothers. He was a good listener.

CHAPTER 13

Desert Fox

More bombs over Baghdad.
The President suffers from corns and
his wife and sister-in-law join the
corruption carousel.

I had warned him time and again. His shoes were too small, too narrow and now he was suffering.

The twenty-eighth of January 1999: it was a mild and sunny winter's day in Baghdad and the Bin-Sina director, Zuhair al-Azzawi, came to my office and warned me that the President was en route to the hospital. We were all surprised. This was the first time he had notified us of his arrival. But Saddam was in pain. A corn under his right foot was driving him mad. Now he wanted to have the thick corneous skin removed.

'You were right,' he said when he arrived. 'Where do you want to operate?'

I suggested the outpatient department but when we arrived the President spotted a dirty towel lying on the operating table. He looked at al-Azzawi. 'Did I not inform you that I was coming?'

The director rushed to change the towel for a clean one. He was petrified.

'If this can happen to me I hate to think how you treat your other patients,' the President said.

Al-Azzawi mumbled an apology but surprisingly enough kept his job. That surprised the rest of us too.

I gave Saddam a local anaesthetic and removed not one but two corns. When I bandaged the foot I advised him to keep it quiet and up for a couple of hours. But less than one hour later two of his bodyguards rushed in, panicking. Please would I bring a new bandage and come with them to the Republican Palace immediately.

The President was lying on a double bed, a rather bloody double bed. The bandage round the foot was soaked through and there was blood on the floor. He was pale. 'It's not your fault, Dr Ala,' he said. 'I didn't follow your advice but went straight into a meeting with some compatriots. Suddenly it started to bleed like hell.'

I changed the bandage and said no damage had been done. 'I will of course check on you from time to time, sir.'

Four days later I checked the foot again. This time he was waiting for me in a small house under some large trees near the suspension bridge over the Tigris. He constantly changed his place of residence for security reasons.

'I will never forget this day, February the first, when you operated on me after the car collision in 1991,' he said.

I examined the foot and applied another bandage. When that was done Saddam asked me to come into an adjoining room. A staff engineer rolled out a map showing the Republican Palace and all the buildings in the vast complex.

'Look here,' said Saddam, 'this office building was bombed during the last American missile attack. I have decided to rebuild it, but twice as large.'

Between 17 and 20 December 1998 American and British bombs and missiles had once again rained down over Baghdad and other Iraqi towns. I continued to drive between my shifts at Bin-Sina and al-Wasiti as usual during these days and nights. It struck me as surprising that my chauffeur and I wound our way through the streets of Baghdad, surrounded by fire and smoke and explosions, without ever even giving it a thought. 'If you are wet you do not fear the rain', is an Arab saying. We were soaking wet.

President Bill Clinton called the punishment Operation Desert Fox. This time the reason was as follows: UN weapons inspectors, hunting for the regime's alleged weapons of mass destruction, had left Iraq in December. They had been at it, on and off, for seven years and now their leaders claimed that their activities were being progressively curtailed. Saddam for his part was fed up with them – not least because it had become apparent that the relationship between the UN inspectors' work and the American CIA was not watertight.

Approximately a hundred different sites were targeted during the four days the air strikes lasted, most of them offices and buildings belonging to Saddam's security and intelligence agencies. Several of them were attached to the Republican Palace near the Tigris.

The sunshine entered through a small window. The rays glanced off his chest and the elegant pin-stripe suit. 'During the war with Iran' – Saddam pointed to one of the buildings on the map – 'I used this house for planning meetings before important battles. I called it "The House of Victory". It was partially damaged by American bombs in February nineteen ninety-one, and I ordered it to be rebuilt, twice as large. Now it has been targeted again and I have ordered my planning office to rebuild once more, like a palace with plenty of room for statues and works of art – the ceilings will be high.'

On the morning of 8 February, the President demanded a rebandaging and I was once more fetched to the little house by the Tigris. He appeared cross and out of humour and asked me, and his bodyguard, to wash our hands. Another bodyguard, standing in the corner of the room, was for some reason also asked to wash his hands.

Saddam was silent during the bandaging, completely preoccupied with his own thoughts. 'Is the wound healing?' he asked when I had finished.

I confirmed that all was well and watched him while he walked around to make sure the bandage was comfortable and not lumpy under his foot. His face was drawn and his eyelids heavier than usual. He asked me to wash my hands again, then shook hands and said goodbye. He wanted to sleep.

Rumours were rife in Baghdad that the last air-raids were a

signal to Saddam's generals: initiate a coup d'état and get rid of him. It was an invitation inciting unrest.

That evening I heard on the news that King Hussein of Jordan had passed away. Also reported was the liquidation of General Kamel Sajed and several other officers. The general was one of Iraq's greatest and most respected war heroes. He had repeatedly been decorated for his courage and daring on the battlefields and his reputation amongst the armed forces was exceptionally good. Now he was accused of planning a coup with other conspirators.

It was alleged that he had received a letter from General Nizar Khazraji. Khazraji had escaped to Europe a few years after I had patched up the wounds he had sustained when he was shot by Shia Muslim rebels in Nasiriya in March 1991. The former Chief of Staff had been helped over the border to Turkey via the autonomous Kurd territories in Northern Iraq by Masoud Barzani and the KDP.

So, time for yet more reflection. The execution of Kamel Sajid and his officer colleagues was a new reminder of the sort of regime under which I lived; and how short was the distance between life and death.

Despite everything, we Iraqis were materially better off as we approached the millennium. Two years before Saddam had given up his resistance to the introduction of the oil-for-food programme under UN auspices. Under strict control by UN inspectors from New York, large amounts of Iraqi oil were shipped out to the world market. Income from the sale was deposited in a frozen UN account, which the authorities in Baghdad could draw on to pay for the import of, in the first instance, food and medicine.

This gigantic humanitarian project got going in 1997. It had to feed a population of over twenty million, and within Iraq the organisation exceeded all expectations. Relatively quickly all families in need were assigned rations of staples and foodstuffs twice a year: flour, rice, sugar, oil, tea and soap.

The UN programme curbed hunger but did nothing to solve Iraq's fundamental economic problems. It stifled all healthy economic growth and killed initiative. It was no longer necessary to work to eat. Nor could the oil-money finance absolutely vital repairs to power stations, pumping and treatment plants for water and sewage or pay for restoration of the neglected national grid. The purchase and importing of new pumps, filters and pipes might have been given the all-clear by the sanctions committee who were sitting on the frozen account in New York, but it was impossible to free up parts of the oil-money to pay entrepreneurs or companies inside Iraq who might have carried out the necessary work. And as no priority was given to these projects by the ever more incompetent authorities in Baghdad, many of the streets in our towns ran with sewage because the outlet systems were blocked.

The pollution situation in Southern Iraq was especially precarious. Water and sewage distribution systems had broken down after the wars in Iran and the Gulf. The pressure in the broken sewage pipes was higher than in the water pipes, which were also leaking, and both sets of pipes shared the same ditches. The sewage mixed with the water, which was taken straight from the wells, and drunk without being distilled or boiled. Dried milk too, given to thousands upon thousands of ignorant mothers through the oil-for-food programme, was mixed with the sewage water.

In Basra, for example, I am sure that at least half of all infants were suffering from diarrhoea at any one time. The mortality rate was shockingly high.

Worst of all there was no concerted national plan to tackle the nation's health problems. Neither Saddam, the party bigwigs in the Revolutionary Command Council nor any of his ministers had any idea of the battles we were waging on the medical front. It was like tilting at windmills whenever we suggested concrete, practical improvements to the national health system. The distrust of doctors, and what our profession stood for, had long been deep-rooted and widespread.

For example, early in the eighties, while the Iran war was raging, more than forty of Iraq's very best specialists were given notice. A clean sweep was made of the medical faculties where professors and chief physicians worked and lectured. It mattered

not that most of them had been educated and received their
PhDs at the best universities and hospitals in Great Britain and
France. No explanation was ever given as to why Saddam
removed the very backbone of medical research and progress in
Iraq. Apparently, a Baath Party committee delivered a report
pointing out that it took a very long time for newly qualified doctors to become chief physicians in hospitals or professors at
universities.

Saddam's guillotine action was in many ways typical of the
way he solved difficult problems.

Medical research in Iraq boiled down to quackery – under the
President's patronage. One day at the end of the eighties my
then Health Minister, Abdul Salam Muhammad Said, phoned.
He said that Hussein Kamel al-Majid wanted to see me. He had
a news cutting and a short video piece about a new miracle cure
for cancer. The inventor had been to see the President who was
enthusiastic and had given him his full support.

That's why Hussein Kamel consulted me. The video recordings showed how several cancer patients revived miraculously
after having drunk a few glasses of the inventor's history-making,
herb-based elixir, brewed in some pots in his kitchen. 'I have to
admit that I'm slightly dubious about this,' the minister said. 'but
the patient on the video does look better after the herbal drink,
doesn't he?'

'I think the inventor has mixed a large dose of cortisone in
with his wonder cure,' I said. 'That can make cancer patients
feel much better for a short while, but doesn't stop the illness
spreading. To be quite honest, I would be very cautious about
trusting a cancer researcher who doesn't even seem to have a
microscope in his kitchen.'

Hussein Kamel thanked me for the advice.

Two months later the quack was exposed. Cortisone was
indeed the main ingredient in the wonder medicine which
Saddam was so keen on. The cancer patients on the video died
shortly afterwards. It also came to light that the inventor had
been dismissed from the army. He had mental problems. But in
the meantime the ministry of health had ordered our hospital

and other hospitals in Baghdad to put all our facilities at his disposal and help him any way we could with his important research work.

Saddam's word was law.

It was not just the herbal brewer who took Saddam for a ride. At about the same time I was looking after his corn a pharmacist popped up at our hospital. The hospital had been renamed Saddam's Centre for Plastic and Reconstructive Surgery. The pharmacist had researched and developed a wonder ointment against gangrene. Now she wanted to have it clinically tested on our patients.

We had many of them. Diabetes is endemic in the Middle East, and a common symptom is atherosclerosis, specifically in the legs. The reduced blood supply that ensues can develop into gangrene, with amputation as the end result.

The pharmacist would not tell me what was in her salve, but when smeared on to the gangrene she insisted it would stop the disease from spreading, the patient's blood supply would increase drastically and amputations could be avoided. Many legs would be saved. It would be a world sensation, worthy of a Nobel Prize.

She had written to Saddam about her pharmaceutical breakthrough and he had written a nice letter back. 'But from experience I know that many new ideas are unable to penetrate our country's bureaucracy,' the President wrote. 'You will meet opposition.'

She also presented a letter from his office in which Abed Hamoud made it clear that Saddam wanted us to give her all possible support and help.

'OK,' I said, 'you can try out your ointment. But on one condition. You must sign a declaration that you – and only you – accept all responsibility for what happens to the patients after you have started treating them. We haven't a clue what's in your salve and we don't know what the side effects might be. But if you take personal responsibility, that's OK by me.'

'I'll be back tomorrow,' she said, but she never turned up again.

However, she did turn up at the offices of Brigadier Riyadh Muhammad Saleh, director and responsible for Saddam's Centre for Heart Diseases in Baghdad. Dr Saleh was Iraq's foremost heart specialist and had long been part of the President's medical team. One day he was dismissed, and the reason why became clear soon.

Dr Saleh had tested Saddam's blood pressure. It was on the high side, and the President had been advised to eat less fatty food, cut down on salt and smoke less.

The next time Saleh came to examine him one of Saddam's bodyguards said that he was puffing away as much as ever, and he had not followed the dietary advice given either. 'Well, sir,' said the heart specialist when he tested him again, 'I must remind you that smoking is not good for blood pressure. You must try and give up.'

Saddam was furious. 'Shut up! You told me that the last time you were here. You don't have to repeat yourself. It's up to me if I smoke or not. I don't need you any longer.'

The brigadier kept the job as hospital director but even that was hanging by a thin thread when the pharmacist turned up. Amongst other things she demanded to take over the care of Major General Hisham Sabah al-Fakri, another of the great commanders of the Iranian war. Both the general's legs were gangrenous owing to advanced diabetes.

'I just didn't dare refuse. She arrived with one of Saddam's bodyguards,' Dr Saleh told me when he phoned to pour out his troubles. 'She'd told Saddam that she was being sabotaged by the doctors she came into contact with, and he wanted it to stop.'

One day, after she had rubbed the miracle ointment into the general's legs, Dr Saleh sneaked in and took a sample to check the bacteria content. The report from the laboratory showed that the salve was not sterile. It was oozing with bacteria. When confronted with the results the pharmacist hit the roof.

'How dare you send a sample of my ointment to the laboratory without my consent!' she screamed before rushing out of the door. She went straight to the Republican Palace to an attentive Saddam. Here was her proof. Her work was being sabotaged. The doctors would not cooperate.

Dr Saleh was told he need no longer consider himself director of Saddam's Centre for Heart Medicine: he could retire.

It was now the turn of Yarmouk hospital in Baghdad. Saddam convened a meeting with the pharmacist, the Health Minister and four gangrene specialists in his office. He demanded that Yarmouk establish a fully staffed laboratory to research further into the ointment.

Major General al-Fakri's legs could not be saved. They were both amputated.   .

On 10 February I was driven to yet another small house near the suspension bridge. I was to meet the President at five to check his right foot and apply a new bandage. I had to wait a considerable time before he turned up.

When he did he apologised for making me wait. He had had an important meeting with some officers and it had all taken longer than expected. The officers were developing an air-defence system in the no-fly zones in Northern and Southern Iraq.

'They're professionals and are making progress, but they need money and the sanctions imposed on us mean that we don't have enough. Like Karl Marx used to say: "Money disappears in critical moments."'

The first no-fly zone had been established in the north. It was meant to give Kurdish refugees who had sought protection in the so-called safe zones after the 1991 rebellions a feeling of security. The USA, Britain and France informed Baghdad that from now on no Iraqi planes or helicopters would be allowed into air space north of the 36th parallel.

The next year the three superpowers decided to introduce a similar no-fly zone in the south, initially south of the 32nd parallel. The Marsh Arabs were fighting a desperate and hopeless guerrilla war against the government forces in the marshes, which were drying up thanks to Saddam's large drainage project.

But as far as I could see the main reason for establishing the no-fly zones was not out of humanitarian concern for the Marsh Arabs or the Kurdish refugees. It was quite simply to monitor us Iraqis.

The two zones – the southern one was soon extended north to the 33rd parallel – covered the larger part of Iraq. American, British and, until 1998, French planes patrolling the air space were thus a continuous reminder to Saddam that he was no longer master in his own house. Every day during this period of psychological warfare 50 to 100 overflights took place; any endeavour to shoot down the allied fighter planes promptly led to the Iraqi cannons and missile batteries being bombed to smithereens.

Many hundreds of Iraqis were killed, and thousands wounded, during these air attacks in the no-fly zones, and attempts at defending Iraqi air space were unsuccessful. Not a single American, British or French plane was ever shot down.

'If we don't have money for a decent air-defence system, that makes our sense of patriotism even more crucial,' Saddam continued.

'Patriotism is a relatively loose concept,' I said.

'Why's that?'

'Because patriotism is usually related to how people express the concept and not to what they have done for their country. People believe that those who demonstrate in the streets are more patriotic than a scientist who spends most of his time in a laboratory making scientific advances.'

'I think Iraqis know what they are doing when they demonstrate,' said Saddam. 'It's ingrained in our civilisation's long history: patriotism increases when the country is threatened from outside.'

I looked at him. How far could I go? All the jumping around and dancing and sloganeering praising him were false. 'The royal family was hailed before the monarchy was toppled in 1958,' I said. 'Abdul Karim Kassem experienced exactly the same before his fall in 1963 and sheikhs and tribal lords from the whole country glorified Abdul Salam Aref as long as he was president. Those very same people rushed out on to the streets and shouted laud and honour after the Baath Party coup in 1968.'

The President was silent. 'The problem is that the sense of patriotism disappears when the danger has gone away. Then most individuals revert to being passive and weak,' he said.

While the oil-for-food programme certainly fed millions of Iraqis, at the same time it proved a veritable goldmine for

Saddam's close relatives, party brass and ministers who wished to enrich themselves even further. Huge contracts were circulating. From 1997 until the regime broke down in April 2003, food, medicine, goods and products worth more than 16 billion pounds were bought in. Even low percentage commissions added up.

The purchases were of course approved and the invoices controlled by the sanctions committee in the UN's Security Council. The committee's first job was to prevent Saddam from buying new military matériel or components and equipment which could be used to develop weapons of mass destruction. Its grip on questionable deliveries and contracts, and the stream of 'bonuses' which followed in the wake of them, was less strong: it was obviously very easy to fool it.

The system was simple. Uday, Qusay and the other vultures in Baghdad who were lucky enough to be part of the corruption simply had to deal only with suppliers who were willing to hand out the largest 'bonus' under the table. The 'bonuses', which were agreed on in advance and which the suppliers transferred via various secret channels to the recipient, were added to the final total in the contracts before going to the UN sanctions office for approval. The more expensive the goods, the higher the 'bonus'.

The health sector was no exception. While we screamed ourselves hoarse after scalpels, bandages, antibiotics, anaesthetics and other medicines vital to our daily work, extravagant and advanced medical equipment was purchased instead. Suddenly every hospital in Iraq had a CT- and an MRI-scanner. In most cases they had neither the staff nor the necessary medical competence to operate them. We were witnessing cynical, brutal and completely grotesque corruption.

Patients died on the operating table because our anaesthetists no longer had enough drugs to treat them before and after operations. In desperation they resorted to alternative anaesthetics, which produced side effects, often with fatal consequences. The Health Minister of the time, Omid Midhat Mubarak, was trapped between the corrupt system, which invaded the ministry of health

in particular after the oil-for-food and medicine programme, and
the increasing demand of hospitals for urgent and life-saving drugs
and equipment. Although he had been rebuked several times,
Saddam had on many occasions said that he considered Dr Omid
a reliable mediator between the government and the Kurds in the
north.

Even Saddam's wife Sajida threw herself onto the corruption
carousel with her sister, Ilham, who was married to Watban.
Everyone wanted a piece of the cake.

Ilham phoned one day and asked me to come to her house.
Apparently it was about some matter of national importance.

'Sajida and I want to do something to help our country
through these difficult days,' she began when I had sat down and
we were being served tea by her servants. 'We know that MRI-
scanners are being bought in for the hospitals for large sums and
we have been contacted by a company that can deliver such
equipment at a much lower price than the one the health ministry
has negotiated with its suppliers,' she said. 'Our supplier is well
known and anyhow, they are better and more effective.'

I was told that some representatives of the company would
come to my private clinic the next morning to discuss the matter
further.

'We are in a hurry. It would be wrong to miss such an opportunity,' the President's sister-in-law and cousin stressed.

The plan the two sisters had devised entailed that I, whom
Saddam trusted, would write him a letter explaining that the
MRI equipment from the specialist company was superior in
price and quality and that therefore it should be the one to supply
all Iraqi hospitals.

'But this isn't my specialist field,' I said to Ilham. 'You should
ask a radiologist instead.'

'No, it's you Saddam trusts. Sajida wants you to write the recommendation after you've read the brochure and spoken to the
reps.'

The reps came to the clinic the next afternoon and, as I anticipated, pontificated about the superior quality of their MRI
machines: apparently there were none better on the international
market.

'You can personally make a great deal of money out of this,' they said. One salesman was from Iraq, the other from the Lebanon.

When they had left I phoned Ilham. 'I'm sorry, but I don't intend to write that letter to the President.'

'OK,' she said, finishing the call. But she phoned back after a short while, having spoken to her sister. 'We want you to come to Bin-Sina this evening.'

I went to the hospital, where one of Sajida's bodyguards was waiting with a letter for Saddam. In the letter I suggested that the health ministry purchase MRI-scanners from the firm Sajida had mentioned as they were cheap and efficient. All that remained was for me to sign.

Another telephone call to Ilham. 'I've read the letter. Why do I need to sign it? This is not my field of medicine. I am not going to recommend anything, either to the President or anyone else.'

'You are behaving most oddly. Sajida is simply asking for a favour. She is married to the President and she is asking you personally to help. She knows that Saddam respects your opinions and trusts you not to lie.'

'I'm sorry, please forgive me, but I am not signing.'

Ilham was furious and flung the phone down. Three days later she was at it again. 'We've got hold of a radiologist. He's already signed the petition to the President so you only need add your signature.'

'It's out of the question.'

She cursed me again, but stopped phoning.

Two days after the sisters' failed attempt, Saddam's mighty secretary came to see me at Bin-Sina. Abed Hamoud got straight to the point. 'It was wise of you not to sign the letter about the MRI-scanners.'

'How do you know about it all?'

'That's my job,' he said.

On 16 February 1999, two weeks after having removed the corn from under Saddam's foot, the wound had healed. I was taken to yet another house in the palace complex in Radwaniya. It was cold and miserable and windy.

The President's blood pressure had been checked by one of his heart specialists, Dr Taher al-Tikriti. It was normal and Saddam was puffing away at his big Havana cigar. He seemed tired and depressed. 'Dr Ala,' he said after Dr al-Tikriti had left, 'how do you see the UN sanctions? How do they affect ordinary people?'

'No doubt the trade blockade the USA and Great Britain are insisting on is harming us. But it's only responsible for about fifteen to twenty per cent of the economic difficulties we are experiencing. All the rest is due to the catastrophic mismanagement by government ministers and civil servants. They must take the responsibility.'

The President's closest bodyguard, Captain Sarmad Sufar, was standing in a corner of the room. Saddam waved him away; I could see he didn't like what he had just heard. 'Why are you saying this?' he asked.

'This is what I hear when I meet people and when I talk to my patients. It's also what I myself observe.'

'Can you substantiate this?'

I explained that if an Iraqi wanted to set up a business and had to seek official approval, a purgatory of officialdom awaited him before he was through. 'You have to be prepared for the worst and your case won't be heard unless you are prepared to pay a substantial bribe. It's hellish.'

Saddam sat quietly for a moment. Then he said: 'My personal dilemma is how to find the right people for the important jobs. I know that the ministers aren't all that efficient. They're not really very intelligent either. That goes for the leaders of the Baath Party too. When I meet with them and discuss complex issues it takes me ages just to get them even to understand what I'm talking about. I can tell from their faces that they haven't understood a thing. Their expressions make it pretty obvious.'

The President fell silent again and lit another cigar.

'I've tried to appoint new people, people who are unknown quantities, to the various departments as under-ministers and deputy secretaries, hoping to curb the corruption. I always thought that party members were not quite as dishonest as the civil servants. But I realised very quickly that the new brooms were as venal, if not more so, than the ones they had replaced.'

There was really no explanation for it, but when the dictator left I actually felt sorry for him, a victim of his own power.

In conversation with the President and Abed Hamoud in 1998.
(Author's Collection)

CHAPTER 14

An Artist's Life

Saddam cooks a meal and orders a monument. Unknown benefactors phone from Hong Kong.

'Never tell a Bedouin where you live,' the President said.

We all know what that means in Iraq. If you are too friendly and willing to please there will soon be no limit to what is required of you.

It was Friday and a holiday one morning in late 1999 and yet again I had been fetched to one of the small houses somewhere in the Radwaniya palace complex.

'I apologise for having to bother you with this foot, but I would be grateful if you could change the bandage.' He was in a good mood. The weather was beautiful; the winter sun warmed the air. The sore resulting from the operation to remove the corn had healed. No new bandage was necessary.

'But let me remind you to make sure your shoes are not too tight.'

'Will you have lunch with me and my bodyguards?' Saddam asked. 'It's my turn to cook today.'

A kitchen had been rigged up outside the little house and the President had prepared no less than ten pots with meat, chicken, gravy and rice, bubbling over the gas jet. From time to time he stirred the dishes and tasted them, seasoning them with salt and spices.

'Here,' he said, and helped himself from one of the pots after we had seated ourselves around a refectory table in the sunshine. 'Here's a nice piece of meat.'

'It's too much,' I protested. 'My cholesterol is too high and I'm trying to cut down the amount of meat I eat.'

'This is young lamb. It won't hurt,' Saddam said.

I thanked him and said I wasn't really too worried about all the warnings I had had. But a few days before at Bin-Sina I had overheard a conversation between two heart specialists about cholesterol, I told the President. I felt at death's door, contemplating all the cholesterol I ate, and interrupted them: 'Apart from accidents, we usually die from three things: heart stroke, stroke or cancer. Stroke, followed by paralysis, adds enormously to your relatives' burdens, because they have to nurse you for the rest of your life. Cancer and all its ramifications is nothing you'd want to strive for. In my opinion, heart stroke is easily the best way to go. So what are you guys really worried about?'

Saddam seemed to like that.

Grey hairs had started to appear in the neat moustache of one of the President's bodyguards. Saddam joked about this obvious sign of ageing: why did it appear in the moustache before one's hair?

I explained that we were talking about two different areas of the head and that grey hairs appear a lot sooner in a moustache or beard than on top of the head. 'The solution is to shave off your moustache and beard or just give up worrying.'

Saddam looked at me; he wasn't too happy with my suggestion, I could see. I realised I should have kept my bloody mouth shut. I knew he dyed his moustache.

When I got up to go he asked me to wait a moment. He wanted to know if I had ever had a statue or monument erected in Baghdad. 'Why can't you enlarge one of your small sculptures? I'll leave it to you to choose where you want to put it.'

I thanked him and said I would like that.

'Come back when you have made your choice,' he said.

It didn't take long. I had called my 1992 exhibition 'Grains of Thought'. One of the sculptures symbolised a man and a woman embracing each other. I'd called it 'The Union'. A few days after the Radwaniya lunch I took it to show Saddam. It was obvious he didn't like it, but he didn't demur. 'If that's your choice, get going,' he said, without asking what the sculpture represented.

'Have you any suggestions for alterations?'

'No,' he replied.

Saddam's bodyguard Captain Sarmad Sufar went with me to the President's architectural and engineering office, from where his grand building projects were administered. The head of the office, Mazen al-Alosi, was expecting us.

We decided to erect the monument near some large crossroads in al-Mansour, where the desert motorway hits Baghdad. The monument would be twenty-one metres high; the two embracing figures would be sculpted from white stone quarried in Mosul. The stone was the same as that used by the Assyrians in Mesopotamia, three thousand years ago, for their amazing carvings and statues.

'That's fine,' al-Alosi said, 'but what is the monument called? We need to discuss this with the President's secretary, Abed Hamoud.'

'"The Union",' I said. 'It depicts the essence of life: the coupling of man and woman.'

For me it was a busy year. Following some prompting, which must have originated with Saddam, the department of culture decided that twenty of my paintings and a similar number of sculptures were to be exhibited in Paris, London, New York and Vienna. I requested a meeting with the Minister of Culture, Dr Humam Abdul Khaleq, one of the regime's most organised and straightforward men. I wanted to know who would write and edit the exhibition catalogue. I was terrified of being used for political purposes.

'You can edit the catalogue and chose whomever you like to write it,' Abdul Khaleq assured me.

This time, too, the catalogue was devoid of portraits and the usual eulogy about the President's role in encouraging Iraqi cultural life. I was on my way.

First stop was the Arcima Gallery in St-Germain in Paris. Thereafter I continued to London and the Bolton Gallery in Mayfair. The theme running through the exhibition was man's suffering from the time Cain murdered his brother Abel. Three days after the opening a stranger phoned to say he very much appreciated my art. I was taken aback. My mobile phone was borrowed from a friend and only he knew I had it. The man wanted to meet me. I was en route to visit my son in Northern England and would be back in London in five days.

'Phone me then, at six,' I said.

He phoned right on six o'clock, on the day arranged. I invited him to have breakfast with me at the Gloucester Hotel. He was young, slim and elegantly dressed in black. As soon as we sat down he started to praise the exhibition in the Bolton Gallery. My style had made a strong impression on him. 'But is the exhibition your only reason for coming to London?' he asked.

No, I said, it was as important to visit hospitals and clinics to research the latest developments in plastic surgery, and to buy instruments and medical equipment for my Baghdad hospital. That was actually true. Then: 'I apologise for asking, but how old are you?' I asked. He looked about the same age as my son.

'Thirty.'

'Listen,' I said, 'I'm twice your age, but that doesn't really matter: age is no guarantee of wisdom, but what it does bring is experience. Fortunately – or unfortunately – I have lived in a country where, since 1958, we have experienced nothing but bitterness and hurt. That's taught us, however stupid we are, how to discern people's intentions when we meet them and we can do it without much effort.'

What I wanted to say was that if he wanted to haul information out of me, it was better to come straight to the point. And for heaven's sake, not to proceed in a manner which, with my Iraqi background, I could not stand.

'You phoned my mobile and I never asked how you got the number. I immediately knew that you belong to the British intelligence services. I couldn't care less – I really don't care *who* you are, but please don't insult my intelligence.'

The young man looked chagrined.

'But go ahead, I'm ready to answer.'

My young breakfast companion tried to pull himself together and reiterated what an impression the exhibition had made on him. 'What is it like to be an artist under Saddam?' he managed to ask.

I looked at him again. 'I'll give you some advice which you can take back to your employers. Saddam will sooner or later disappear; even Baath Party members themselves have had enough of the corrupt and incompetent regime. But the Iraqi people will remain, as will the old traditional ties to Britain. So go and tell your bosses that if the question is how to win our hearts and minds and maintain the ties, something must be done at the Home Office to make it easier for Iraqis to get visas. Some of my patients have died waiting in Amman for visas; they could have survived if they had got to a hospital in this country.' Two of my friends, and very well known surgeons, Dr Talal al-Jalabi and Labib Hasso, died in Amman after having waited three months for a UK visa.

He thanked me for my advice and gave me his visiting card before leaving.

In the USA the paintings and sculptures were exhibited in the UN building in New York. Several ambassadors came to the opening. I gave a small speech about my experiences as doctor and artist in Iraq, and took the opportunity to air my opinion of the manner in which I was treated when I landed at JFK airport.

'I have always admired the USA for its scientific and cultural achievements. But to have my fingerprints taken and be photographed from three angles as though I were a common criminal, does not accord with my impressions of this country's strong and civilised society. That's the behaviour I associate with other regimes,' I said, without mentioning which ones. I also reminded those present of the values I associated with having a Statue of Liberty in New York Harbour.

A representative of the American UN delegation came over to me and deplored my treatment at the airport. 'You are more than welcome to stay in our country,' he said. 'Permanently.' I thanked him but declined.

I was then interviewed by CNN, and I talked about how the Iraqi people had suffered, and especially during the war against Iran.

'Ala Bashir's work shows the Saddam regime's great cruelty,' the news anchor reported when the news item was broadcast.

Where she got that from was a mystery. I never said it but it was true. In Baghdad the story passed unnoticed and there were no reactions when I returned.

Whilst in New York a charming representative from Pennsylvania University contacted me. She wanted me to exhibit in the Esther M. Klein Gallery in Philadelphia, but I heard no more. It turned out that the letter from the university with the official invitation to exhibit lay for more than a year with Iraq's UN ambassador Said al-Musawi. The gallery had given advance notice of the exhibition for February 2000, but the ambassador never informed me.

Moscow and Vienna followed New York. In the Russian capital I showed in the well-known Manezh Gallery on Manezhraya Square near the Kremlin; in Vienna in the prestigious Palais Palffy. The latter gallery's director was very friendly and obliging and couldn't have been more helpful during my Austrian stay. Iraq's ambassador, Naji Sabri al-Hadithi, also bent over backwards to make the exhibition and the opening night a success. Virtually the whole diplomatic corps were present at the private viewing.

A few months later a contact that I had met at the exhibition sent al-Hadithi a letter which he asked him to pass on to me. It contained an exciting proposal which he wanted me to consider. A well-known South African conglomerate – my contact could not say which one – wanted me to accept its cultural patronage and ensure that my art was exhibited not only in Europe, but also in South Africa and the far East. The firm's HQ was in Hong Kong. They were willing to donate an operating theatre with all modern equipment to our hospital.

'This will ensure a bright future for you. Every door will open and your name become known all over the world,' wrote my contact.

Ambassador al-Hadithi sent the letter on to me, but a copy only. The original he sent to the Foreign Office in Baghdad. It didn't take long for me to be called in to Foreign Minister Muhammad Said al-Sahhaf. 'Do you know this South African company?' he asked.

'Not at all,' I said.

Al-Sahhaf sent the letter on to Saddam's Chief of Staff, Ahmed Hussein Khudair al-Samarrai. He phoned me three days later. 'If you can vouch for the South African company it's OK for you to let them help with your exhibitions,' said the Chief of Staff.

It was a trap, and an easy one to see through. 'No,' I said. 'I haven't a clue who they are, and I can't vouch for them.' If I had said yes, jumped in with both feet, that would have been the end of me.

'I'm glad you said that,' Ahmed Hussein Khudair said. According to the Chief of Staff, Mukhabarat, our own intelligence service, had smelt Mossad, their Israeli counterparts, a long way off.

Whoever they were, the men in the charitable South African firm continued their overtures. One day someone phoned from Hong Kong. Or at least that was where the man said he phoned from. 'As we operate our charitable activities anonymously, I am afraid I can't give you our name,' said the voice from the Far East.

I was frightened. My phone was undoubtedly tapped. 'It's better not to contact me,' I said. 'You can talk to my son in Great Britain, but never phone this number.'

My son kept on receiving calls from 'Hong Kong', but three months before the fall of Baghdad in 2003 they stopped. Since then it has been quiet from that part of the world and luckily I never heard anything from Mukhabarat or our other intelligence and security services following the – for me – perilous phone calls from 'Hong Kong'.

Saddam believed that it was excellent propaganda for modern Iraqi art to establish itself on the world scene. But for the most part he preferred that I stayed at home. 'Your paintings and sculptures are a national treasure which must not be sold abroad,' he said and placed a ban on my going abroad with any works. He even disliked me taking on art projects outside Iraq.

In the summer of 2000 I was visiting Ghazi al-Zibin in Jordan. He is a plastic surgeon, and also a member of the Hashemite Kingdom's National Assembly. I told him about 'The Union', which was going to be erected in Baghdad.

'Why can't you sculpt a monument here in Amman?' he asked.

The mayor of the Jordanian capital had several times asked him to submit ideas to improve the town's cultural environment and al-Zibin had promised to contact me. I was excited by the prospect and following conversations with Amman's planning authorities it was decided that I would send them a sketch and a proposal for a monument to be erected by one of the town's big roundabouts.

In Baghdad I happened to mention the project to Saddam's trusted bodyguard, Captain Sarmad Sufar.

'Don't do anything before you have the President's blessing,' he said.

I saw no reason to have to ask the President, but from experience I knew that I had better follow the advice, especially as it came from such a close companion. I wrote a letter describing the Amman project and gave it to the Captain. The answer arrived three days later.

> Brother, Dr Ala – peace be with you – to erect a
> monument in a capital city is exceedingly time-consuming
> as it demands the artist first gains an intimate and deep
> understanding of the country's specific cultural and
> historical heritage. As it concerns only one sculpture or
> one painting you should be spared from, and rise above,
> demands such as these. Leave them to colleagues who are
> first and foremost interested in making money. But of
> course the choice is yours.

There was no misunderstanding his answer. The project in Amman was shelved.

It was not always easy to get things done inside Iraq either. On New Year's Eve 2000 I dreamt that I was in Karbala, inside the sacred memorial to Imam Hussein, the great martyr and Shia role model. In my dream I painted a large abstract painting of the battle of 680 when Hussein was killed on the plains outside the town.

The cause of the battle of Karbala was the bitter disagreement as to who, in the wider Muslim world, was to be Muhammad's heir. The religion had spread like a vast empire from Persia in the east to Egypt in the west, from the Arabian Peninsula in the south to Armenia in the north. But Muhammad's death in AD 632 caused a great deal of confusion amongst his followers. He had no sons. The question who was his rightful successor, the next Caliph, brought terrible internal strife, and developed into a sequence of uprisings, killings and attacks in the years that followed.

Muhammad's close friend, adviser and father-in-law, Abu Bakr, was his first successor. He died just two years after having been elected. The next Caliph, Omar bin al-Khattab, was also the deceased Prophet's father-in-law. He was killed by a slave in 644. The third Caliph, Uthman bin Affan, was Muhammad's son-in-law. He was murdered by a gang of discontented Egyptians in 656.

Ali bin Abu Talib took over and became the fourth Caliph. He was the Prophet's cousin and son-in-law and his followers, 'shi'at Ali' (Ali's party) considered him the first lawful religious and political leader – Imam – after Muhammad: the kinship was very close.

But Aisha, one of the numerous wives who survived Muhammad, opposed him; so did Muawiya bin Abu Sufyan, the governor of Syria. They both insisted that it had been the Prophet's will to proclaim Abu Bakr as his first rightful successor. Thus Imam Ali had no claim to the caliphate.

Rebellion and riots ensued. Ali was killed in 661 by a poisoned sword during an assassination attempt in Kufa in Mesopotamia. The question of who is Muhammad's lawful successor – Abu Bakr or Imam Ali – divides the Muslim world today into Sunni Muslims and Shia Muslims.

The governor of Syria, Muawiya, who founded the Ummayad dynasty in Damascus, became the fifth Caliph when Ali died. He was succeeded by his son Yazid bin Muawiya, in 680.

Hussein, Ali's son and the Prophet's grandson, who lived in Medina, was asked to recognise Yazid's appointment, but hesitated. Clear signs from the Mesopotamian Shias indicated that they didn't approve of Yazid as Caliph. And the inhabitants of Kufa, capital of the Muslim empire under Ali, were clearly prepared to fight for Hussein if he rose against the new Caliph in Damascus. To be on the safe side, Hussein sent his cousin, Muslim bin Aqil, to Kufa. Bin Aqil managed to gather several thousand written declarations and sent them back to Medina.

Based on those Hussein decided to break camp and set out for Mesopotamia with his whole family, seventy-two able-bodied men and their families.

In Damascus Yazid sensed the approaching rebellion. He sent a large number of troops from Basra to Kufa. The soldiers were brutal and the will to resist amongst Hussein's followers ebbed away. Muslim bin Aqil tried to escape but was caught and hacked to bits by the Caliph's soldiers.

He never managed to warn his cousin – who was now en route from the Arabian desert with his entourage – that the welcome in Kufa might not be what he had expected when he received all the declarations of support from the town's inhabitants.

Hussein and his followers met the Caliph's soldiers – there were more than three thousand of them – on the plains outside Karbala, not far from Kufa. They were thirsty after the long and strenuous trek through the desert but the soldiers blocked their access to the Euphrates. They could not get at the water. The Prophet's grandson asked the captain of the Caliph's soldiers permission to return to Medina but was refused. He was asked to surrender with his entire company. They would be taken to Damascus as captives.

Hussein decided to fight the heavy odds and told his seventy-two soldiers to save themselves before it was too late; all declined.

The battle was fought on 10 October 680. One by one Hussein's brothers, sons, cousins and followers were cut down and killed in front of horror-struck and crying wives, sisters, cousins and small children. Hussein was the last to die. He was decapitated so that his head could be taken to Damascus. The captain of the Caliph's troops then commanded ten horsemen to have their horses trample on the Imam's corpse.

This humiliation of the Prophet's grandson was not the last. When his head was paraded in triumph before Yazid in Damascus, the Caliph's commandant, to be on the safe side, knocked out his teeth with a stick.

The surviving family members from the battle of Karbala were led through Kufa on their way to Syria. The streets were full of people crying over the fate of Hussein's nearest. That did not, however, stop them from looting the prisoners of everything they had.

'Why do you do this, yet still cry over our fate?' Zainab asked. She was Imam Hussein's sister.

'If we don't take it, someone else will,' was the answer.

I had been brought up on the legend attached to the Imam's death; it has always fascinated me. The account of how his close family were treated in Kufa haunted me as Iraqi society started to disintegrate after two wars: the war against Iran and Saddam's tragic failed military adventure in Kuwait.

My cousin, Muin Kasem, the entrepreneur with several commissions in Southern Iraq, once told me what happened to him on his way from Basra to Baghdad in 1994. Outside Amara, about four hundred kilometres south of the Iraqi capital, a car with father and mother and five children left the road. The car landed on its roof and the father, who was driving, was killed instantly. The mother was thrown out and suffered life-threatening injuries. Two of the five children were killed. The three other children survived but were seriously hurt.

People from the village nearby rushed to the scene of the accident.

'While I tried to pull the father out of the wreckage, I saw the villagers throw themselves at his wife. They removed her ring, necklace and everything else she had of gold. The pockets of the dead children were also searched for anything of value.'

In the course of a few minutes they had even managed to loosen the four tyres and run off with them. If they didn't take them, someone else would, no doubt.

My head was spinning when I woke on the first day of the new millennium; my dream about Hussein's death outside Karbala and the painting I had started in the Imam's magnificent mausoleum were fresh in my mind.

I travelled to Karbala to talk to the guardian of the tomb. He

was a so-called sayeid, one who is directly descended from Imam
Ali. Initially he was not against my painting something from the
historic battle outside Karbala; the painting would fit in well on
the wall of a hall rarely visited by pilgrims.

'But you must ask the President for permission,' he said. The
mayor of Karbala, who had been pulled into our deliberations,
agreed.

'I don't understand,' I said. 'There are masses of paintings in
the sanctuary already, by both Iraqi and Iranian artists. Surely
they haven't asked the President's permission?'

'You must,' they both insisted.

Having thought the matter over for a couple of days I wrote to
Saddam and explained my plans for a painting in Karbala.

On 20 January 2000 he replied. The answer was neither yes
nor no.

What is at stake here, my brother, Dr Ala, is that we need
the spirit of history as an example and encouragement.
But as you so well know, history does not proceed without
some conflict. Results are judged in the light of its values,
those that we can attribute to the principles the people
and the nation have inherited, and which we strive to
emulate. The nation's sons must be aware. History must
not be so interpreted that the thesis weakens the antithesis
where charity and great achievement are concerned. The
people of today must not rise up against the past. At the
same time we must not ignore the learning of yesterday if
we want to achieve a balanced and responsible
interpretation.

Thus it is not the drama around Hussein's martyrdom
which is important, in spite of it being as sad today as it
was then. The most important thing is what,
fundamentally, we can learn from it: how the pure, faithful
human being can devote himself to keeping alive what he
believes in, in a time when preserving one's own life would
put a stop to what one believes in and thereby extinguish
the shining example.

We must in any case remember that when a national

and indisputably correct objective is at stake, consensus among the people is more important than any conflict which might seduce those who believe the saying that strife enriches life.

Differences that enhance people's lives are not the same as those which engender aggression and stoke up strong feelings which they then cannot control.

Our thoughts, our conscience, our opinions need to be in harmony. Solidarity, based on our nation's strong historic heritage, is what will take us into the future, as we at the same time are filled with confidence in the present and its strong influence. It is the prerequisite for the nation to progress in the right direction and conduct itself in the right way.

For your country, brother. Peace and God's grace be with you.

Your brother, Saddam Hussein.

That's how he used to express himself. But the message was clear. The Shia rebellion in the south, which followed the defeat in Kuwait, had not been forgotten. It had hurt and shocked him; it wasn't how he thought a popular and beloved leader should be treated.

I had better drop the project in Karbala too.

Fortunately, in Baghdad work on the 'The Union' proceeded apace; the sculptor Mustafa Khalib was responsible for its execution. But the name plaque on the monument was causing concern in higher circles. The all-clear only came after long deliberations. Abed Hamoud phoned me.

'It's OK,' he said. 'You can call it "The Union", but it symbolises the people embracing the President, not the union between man and woman.'

'Yes, sir,' I said.

A ladies' man with a steady hand and a love of cigars.

CHAPTER 15

Marriage

Saddam builds up a network of women
spies and finds Uday a wife. His elderly
aunt becomes increasingly difficult.

The years marched on and age was also leaving an impression on
Saddam's nearest and dearest. One summer's day in 2000 I was
asked to pop over to see Samira Shahbandar. She lived in an
average house simply furnished near the resurrected suspension
bridge over the Tigris. The President's second wife had seen a
programme via satellite on her TV about cosmetic surgery. She
now wanted my opinion on the success rate of such surgery.

I told her not to take everything she saw on TV as gospel
truth. Cosmetic surgery was big business all over the world and it
was easy to be duped by doctors and clinics who promised more
than they could deliver.

'My face and neck have started to wrinkle,' she said.

Samira Shahbandar was still a beautiful woman. Her hair was
blonde and her eyes blue. She was by then between fifty and sixty
years old and in my opinion she didn't need a facelift urgently. But
having looked at her more closely I said that an operation would
of course take years off her age.

We made an appointment to perform the facelift on the following Friday. As everywhere in the Muslim world the day is a
holiday, so there would only be a skeleton staff at Bin-Sina and
the operation could be completed without too much fuss and
gossip being generated.

All went according to plan on the Friday morning and the President's wife was settled in a special suite earmarked for Saddam and his closest family. I returned to the hospital during the afternoon to make sure that no complications had arisen. All was well.

'By the way, does your husband know about the operation?' I happened to ask her.

'No,' she said.

My blood ran cold. Saddam had issued clear instructions that he was to be informed immediately of any medical treatment carried out on his family.

'I don't think you realise the implications for me, not telling the President about this facelift,' I said.

Saddam demanded complete loyalty and openness from the medical team he had chosen. Nevertheless, he never trusted us. He kept us constantly under surveillance, and he – or one of his close collaborators – had the gall to try and trap us from time to time.

Just after I had joined the President's team at the beginning of the eighties one beautiful woman after the other began to appear at my private clinic. They all asked to have their hymen repaired.

It is well known that virtue commands a high price in the Muslim world. Catastrophic consequences can result from the non-appearance of blood on the sheets during the wedding night. The women of the family sit like vultures outside the bedroom door, ready to grab the evidence and wave it triumphantly around for all to see the next morning. Lack of such evidence can bring great danger to the bride because a father, brother or cousin often intervenes to restore their family's honour. You can lie and cheat, steal and kill and keep your honour intact. But you must never give away a daughter who is without virtue. That is the worst sin you can commit.

All is not lost, however, as there are medical means for a bride to resort to if she has ventured out on thin ice before the wedding night. The simplest and most common is to pay a visit to a gynae-cologist immediately before or on the wedding day. A few well placed stitches, which will trigger off some bleeding when they are pulled loose in the decisive moment, usually do the trick and will ensure that family happiness is kept intact too. In Iraq and most other Middle Eastern countries doctors are forbidden to undertake these little adjustments. In exchange for the necessary insurance money, however, many of my colleagues are prepared to step in at a time of need.

But I smelt a rat at this stream of girls who came to my clinic to have their virtue restored. None of them were embarrassed when they presented their requests. They got completely undressed in next to no time and jumped up on to the examination couch without hesitation. They never argued when I said no, asked them to dress and threw them out, informing them that I was not that sort of a surgeon. If they had been in real trouble they would have behaved differently and implored me to help them. It was all too clear that they had been sent to lead me into temptation. Before being allowed to join the President's inner circle my ethics were being tested.

Many young and beautiful women circulated within the regime's secret services. Some of them worked directly for the President independent of the official intelligence agencies. Saddam used to select them when on visits to universities, research institutes, various businesses or from central or regional administrative bodies. They were asked to come to his office, praised for their efficiency and competence and then promoted to key positions within the departments, directorates and other state administration.

There were quite a few of them. Saddam's bodyguard told me that Saddam rendezvoused with them on set days and at set times month after month. Some became close to him, for variable periods of time. Apparently he treated them courteously and with charm and generosity. He always listened attentively to what they had to say.

Several of them came to the clinic for nose jobs or other plastic surgery. The President was never very happy when they said they needed my help but he usually gave in when they had nagged for some time. They nearly all spoke kindly of him; very few experienced any unpleasantness. But they have to be careful, one of them told me. One of them said to me that she had been shown the door one night when she said she thought that invading Kuwait had been a calamity for Iraq. The President saw red, screamed and shouted and told her never to show her face again. The next morning a tidy little sum arrived from his office, so that she would not suffer in the immediate future.

However, the great majority of women with whom Saddam had close and frequent contact never took on the role of mistress. He was interested first and foremost in the information and gossip they brought him. Several were asked to ingratiate themselves with their bosses. Confidences leaked during intimate encounters proved disastrous to many lovesick ministers, high-ranking officers and party bosses when passed on to Saddam by his network of women. This no doubt explained certain dismissals, arrests and executions which arrived like a bolt from the blue.

Treading unawares on the toes of one of Saddam's women could be fatal too. Mazen al-Alosi was for many years the President's favourite architect, unrivalled and highly esteemed. He had a civil engineering degree from America in addition to his other academic qualifications and he designed and supervised the construction of many palaces, residences, mosques and resort villages for the elite in Baghdad and elsewhere in Iraq. The projects were always completed on time and on budget and Saddam decorated him with every medal and order and honour that could be crammed around his neck. I got to know al-Alosi when the President chose his office to erect 'The Union' along one of Baghdad's main approaches. But when the time came to unveil the sculpture in the spring of 2003 he was not there. He had fallen into disgrace.

While networking Saddam had caught sight of a female civil servant on a building site in Baghdad. He had asked al-Alosi to employ her. After being taken on she arrived late and left early while the other staff wore themselves out trying to complete the many and large building projects. Al-Alosi decided to give her a written warning stating that if she continued the way she had started, he would have to give her notice. That was the end of him as far as being head of the presidential architect's office was concerned.

He was called in to Saddam who demanded that he withdraw the letter and apologise unconditionally. Subsequently he was demoted and moved to one of Baghdad's more anonymous project offices.

The female architect was about thirty and in my opinion not particularly pretty, but men seemed to find her attractive. Saddam sent her to me one day, accompanied by one of his bodyguards, so I could examine one of her eyelids. It was not as perfect as she wanted it to be, owing to a minute congenital defect. However, plastic surgery would leave its traces and I advised against doing anything to the eyelid.

She was content with the verdict and I thought no more of it until September 2000, when I was en route to an international medical conference in Düsseldorf via Vienna. As usual, when in Vienna, I stayed with our ambassador, my good, hospitable friend Naji Sabri al-Hadithi and his wife, whom I had known for many years.

One evening the ambassador mentioned that an Iraqi architect had arrived in town together with her husband. He did not know them, they weren't members of Saddam's family, but Abed Hamoud had telephoned and asked the ambassador to pay them special attention. Al-Hadithi was slightly confused: the two visitors did not seem particularly important.

I asked her name and the ambassador gave it to me.

For God's sake, roll out the red carpet and turn on the charm, was my immediate advice. I wanted to make sure he didn't walk into a trap; she could get him into trouble if his behaviour wasn't up to scratch.

No sooner said than done. My friend the ambassador followed the advice and took care of the couple. There followed lunches and dinners at Vienna's best restaurants, major shopping in the town's most fashionable shops and department stores.

She appeared delighted when she and her husband were driven to the airport, loaded down with clothes and presents to take back to sanctions-hit Baghdad. A few of her suitcases were stuffed with exclusive outfits, shirts and ties more suited to someone of Saddam's size than her husband's.

The couple's successful autumn holiday was no doubt a positive factor in support of Saddam's already-taken decision to appoint Naji Sabri al-Hadithi as Foreign Minister.

Al-Hadithi had his own theories regarding his appointment as the regime's last Foreign Minister. In the early eighties his brother, Muhammad Sabri al-Hadithi, was Iraq's Deputy Foreign Minister. Following intelligence and pressure from Hussein Kamel and Chemical Ali, Saddam was led to believe that the Deputy Foreign Minister, together with a number of other conspirators, was planning a coup. He was arrested, tortured and killed with the other alleged offenders. Al-Hadithi's third brother was also held and maltreated, but released after a long stint in prison.

When Naji al-Hadithi was installed as Foreign Minister in 2001 – his predecessor, Muhammad Said al-Sahhaf was appointed Minister of Information – Saddam came over to him. 'I hear that your brother was killed,' he said. 'I knew nothing about it.'

Of course he did. But al-Hadithi got the feeling that his appointment as Foreign Minister came about because Saddam had started to think of his posthumous reputation and because he wanted to apologise somehow for what that had happened twenty years before. Nor did the President content himself with the actual appointment; he made al-Hadithi a present of a farm and an impressive house immediately outside Baghdad. His elder, once-tortured brother's pension was increased and he was given a new car.

I feared the worst at Bin-Sina when it became obvious that Samira Shahbandar had failed to clear the relatively innocent cosmetic surgery with the President. I was still discussing it with her when I heard footsteps outside in the corridor and Saddam entered. He appeared uneasy and apprehensive.

'Is anything wrong?' he asked.

'No,' she said. 'I've just had a small growth removed from behind my ear.'

Saddam looked at me.

'Is it dangerous?'

'No,' I said. 'There was a small lump on the left side of the throat which has now been removed. But I have transferred some skin from the left cheek and repeated the procedure on the other side so there will be no difference between the two sides of the face when it heals. All is well and she can leave the hospital this evening.'

Saddam looked at me and smiled. He said nothing, but I was not stupid; I realised that he knew what I had done for his wife.

Officially Sajida was the President's only wife. She was the daughter of his uncle, Khairallah Tulfah. The two cousins got engaged during Saddam's stay in Cairo following the unsuccessful assassination attempt on President Abdul Karim Kassem in Baghdad in 1959. They married when Saddam returned from Egypt after Kassem's fall in 1963.

Saddam was not straight with Sajida. There were rumours circulating that he had also married Samira Shahbandar (which was true), but the subject was taboo in family circles. I spoke one day to Sajida's sister, Ilham, who told me that she personally was convinced that the President was lying and that he had taken another wife. 'But Sajida refuses to listen and the President refuses point blank too!'

Life was not easy for Sajida. I remember being called to the presidential palace on the west bank of the Tigris one winter's morning in 1993. Sajida had a skin lesion on her arm which she wanted removed. A room in the palace had been converted into a small surgery and we decided to go ahead with the operation the next day.

When I returned I forgot to give her a local anaesthetic before starting the procedure. This is the one and only time I have ever made such a terrible mistake. But not a sound escaped her lips. I only realised something was wrong when more blood spurted from the cut than was normal. As a rule anaesthetic controls the blood flow.

'Does it hurt?' I asked her.

'Yes,' she said.

'Why didn't you ask me to stop?'

Sajida looked at me. 'If you can put up with Saddam Hussein you can put up with anything,' she said.

On the whole it was both pleasant and straightforward looking after the President's wives. Far more difficult, however, was the task of looking after his aunt, Hajia Badra. 'Hajia' meant that she had completed the great pilgrimage to Mecca, the Haj, in her youth. Now she was old and wizened and mummy-like, and drove me and all the doctors at Bin-Sina insane.

She was Saddam's mother's sister, a spinster and loved operations. Her normal routine was to call us around midnight to say something was hurting somewhere. She lived in a large house in Baghdad and her nephew had furnished her with servants and bodyguards and everything else she needed. But she loved, and demanded, operations. It did not matter what the trouble was. If her arm was itching she demanded surgery to stop it. I lost count of the number of bits of skin I cut off to make her happy. Happiness for her was a general anaesthetic. We cut her up and then sewed her up again for one imaginary ailment after the other. Not a week went by without her demanding endoscopic surgery. Nothing was wrong with her stomach; but no throat in the world had had that fibre-optic snake – which normal people hated – pushed down it as many times as Hajia Badra's. Of that I am certain.

She was lonely, and just wanted to be the centre of attention for a brief moment. But we knew she could be deadly: two of her servants disappeared and were executed after she accused them of stealing from her. We quite simply dared not stop the nonsense and say enough was enough.

Sajida lost her temper one morning when she passed Hajia Badra's house. The old trout had got it into her head that she was going to be the target of an assassination attempt. She had made her bodyguards put up two checkpoints fifty metres apart in the road that passed her house. No one was allowed through without accounting for their errand in the neighbourhood.

Sajida, who passed this way en route to the presidential palace, was enraged when she was stopped. She demanded the checkpoints be dismantled at once. 'If they aren't I'll stuff you into my boot and drive you straight to gaol,' she said to the two bodyguards who came rushing out of the guardroom in front of Hajia Badra's house to let the President's wife through.

They did as they were told.

Next morning Hajia Badra was on her way to Bin-Sina for another operation. When she realised that the checkpoints had disappeared she exploded. She cursed and railed and threat-ened the guards with eternal incarceration in Saddam's most terrible dungeon if they did not immediately close the road once more.

They did as they were told – again. One of them told me they dared not disobey her. The checkpoints were resurrected.

A few hours later Sajida passed again. Her explosion was, if possible, stronger than Hajia Badra's. The two poor guards were stuffed into her boot and went to gaol for a week. But the check-points in front of Hajia Badra's house were never resurrected.

Early one morning, before daybreak, the President's aunt phoned me. Her right index finger was hurting and please could I come immediately.

'How long has the finger been painful?' I asked.

'Three months. You must operate.'

She considered my response rude and accused all doctors of working only for money or when they were coerced into it. I managed to persuade her that I would see her the next morning at Bin-Sina.

To be on the safe side I took Bin-Sina's director and two nurs-ing staff with me. There was of course nothing wrong with her index finger.

'I want you to operate on it,' she said.

'Why? There's nothing wrong with it.'

Hajia Badra flew into a rage. 'All you doctors think of is making money and becoming famous. Just you wait, I'll show you!'

'It won't help that you are Saddam's aunt. I wouldn't operate on your finger for ten million dinars.'

Sajida phoned me during the afternoon. She was polite and apologised on behalf of Hajia Badra. 'But please perform the operation. Even if it is not necessary.'

'But what if there are complications?'

'Never mind, just operate.'

Thank God, she also pestered many of Saddam's ministers with her demands. They plucked up enough courage in the end and complained to the President. He cut Hajia Badra's telephone lines. Peace reigned at last!

*

Hajia Badra apart, the small hospital was always busy. Saddam was not alone in having two wives or more. Take Izzat Ibrahim al-Douri, Vice-President of the Revolutionary Command Council and Saddam's right-hand man. He had four wives and countless children, all entitled to be looked after by us when necessary. The vice-president lived on an estate by the Tigris, where his first wife lived in the original house, the other three in their own identical houses.

Barzan, Saddam's half-brother, explained to me how it was al-Douri got the fourth one. One day, when the Vice-President was visiting his farm in Tikrit, he caught sight of one of the daughters of his tenant farmer. She was a stunning beauty and only eighteen years old. Al-Douri immediately asked her father for her hand and consent was naturally forthcoming. Al-Douri no longer slept with his first wife (she was too old for his liking); instead she had been allocated the task and honour of cooking for the three other wives and children. Meals were prepared in the main building and carried round to the other houses according to strict rules. Like all good Muslims, the Vice-President kept a strict routine concerning where he went to bed at night.

Living like this naturally produced lots of children and one day Izzat Ibrahim arrived unannounced in Bin-Sina with three of his sons. He wanted them circumcised. They were between three and four years old and he had forgotten one of their names. I refused to operate: the three sons had eaten breakfast that morning and it would have been impossible to give them anaesthetic in case they vomited and suffocated. It is exceedingly painful to be circumcised without anaesthetic. Al-Douri was absolutely furious, but when he realised he was getting nowhere, he took his sons later on round the corner to a barber who dealt with the matter. The little ones must have suffered agony.

Samira Shahbandar's convalescence ran its course without problems. I popped into her house from time to time to make sure there were no complications. She was obviously pleased at these visits and I spent time chatting to her. It was plain to see that she led a lonely life.

She spoke often and at length of her admiration for Saddam.

'I never can understand how he has managed to get where he is given the wretched and primitive circumstances in which he was brought up.'

She had two sons and a daughter from her first marriage. Her two sons and daughter and the daughter's husband lived with her. A little granddaughter had just arrived and the President had grown fond of the child. He made a great fuss of her whenever he visited. 'He always wants to see her. He tosses her in the air and loves playing with her.'

But the visits grew rare and now – in the summer of 2000 – Saddam had become increasingly concerned about his safety. He constantly switched homes, both day and night-time.

Samira Shahbandar suddenly had trouble keeping a straight face. By the door were two red suitcases. 'Look at that,' she said. 'That's my existence. I have to be ready every evening in case his bodyguards come to pick me up. I never know when he'll want to see me or in which house we'll spend the night together. This is no life. And yet people envy me . . . but I know God will punish them,' she said.

When I left I spotted a tiny photograph of her first husband in the bookcase.

There were several reasons why she was not entirely happy. Her oldest son was an aircraft mechanic and had requested a transfer to Jordan so he could work and live in Amman with his family. The real reason was that Uday had started to pester him and Samira's son feared how it might end.

Initially Saddam had refused him permission to go, but eventually he changed his mind. 'I'll agree to it on one condition,' he said to Samira. 'You must never ask me for permission to go abroad to visit him. I am sure your son will never return to Iraq.'

'Well, I'm sure he'll come back!' she insisted.

But Saddam was right, and she found it increasingly difficult to bear her oldest son's absence. There were other things bothering her too. She was an intelligent and well-educated woman who had worked in the secondary educational system before she married her first husband. She was waking up to the madness that was developing around her and realised that the regime was heading for a fall.

*

At about the same time Samira had her face lifted the President wanted me to examine his feet again. He did not wish to suffer from more corns; one was enough. I was fetched and taken to one of the big palaces he had built in Radwaniya. It was large and surrounded by a park-like garden with several small ponds used for pisciculture.

When I had checked his feet and praised him for beginning to wear shoes a size up from those he used to have on, Saddam asked one of his bodyguards to catch and give me five large carp from one of the fish farms. In contrast to the rest of the family, who were skinflints and misers to a man, Saddam was often very generous.

'That is too much,' I protested when the bodyguards arrived with the fish.

'Take them home to your wife. She'll be happy. Women always want more than they need: you see it in the market every day. They're never happy with what they have. It's innate. It doesn't matter whether they're stupid or intelligent, whether they come from the country or were brought up in Baghdad. They're the same everywhere and there's no use trying to change them,' said Saddam.

'I think you should try even larger shoes, up another number,' I interrupted, but the President was more interested in the weaker sex and continued:

'They're sentimental and romantic and find it hard to make up their minds. But having said that they can be man's best friend. They're more honest than men and once they *have* made up their minds they'll sacrifice everything for their decision. They deserve to be heard and to be influential and to have the same rights in society as us men. Of course, all within the framework of our religious and cultural traditions. Throughout our proud history morality has always been preserved,' he said.

I let the bodyguards keep the carp when I left.

By Middle Eastern standards Iraq's head of state was more progressive than most with regard how women were viewed, at least officially. He had already pushed through legislation in the 1970s to end illiteracy in the country. School attendance became compulsory for girls as well as boys. Parents who found it unnecessary and kept their daughters at home were punished.

Early in the 1990s the regime passed a new law which opened the way for women to divorce without the man's approval, which was unheard of and approaching blasphemy in the male-dominated Muslim world. In addition he gave women rights following a divorce. Sheikhs and mullahs in the strongly religious, tribal-oriented society were horrified when they were told that from now on a man would be obliged to support his ex-wife financially, that he would have to wait three years before throwing her and any children out of the family home and that furniture and personal chattels were hers automatically once the divorce was final. The protests were vociferous but Saddam forced it through. It wasn't long before the new legislation was put to the test, in the President's own family.

In 1994 Saddam's half-brother, Barzan, had just returned from Geneva, where he was Iraq's ambassador to the UN, when the President came to visit. The visit concerned Saja, the ambassador's daughter. Saddam wanted her to marry Uday.

Of all possible prospects for a sweet, educated young girl, this was the worst. A worse psychopath or more profligate fornicator would be difficult to find in Baghdad than the President's son. But Barzan dared not say no. His big brother, Saddam, sixteen years older, was like a father to him. His wish was law in the family.

'I will give Uday my daughter. But you must be her father and protect her personally,' Barzan said.

Two months later Uday and Saja became husband and wife. Four days after the wedding the newly-wed President's son hired a suite in the Hotel al-Rashid and took up residence in the company of a gaggle of prostitutes. Baghdad had another scandal to gossip about.

Saja moved in with her aunt Sajida, Uday's mother. She had nowhere else to go. Her parents were in Geneva. In vain she tried to get her father-in-law to agree to a divorce. The President avoided the issue. 'You'll have to discuss it with Uday,' he said.

But Uday would not hear of a divorce. 'We don't get divorced in our family,' he said. There were well-established practices for instances like this. When spouses no longer got on the husband, like the Bedouin, found another wife. The old wife could stay, and was fed clothed and sheltered. Uday thought Saja should adapt herself to those conditions.

The sojourn with her aunt and mother-in-law was a veritable prison sentence for Barzan's daughter. I saw her from time to time when I called on Sajida. It was agony to look into her tear-stained eyes. They cried for help. Luckily her father eventually saw the urgency. He came to Baghdad and the daughter stole out to meet him. Together they got out of Iraq and back to Geneva.

Barzan's relations with Saddam had already taken a serious blow in 1983 when he was dismissed from his post as Iraq's head of intelligence. They did not improve after the disastrous marriage forced upon the his daughter and they deteriorated further when the President called his half-brother home from Geneva in 1998. Barzan's wife Ahlam was dying of cancer, but Saddam insisted he return home. The UN ambassador fought hard to convince Saddam that he could not leave her alone in the Swiss hospital where she was fighting for her life.

In my opinion Ahlam was the bravest and most upright of the women in the family. She was smart, intelligent and never flinched from criticising her brother-in-law. Many times I heard her deplore the one-party system, the dictatorship and the lack of freedom of press, opinion and expression.

'Sooner or later the regime will collapse,' she said.

Saddam loathed her. He called her 'the yellow snake'.

Barzan, on the other hand, loved her deeply. When she died he began building a mausoleum for her in Tikrit. It was planned to be fifty metres tall and surrounded by seven houses, one for each member of his family. The project was unfinished when the regime collapsed.

On his return from Switzerland in 1998 Barzan became the president's adviser. But he never advised about anything. Nor did his brothers Watban and Sabaawi, both of whom were given 'advisory' jobs after they were sacked as Minister of the Interior and head of the secret police respectively. In reality they were sidelined in the mid-nineties, but kept their bodyguards and bullet-proof Mercedes cars and were shown at least some respect.

At the end of April 2001 Barzan phoned me. Please would I come over? He had something important to tell me. 'It's between God, you and me.'

I was so curious that I complied immediately.

'I have made a serious decision today and I want you to help me implement it,' he said when coffee was being served. He was sweating and very pale.

I immediately wondered whether a coup was in the offing: perhaps he needed me to join him. I was prepared for the worst.

Barzan said nothing more but asked me to come in his car to the al-Mansour area where we stopped near the house of the former intelligence head Fadhil Barak, who had been accused of treason by Saddam and executed some years before. We went into the neighbouring house and were met by an elderly, kind gentleman who had been a highly thought-of judge all his life. He was a pensioner and the father of Fadhil Barak's widow.

Barzan was courting.

'As you see,' said Saddam's half-brother, 'I come with one of my best friends. I admire and value him more than any of my brothers. He is the only one with me but he is worth more than a hundred other respected men.'

The judge nodded understandingly. Ordinarily Arab tradition calls for a large delegation of male relatives, friends and tribal members to accompany a suitor seeking a woman's hand in marriage. In this way he shows his respect for the future wife's father and family. 'It is an honour and a pleasure to welcome you to my home,' said the judge.

Barzan then told him about his situation, and how times had become difficult since he lost his wife whom he had loved dearly. 'Your daughter, Jenan, has also suffered recently. I have great respect for her and I ask you for her hand in order that I may marry her.'

'May God bless you both,' said the judge.

Jenan was an attractive woman in her forties. She, her two

sons and three daughters, all university educated, welcomed us into the house. They were in their finery: we were expected. They served us tea and cakes.

In the car on our way home after the proposal, I asked Barzan if the President knew about this new marriage.

'No, why should he?'

'If I'd known that he hadn't been informed, I wouldn't have come with you.'

'Why? I'm a free agent. Saddam doesn't ask anyone's permission to do anything – he certainly never asks me.'

'This is different. What would you have said if your son married without letting you know?'

'I am totally sidelined politically and socially where family matters are concerned. I'll do as I like.'

'I know this is going to cause me problems,' I said.

The marriage ceremony took place seven days later. As expected I got Saddam's family on my back because I had sided with Barzan.

'You shouldn't have done it. He's disgraced the whole family by marrying the widow of a traitor,' said Sajida.

I never heard a word from Saddam, thank God. But he called his three half-brothers together to discuss the matter. 'Get a divorce immediately, or you are not our brother,' he insisted.

Barzan refused; divorce was never mentioned again.

A do-gooder – in his own eyes.

CHAPTER 16

The Lift

Uday wants to run his own hospital. The Health Minister gets into trouble.

Meki Hamodat was a lieutenant general. He was short, grey-haired, fiftyish and, in his own eyes, exceedingly important. He was Uday Hussein's military adviser. But when he arrived at the hospital on the morning of 20 June 2001, he hadn't come to discuss matters of defence. There was something else on his mind.

'The President's son wants your lift,' he said.

There was only one lift at al-Wasiti – the name most people still used despite the hospital having been renamed Saddam's Centre for Plastic and Reconstructive Surgery in the mid-nineties. But our building was only two storeys high, and that was the whole point of the lieutenant general's visit. A kilometre to the east was the maternity hospital al-Haydari, and it had three storeys. And no lift. Hamodat was of the opinion that the obvious thing to do was to move our lift. We would have to make do with the stairs between the ground floor and first floor.

Uday had acquired al-Haydari on the quiet a few weeks earlier and was now in the process of converting the old delivery rooms into Iraq's most modern private hospital. He saw the money-spinning potential of the health sector; but because no one must know that he had involved himself in the hospital, he was finding it difficult to lay his hands on the technical and medical equipment and other paraphernalia he needed to get the new project going via the official procurement channels. Accordingly,

explained the general, he needed a lift, and he gave me to understand that he took it for granted that I would concur.

I permitted myself to argue that the lift was doing splendidly
where it was and that it would be wrong of me to let go of a piece
of public property without an order from a higher authority.

The general fished out a small piece of paper from his inside
pocket and laid it on the table. It was a request from my Minister
of Health, Dr Omid Midhat Mubarak. 'Dr Ala,' he had scribbled
on it, 'would it be possible to move your lift from your centre to
Uday's new hospital?'

'But this isn't an official letter,' I protested. 'The request is a
question, not a demand to dismantle the lift and hand it over to
you.'

The general became angry; his face turned red and he
slammed the door in disgust as he rushed out empty-handed.

I feared the worst, not just for myself but also for my minister,
Dr Mubarak himself.

It is not difficult to understand that very special characteristics
were needed to find one's way through the Byzantine labyrinth of
Iraq's bureaucracy: personal, political and commercial stumbling
blocks were positioned everywhere. I can only take my hat off to
my last Minister of Health, Dr Mubarak, who managed to cling
to office from the moment he was appointed to the job immediately after the first Gulf War until the American invasion pulled
the carpet from under his feet in April 2003.

Dr Mubarak, who is my age, was socially and politically
extremely adaptable. He was born and grew up in Sulaimaniya in
Northern Iraq, where he first made his mark as a guerrilla soldier
for the then Kurdish leader Mustafa Barzani. Mubarak says that
he is a Kurd, but some believe that he originally came from the
Arabic tribe called al-Nuami which is a well-known tribe.
Anyhow, he changed sides when a young doctor and was
appointed to the position of director of the regime's republican
hospital in his home town. Kurdish resistance groups tried to kill
him twice and during the last assassination attempt he was hit in
the chest by several bullets from a Kalashnikov and badly
wounded.

Life was obviously safer in Baghdad where he became medical

adviser to the presidential staff. Membership of parliament soon followed and, via a short interlude as Iraqi Minister of Social Affairs, he was made Saddam's Health Minister. As a cabinet minister his ability to swallow insults and humiliations from above was unsurpassed. But, as I suspected, the question of our lift very soon hit him like a ton of bricks.

'Can you come over immediately?'

It was scarcely seven o'clock on the morning after Uday's military adviser had paid me a visit. The Health Minister said nothing more, but, in view of the time of day – he was never at his office that early – I realised that all hell was about to break loose.

His face was ashen and drawn when I walked in. 'Saddam knows about the lift,' he stammered. He didn't know how, but just before midnight the President's office had phoned him and told him to go straight to his place of work. Three officials from Saddam's staff were already awaiting him and they interrogated him until early morning. They had with them a handwritten letter from the President. He wanted an immediate explanation as to how it could be at all possible for a trusted minister to even contemplate the removal of a lift belonging to the Health Authorities to a private hospital. Mubarak showed me the letter. It was full of deletions and had clearly been written in a state of excitability.

Mismanagement and corruption had spread to such a degree that, although he pretended not to, Saddam saw pretty much everything that Uday, Qusay and the rest of his inner circle did. But theft of public property was evidently too much, even for him.

'What shall I answer?' My minister begged me to help him.

I explained that I had not tipped Saddam off, if that is what he thought. The President had his own channels of information – everywhere. It was therefore no more than could be expected that he was tackling the problem personally, and that he, who always had the nation's welfare at heart, had taken an interest in the lift. It was, after all, being moved from an important Baghdad public hospital. I knew that the minister's office was bugged, so there was no harm in laying it on thick. 'But,' I finished, 'the lift stays. It hasn't actually moved for ten years anyway.'

Saddam's Centre for Plastic and Reconstructive Surgery was situated three hundred metres north of another, totally different type of centre. This was housed in a large three-storey building; there were only a few small windows. The building was out of bounds but we all knew what went on there.

During the air attacks against Baghdad in 1991 the Americans bombed the torture centre, the regime's most brutal and darkest, to pieces. And as there was open country between them and us the powerful explosions caused us great damage too. The lift doors were especially badly hit. During the ensuing chaos the hospital was looted. The steering mechanism disappeared together with other important parts and during the subsequent ten years the purchase of new doors and spare parts never reached high enough up the Health Minister's list of priorities. This was his salvation.

'Why don't you tell the President that the lift is broken and the ministry is about to replace it,' I suggested, 'and that you are considering leaving Uday the old, broken one, which is only fair and proper, as he has shown such interest in it.'

I could tell that the skilled survivor glimpsed a ray of hope at the end of the tunnel. Saddam would probably accept the explanation.

It was more unfortunate, however, that further raids on the Iraqi health services, initiated by his son, had been sniffed out by the President. In order to establish the new hospital in record time, it wasn't only a lift Uday was after. He chose to fleece most of the public hospitals in Baghdad. He appointed doctors who submitted lists of what they needed for Meki Hamodat to locate and transfer to al-Haydari. It was more straightforward that way. Winter and spring would have come and gone before he could have scraped together the necessary items through the official purchasing channels.

Hospitals visited by the general felt the lash of his whip. Nurses and doctors could only look on while the President's son's envoy stole expensive technical and medical equipment, vital medicines, drugs and surgical instruments. They had to make do with the crumbs left over from the daylight robbery.

Dr Adnan al-Nasiri was a good friend who for a short period enjoyed Saddam's confidence as head of his special complaints office – the ombudsman function set up to help ordinary people when they felt intimidated in the face of officialdom. They could either write to al-Nasiri or make an appointment to see him personally if they had something to say – not, of course that al-Nasiri or his office had any real influence.

But the case of the lift, by great good fortune, had landed on his desk. He had been one of the three men who had interrogated Health Minister Mubarak all night and now I was invited to supply any additional information I could. I assumed that al-Nasiri's office was bugged and gave him the version I had given the minister earlier in the day.

Dr Adnan pushed a piece of paper across the desk. 'I have a copy of Saddam's letter to Uday about the lift,' it said. We always communicated thus inside the administration in Baghdad when discussing sensitive matters. One could never be too careful.

The President's letter followed.

How could you, my son, ever think of taking something from an official building for your private use? [Saddam asked] You don't normally have anything to do with the running of hospitals. Everyone knows that you are behind the al-Haydari project so why are you making it look as though a female doctor has bought it? From now on I insist you, like every other Iraqi citizen, go through the official channels and apply for permission to own and operate a hospital.

By doing such things you are indeed damaging my reputation. People will talk against me but not you. If you had not been my son you would never dare to do what you are doing.

That was how father and son communicated. By letter. They steered clear of the phone which they knew would be bugged. And even Uday and Qusay were obliged to go through Saddam's mighty secretary, Abed Hamoud, to arrange meetings with their father. There was no daily contact between them.

So Uday's military adviser had been snubbed and his father had given him a dressing down. All I had to do was await his revenge. It came therefore as no surprise when two reporters and a photographer from the newspaper *Babel* turned up at the hospital three days later. The President's son was the owner and editor of *Babel*. On arrival the two journalists and the photographer made a beeline for the ill-fated and useless lift. Having photographed it from all angles, they mounted the stairs to my office. I was asked to comment on the obvious administrative fiasco which was here exposed, and which in their opinion was proof of the hospital's disastrous management, nothing having been done in ten years to repair the broken lift. They assured me that the article would appear in the paper.

I said I looked forward to its publication and thanked them for their interest. The hospital needed their journalistic efforts; a bit of publicity would be a great help. 'We've written to the ministry of health many times and asked for money and spare parts in order to carry out the necessary repairs, but our efforts have been fruitless, as you can see for yourselves.'

The reporters and photographer bowed themselves out and I must admit I waited in some trepidation for the article to appear. If it did I could say goodbye to my position as hospital director. The majority of those whose reputations were dragged through the mud in *Babel* might as well resign at once, whether they were ministers or worked further down the ladder, as in my case.

I had been exposed to *Babel* before. That was at the turn of the year 1992/93, after I had been invited to visit Uday at his home late one evening. He talked about this and that and praised my efforts as doctor and artist. What he really wanted was for me to write derogatory articles in his newspaper about various ministers and top executives of the Baath Party. In return *Babel* would both extol my person and print my portrait, as big as the one of the President, whose picture in various poses graced the front pages daily.

I answered that I knew little about the persons concerned and that I had difficulty seeing how this could have anything to do with me.

Uday assured me that this would not be a problem. 'I'll supply you with all the information you need.'

I excused myself and said no thank you! 'I'm not even a good writer.'

Babel struck five days later. A full-page article described how Dr Ala Bashir, in his private clinic in Baghdad, bled patients dry for plastic and cosmetic surgery performed there. The rates asked were far above what was reasonable. Dr Bashir's secretary was especially cunning: she enticed patients into submitting to unnecessary X-rays and blood tests. Moreover, as a human being I was utterly conceited and arrogant. In conclusion *Babel* reminded me that even the Pharaohs were mortal. They lost all they possessed when they died, it said.

No sooner had *Babel* hit the streets than distribution was halted. The next day the Minister of Culture, Hamed Hamadi, phoned me. He told me he had instructions to afford me the right to reply. I could formulate it myself, without interference. The reply would be published in the following day's newspapers and broadcast on television.

I said I wasn't interested as what had been written merited no answer. 'People must be allowed to write and think what they like. Time will reveal what is right and what is wrong. People who know me know that the article is rubbish. And those who don't will soon realise that it is,' I said.

A week later I met Uday's mother, Sajida. She apologised for the article. Saddam had been incandescent with rage when he saw it. 'We're all sorry for what happened,' she said. She went on to say that Uday had disclaimed all responsibility for the article. It had been written without his knowledge, he told the family.

No article ever appeared about the lift and the mismanagement at Saddam's Centre for Plastic and Reconstructive Surgery, and that surprised me. In spite of knowing that Saddam still respected and favoured me, Uday increasingly got his own way with his father. I felt that the President simply did not dare stop his many vendettas, fearing that if he did his son's increasing insanity would gallop completely out of control.

One day, whilst I was operating at the clinic, a young script-writer from al-Shabab arrived. He wanted me for a talk show.

'I can't leave,' I said. 'My waiting room is full of patients. They've come from all over – I can't just ask them to go home.'

'You must,' said the scriptwriter. 'If not Uday will explode. He wants you to take part in the chatshow.'

'I don't even know what the chatshow is about. I'm completely unprepared. I'm very sorry, but I'm not coming.'

'Can you phone the producer?'

'No, I'm not going to phone him. Tell him and Uday that you couldn't find me. I'd rather close the clinic and disappear.' I had recognised the scriptwriter. He was the son of an artist friend. 'Your father is a good friend of mine', I said, hoping he would accept that. Reluctantly he left, but returned almost immediately. 'For God's sake, Dr Ala, please don't make it difficult for me. If I get caught out I'll be in real trouble.'

'Only the two of us will know about it.'

'What about God? Please phone the producer.'

I phoned.

'Well, Dr Ala,' the producer said, 'Uday's sitting in the room next door and he has personally asked for you to come and be interviewed together with other guests. I'm afraid there'll be a lot of criticism of you if you don't turn up.'

I wasn't worried about that, but to defy Uday openly when al-Shabab had actually managed to track me down might cause endless trouble.

There were five participants: a Jordanian singer and her hus-band, an Iraqi singer and one of Saddam's ministers in addition to myself. I was seated beside the anchor, in this case a very beau-tiful woman, who discreetly showed me a piece of paper with questions that I would be asked on it. 'Why is it always difficult to get you to cooperate with al-Shabab?' was the first.

Once I'd answered that I had no problems with appearing on Uday's TV channel the questions continued in the same vein: why did I behave like a prima donna, why was I not very communica-tive, etc. The programme degenerated into a farce, to put it mildly, and when we went off air the anchor woman leant over to me and said: 'Please, ask me to see you out.' She was clearly petrified.

'Could you show me out?' I asked loudly.

We left the studio together, and she walked with me to the main entrance. The young scriptwriter was waiting in a battered Volkswagen and we all drove off together. 'Thank you, we're really grateful,' they said. Uday had demanded time alone with the young anchor woman, which was why she needed to escape the studio. A month later she married the scriptwriter and they fled to Jordan.

Male pop singers suffered especially at the hands of Uday's al-Shabab. He could not bear to see how much easier they found it to pull women than he did.

One morning, during a complicated operation at the hospital, a cameraman, sound man and a reporter from al-Shabab stormed unannounced into the sterile operating theatre. 'What the hell are you doing?' I screamed.

'Uday has asked us to interview you about hair transplants.'

I threw them out but they were waiting when I came out of theatre.

'Three years ago you performed a hair transplant on one of our famous pop stars,' the reporter stated, then poked the microphone into my face. 'We'd like to interview you about him. Was it a successful operation?'

'I have no recollection of such an operation,' I said.

'How could you have forgotten? He's told us about it himself.'

'In that case you don't have to ask me, ask him.'

'No, you have to answer. Uday won't like it if you don't answer.'

'Sorry, but I don't remember such an operation.'

The reporter turned the question around. 'Are hair transplants usually successful?'

'Yes,' I said.

'But you're quite sure that you can't remember having operated on the singer we asked you about?'

'Quite sure.'

The reporter cursed when the cameraman turned the camera off. They were forced to return without the interview.

The pop star got it anyhow. The evening news headlines

screamed the neighbours' disgust at the singer's immoral lifestyle. The local police chief, questioned by the same reporter who had tried to interview me, confirmed that the pop idol lived a life of debauchery and that he was an embarrassment to the neighbourhood. If possible the neighbours and the police would like to see him removed from Baghdad. In addition the pop star had allegedly been a lousy soldier; at least that's what his company commander told al-Shabab's reporter. He had on many occasions been put in the glasshouse for having gone AWOL.

If that were not enough, his female admirers now knew all was not well with his head of hair. The interview with me was given unabridged.

Abed Hamoud phoned me the next morning to congratulate me on withstanding the pressure from the al-Shabab reporter. 'You deserve respect for your professionalism, and for not breaching patient–doctor confidentiality,' he said.

Hamoud hated Uday.

There were many pop stars who fell out of favour. They were usually invited to Uday's parties where they were forced to sing, unceasingly, until the last guests left. Kazem al-Saher, Iraq's most idolised singer, was one who felt the wrath of the President's son.

Al-Saher was famous all over the Middle East and appeared frequently on TV shows surrounded by beautiful women. When he visited Baghdad Uday phoned him and asked him to one of his parties. Muhammad al-Muphraji, Uday's bodyguard, told me how the celebrated singer was treated. Initially he was forced to sing until dawn. Next, Uday asked him to sign photographs of himself. Then Uday gave him his shoe and the pop star was asked to sign the sole. Shoes from other partygoers appeared and the famous pop star signed, between clenched teeth, until his pen ran dry. He never returned to Iraq.

To be exposed to another person's shoes signifies serious degradation in Arab culture. Not for nothing was the entrance at the al-Rashid Hotel paved with a mosaic picture of the American President George H. W. Bush after the Gulf War. It was impossible to enter the hotel without treading on him.

*

So, allegedly, in my spare time I practised hair transplants and other plastic surgery in Baghdad. It is well known that few Arab women are happy with their noses. They are either too crooked in the middle, too large or need a small lift at the front. The nose-job clientele made for very lucrative business.

I had just completed one of these virtually endless plastic surgery procedures when Luai Marza turned up at the clinic. He was on Uday's staff, and I knew him well as I had sewn him together following a traffic accident the year before. And in spite of Arab men also shortening or restructuring their noses all over the Middle East, this was not the reason for Marza's visit, only a few days after my meeting with the investigative news team from *Babel*. It was, of course, to do with the lift.

'Hello,' was all he said when he entered the door. Normally he'd have embraced me and kissed both my cheeks, as is the custom in the Arab world when friends meet. Instead Marza was extremely formal and obviously frightened to be seen as a good friend of mine.

I understood what was going on immediately. He was obviously carrying a concealed microphone and a tape recorder and my suspicion was confirmed when he sat down on a chair close to me.

'Uday is very upset – furious – that you told his father about the lift.'

I said it wasn't true. There was no reason for me to have burdened Iraq's President with such a triviality. 'No one from Uday's staff has forced me into doing anything I did not wish, and nor has Health Minister Mubarak behaved improperly or indeed been anything but correct in this matter.'

Marza was silent and left the clinic.

But it was not quite over yet. Three weeks later, on my day off, I was asked to go to Bin-Sina. Uday had asked for me to come and inspect the leg that had been shot to pieces during the assassination attempt that nearly took his life in December 1996; the leg still troubled him.

We had arranged for me to examine him at nine p.m., but four hours later he had still not turned up. I therefore asked the switchboard to phone Uday's bodyguards and ask whether the appointment still stood. No one dared make the necessary calls for fear of irritating him.

Nevertheless, after half an hour one of his bodyguards arrived with the message that I was expected at Uday's home instead. He had several houses in Baghdad and tonight he was in one of the many houses in which his father sometimes spent the night. When I got there it was nearly two in the morning. The bodyguards made me wait another hour before it pleased the President's son to see me.

'As you were at your clinic until midnight I thought you needed a bit of time to eat and sleep,' he said. He was wearing a white Indian outfit and asked one of the bodyguards for some vodka which he poured down his throat straight from the bottle.

'You don't have to worry about keeping me awake at night,' I answered. 'For eight years as a surgeon during the war against Iran we never had the chance of more than two hours' uninterrupted sleep. After all you know that I usually attend my clinic only for three days a week, between four and seven in the evening.'

Uday asked me to examine his leg. It was unchanged. The scars from the operation were as before. There was no reason for Uday to summon me other than to make me wait as a punishment for the lift business. This was how he always insulted people he didn't like. Ministers, officers and civil servants who did not immediately dance to his tune were summoned to his office in the Iraqi Olympic Committee, where they sat about, waiting for hours on end, before eventually being called in. In the meantime he would order their chauffeurs and bodyguards home, so that the powers-that-be had to walk home or take a taxi when they emerged from his offices.

Uday wasn't alone in his hostility towards me. Saddam's secretary and a few of his guards didn't like me either.

'The devils' – as Saddam used to call his guards – 'they think you rather stiff and unsociable,' Saddam said.

'Yes, I think they are right,' I answered. 'For years I have been unable to detect the line that separates simple courtesy from hypocrisy, particularly in our society.'

Saddam looked at me for a while. 'Yes,' he said.

*

In the end Uday got his lift. It was taken from Rashid hospital, the largest military hospital in Baghdad. But Saddam put his foot down. He forbade Uday to help himself from Iraqi hospitals' much needed technical and medical equipment and their pitiful supply of drugs and surgical instruments.

Al-Haydari changed its name to the Olympic Hospital. The owner was the Iraqi Olympic Committee, whose leader Uday was chairman of the board. The Health Minister blindly endorsed the change of ownership and thus the hospital was entitled to put in for, and receive, the supplies it needed from the medical stores over which the ministry had complete control.

Economically the new hospital proved to be the lucrative business the President's son had hoped for. It was a veritable goldmine. UN sanctions combined with the regime's misrule had made it impossible for twenty-five million Iraqis to be treated satisfactorily at public hospitals for a number of diseases. The Olympic Hospital thus came to the rescue for all those who managed to scrape together enough money to benefit from Uday's health enterprise.

Uday advertised the hospital's services in *Babel* and on al-Shabab, extolling its advanced equipment and French specialists almost every day. Patients flocked there in spite of the prices, which were exorbitant by Iraq standards. The hospital was as a result not for ordinary people, but that did not affect Uday's operating profits. Years of corruption, smuggling and black marketeering had made many Iraqis hugely rich. The customer base was more than big enough.

When the Americans overran Baghdad the Olympic Hospital was sacked in the orgy of looting that followed in the wake of the conquest. It has now risen again as the Sheikh Zaid Hospital following humanitarian relief from the United Arab Emirates. It has been totally renovated and equipped with all facilities and every conceivable piece of up-to-the-minute equipment.

It was not necessary to renew the lift that was taken from Rashid hospital.

PART THREE

The Collapse

Uday's political science doctorate. The people rejoice and laugh uproariously. On the right is the university director Abdul Ilah al-Khasab. (Photo courtesy Zafer Muhammad Jaber)

CHAPTER 17

Countdown

**Regime change draws nearer. Corruption
is out of control and the title of PhD is
the latest craze amongst the power elite.**

'Army Day' on 6 January 2002 was celebrated with a large military parade in Baghdad. Saddam was keen to show the world in general and Iraqis in particular that he was leader of a modern and effective military power. Victory Square was crammed with the regime's most important dignitaries and jubilant onlookers, as tens of thousands of soldiers, tanks, armoured personnel carriers and lorries carrying anti-aircraft missiles paraded through the gigantic monument of crossed swords, a memorial to the 'victory' of the war against Iran.

This flexing of muscles was broadcast live on Iraqi television. What the transmission did not show was the chaos amidst Baghdad's traffic. It had never been worse. All junctions were blocked by tanks and military vehicles which had broken down en route to Victory Square. Several hundred had seized up completely. If anyone had been in doubt prior to Army Day as to the real state of affairs, they were now no longer. The whole of Baghdad was talking about the farce. Jokes proliferated and we all laughed.

The inexorable dissolution screamed at us from everywhere. In more and more parts of Baghdad sewage flowed from pavement to pavement over the whole width of the road; it never drained away, it just kept on reappearing. The bunged-up drains seemed to follow a pattern, rotating from neighbourhood to neighbourhood. On closer inspection the reason was revealed: even the operation of Baghdad's dilapidated sewage network was at the mercy of an ever-accelerating madness of public corruption.

When the basements and streets overflowed, the solution was to be found at the offices of the town engineer. It was never difficult to track down a responsible works manager who – in exchange for a reasonable reward – would redirect the sewage stream to a neighbourhood other than yours. When it re-emerged the farce repeated itself. The sewage was redirected yet again; it was a lucrative business.

The corruption broke ever new boundaries; not even academic life was spared. It became normal for underpaid teachers and professors to pass students through entrance and final exams. Iraqi universities and secondary schools, modelled on the British system and always of a high standard, were, like the rest of the fabric of society, in free fall.

The regime's leaders played their part in the decay. As young Baath Party members moved up the ladder furnished with university degrees and doctorates a feeling of inferiority spread amongst the older guard. Many of Saddam's closest allies had only scraped through primary and secondary school. Now they wanted a further education. Exams and degrees fell into line, one after the other.

Uday took the prize. Like a refreshing desert wind he ploughed through exams and even wrote a doctorate – to the great amusement, not to say uproarious guffawing of the people. In his wake followed Abed Hamoud; Jamal Mustafa – married to Saddam's youngest daughter Hala; Sabaawi – the President's half-brother; and Sabaawi's three sons. Their degrees in political science were taken in record time. At the faculty of political science a system was set up to help the elite succeed. The answers were circulated before the final exams, and when the leaders of society sat their exams, they did so in the dean's office together with a professor or two to supervise, and, if necessary, write for them. Teachers who refused to take part in this special academic exercise were threatened with dismissal, or, in some cases, prison.

Thank God it wasn't quite so bad at the faculty of medicine, although we did wonder what would happen when Omar Abed, son of Abed Hamoud, latter-day doctor of political science, was accepted as a student. We all wondered whether because of who his father was, he would have to pass with exceptional marks. However, before he could take his exams, the regime fell in April 2003.

The President might have wanted to clean up the mess in the institutions of learning, but Saddam was morbidly preoccupied with his own security and became increasingly isolated. Faced with the choice of new and perhaps more suitable candidates for leadership positions, he held on to the ones he had. He dared not dismiss the tight network of villains great and small who surrounded him; he was unable even to do anything about the inner circle of loyal but incompetent and corrupt colleagues surrounding him. 'A bad person whom you know is better than a good person you don't know' is a common saying in our society.

We met at the end of January 2002 to mark the tenth anniversary of the founding of the commission for advanced medical education in Iraq. I was a member of the commission and before the festivities the Education Minister, Dr Humam Abdul Khaleq, asked me to sculpt a small piece to be handed to the President as a thank you for his support. Saddam was very pleased, 'but how is the extension to the Centre for Plastic and Reconstructive Surgery getting on?' he asked.

'Well,' I said, lying through my teeth. It was now over sixteen years since the construction of the extension had begun.

The project had been Saddam's idea. He'd been impressed by our work at al-Wasiti with soldiers and officers wounded during the Iran–Iraq war and he realised we needed updated facilities to continue developing the medical expertise we had accumulated. But all construction came to a halt after the 1991 Kuwait war and the introduction of UN sanctions. By then Hussein Kamel was in charge of prioritising vital imports needed to keep the wheels of defence, industry and society at large going. Air conditioning or lifts for the new hospital did not reach high up his shopping list.

'We'll soon be producing this in Iraq. You'll have to wait,' he said when work stopped.

Back in 1996 Saddam had asked how the new centre was coming along. I told him we were waiting for air-conditioning systems and lifts and without those we were stuck. The President was furious.

'Why didn't you inform me?'

'I realised that you have other and more important matters to deal with.'

'Nonsense. This new centre is vital for the nation. I will take care of it personally,' he said and fired off a circular to the departments concerned. However, when the commission for higher medical education met in January 2002 not much had been done. The shell of the five-storey building stood unchanged from when work stopped in 1991. After the meeting the President approached me and grabbed my arm. A few days earlier he had dispatched some bodyguards to report on the site.

'You said all was well, but that's not the whole truth, is it?'

'With the country in the state it's in I thought it was the right thing to say,' I replied.

I couldn't tell the President about the reccurring problems. That would have raised the question of whose fault the misery was – bureaucrats, civil servants and ministers. That in turn might lead to their punishment – at best a lengthy prison sentence. When the President was angry he was deadly.

'If you wish this centre to be built you must grab the bull by the horns, or those responsible by their shirt collars, put them up against the wall and tell them what you need,' said Saddam. 'If you pussyfoot around you'll never get anywhere.'

I said I wanted to go through official channels and the President in his turn made it clear to me that 'if any problems emerge you know where to turn'. The Minister for Education, Dr Humam Abdul Khaleq, overheard our conversation. He asked Saddam if he could comment, and went on to say that my ambitions and demands were above the capacity and ability of Iraq's directorates and institutions and that was the reason for all the delays.

The President looked at him. 'Are we to accept that Dr Ala

must give up because some people don't understand what he's asking for?' he answered and turned to his omnipresent secretary Abed Hamoud. 'Make sure you issue a directive from me and the Revolutionary Command Council to all departments and directorates that they do everything Dr Ala needs to complete the centre.'

The President then said that from now on Abed Hamoud would deal with the project personally and I would report to him. When they left Hamoud asked to have a word with me.

'It's best not to contact me directly. I'm usually very busy. It would be better if you gave one of my assistants a ring if you run into trouble.' I did not contact him or any of his assistants.

As was to be expected, the hospital extension never materialised.

Right up until the moment the regime fell, all was well, on paper at least, with research and development in Iraq. Saddam liberally doled out orders of merit in gold and silver to researchers and scientists who had excelled in their work. The evening we were celebrating the commission's tenth anniversary I was awarded a gold medal for articles published in medical journals on the subject of plastic surgery.

There were 120 medal awards that evening; Tareq Aziz was in charge. Two of the medal-winners were scientists from Iraq's atomic research institute. I asked one of them whether the allegations that Saddam was in the process of developing nuclear weapons were true and was told that there was absolutely no truth in them and that the project had been shelved many years before. 'But some of our colleagues write elaborate reports and suggest grand development programmes only to be taken notice of and get pay rises,' he said.

When the medal ceremony was over – 40 gold, 80 silver – we were slipped 250,000 dinars each: approximately 100 American dollars.

The Saddam Prize was another award. It was introduced in 2002 and was the highest honour achievable. Six or seven of us were the first to be decorated for our 'lifelong and outstanding contribution in the service of the people'. My contribution, according to the committee, was my work as a plastic surgeon and director of our hospital. But when the committee's decisions were published in 2002 it appeared that my artistic efforts on behalf of the country were to be rewarded. The President had apparently overruled the committee; my award was for art, not medicine. 'Anyone can achieve great things within medicine, but it is rare for someone to create extraordinary art,' he wrote. 'Dr Ala thus deserves to be honoured for his art, not as a plastic surgeon.'

According to the rules the Saddam Prize could be awarded only once in the lifetime of a recipient. But in March 2003, a few weeks before the war, surprise, surprise, I pocketed another one, this time in my capacity as a doctor. The President had decided to break the rules. Again a small group was hailed for its lifelong efforts on behalf of people and country.

What the prize entailed, I never knew. It was up to Saddam to decide but he never got that far before American soldiers captured Baghdad. None of the fifteen recipients received money, medals or diplomas to remind us of the world that had gone – or of Saddam, who in a new general election in October 2002 had performed the incredible feat of being re-elected by one hundred per cent of the electorate for a period of seven more years.

According to Izzat Ibrahim al-Douri, responsible for the referendum, the turn-out had been one hundred per cent too.

On 6 January 2003, the Army Day military parade was cancelled. It was apparent to most Iraqis that the countdown to war with the USA and Great Britain had started and that Iraq would be unable to offer any significant resistance.

On 10 February, while UN weapons inspectors were still looking in vain for weapons of mass destruction and threats of war increased in strength from Washington and London, Qusay asked me to come and see him. His fifteen-year-old daughter was dissatisfied with her nose. The family wanted me to straighten it and make it smaller.

War was lurking round the corner yet this is what occupied Saddam's closest family. It was a simple operation; I had carried out thousands of them.

The next day I was invited to visit Raghad, Saddam's daughter who had been married to Hussein Kamel. Her daughter too wanted a nose job. She was sixteen and thought it was too big. As if that were not enough, Qusay's sister-in-law suddenly took one look at hers – another nose job. By 15 February all three noses had been dealt with. It appeared that the President's family had no idea of what was about to be unleashed, the consequences and how it would affect them.

One month further on, on 13 March, a week before the start of the war, I saw my three nose patients for the last time. I observed how the crystal chandeliers and Italian period furniture had vanished from Qusay's house; it was virtually stripped bare.

Qusay was at home when I examined his daughter and he invited me to have a cup of coffee. His oldest son, Mustafa, was there too. We were good friends; he always stuffed my pockets full of chocolate when I came to visit. The thirteen-year-old was allegedly the one who fought the hardest when he, his father and uncle Uday were tracked down to a house in Mosul, shot and killed by the occupying forces after the fall of the regime.

Today Qusay was elegantly dressed in an ochre-yellow suit with thin, brown stripes. He looked ill, and at times preoccupied. 'How are you?' he asked.

I said I was all right.

'I've been thinking,' he said, 'that when your generation of professors and medical specialists disappear, you will leave a big gap behind.'

'It's there already,' I said and reminded him that in the eighties the government had dismissed more than forty of Iraq's most prominent specialists and professors because a group of young doctors with connections to the Baath Party wanted to be promoted quickly. 'It makes matters worse when people are appointed to important positions without possessing the qualifications to fill them. If I asked you to promote a young army lieutenant to major general and give him command of a brigade or division, would you do it?'

'Are you thinking of the appointment of dean to the medical faculty?' he asked.

'That's one example,' I said.

Qusay reminded me that Abed Hamoud was behind the appointment. As Hamoud's son was working hard to pass his exams it was fitting that he should be advised by a dean. Education Minister Humam Abdul Khaleq was apparently not at all enthusiastic about what had happened.

Then Qusay looked at me. 'We have made masses of mistakes and it will take time to put them all right. It will be especially difficult to get rid of the corruption in the education system.' He told me that he himself had been toying with the idea of getting a PhD, but had decided against it. 'It's all cheating at the university. The only exam I'm proud of is the A I got at high school. I got that without cheating.'

Qusay looked at me for a while without saying anything. Then he said: 'When we are through this difficult period for the country it will be easy to rebuild Iraq. But what to do with all the corrupt people is another and more complicated matter; to restore destroyed human beings is extremely demanding.'

I never saw the President's younger son again.

I asked to be driven to Raghad's home to look at her daughter's nose. The distance between her house and her younger brother's was only fifty metres, but after Hussein and Saddam Kamel fled to Jordan with their families on the fateful eve of the Day of Days in 1995, Qusay had built a high wall between the two properties. I had to make a long detour to get to Raghad and her daughter. One of Qusay's bodyguards drove me.

'The situation is serious,' he said. 'Several men on the staff have disappeared. They fear the war. Two members of the security unit have been executed – they were distant relatives of Saddam's wife Sajida – they were charged with having given American spies information.'

Raghad's house too was empty of furniture. She smiled, but looked sad. 'This is a very difficult time for our country,' she said.

'You can say that again,' I said.

It was difficult not to reflect on what Saddam's daughter had suffered after she and her husband fled to Jordan. When they returned he had been mown down by Ali Hassan al-Majid and the rest of the family. At least her daughter's nose was fine.

*

Barzan al-Tikriti came to see me at Bin-Sina that day. The President's private hospital had moved: its situation near the Republican Palace would not be ideal when the bombs started to fall. One of the wings in the large Kazimiya hospital had been emptied to accommodate Bin-Sina.

Barzan was depressed. There was no longer any doubt what was in store for us. The USA and Great Britain would go to war independent of the other UN Security Council nations. Saddam was not prepared to follow the advice of the American President: to leave the country with his sons to avoid hostilities and spare the country loss of lives and, inevitably, huge material damage.

'Last night I dreamt that you and I fell out,' Barzan said. 'That's why I dropped in. I want to know if something has ruined our relationship.' I smiled. 'It's a good thing you had that dream, otherwise we would never have had this talk.'

We went into my office.

'It's all Saddam's fault. He reacts in the wrong way and always too late to the Security Council resolutions. Abed Hamoud and the gang of four, Izzat Ibrahim al-Douri, Taha Yassin Ramadhan, Ali Hassan al-Majid and Tareq Aziz – they're evil people and appalling advisers. Time and again I've told him to get rid of them. They're responsible for the war but Saddam will be the one who is blamed for the corruption and having led our country over the precipice.'

I told Barzan about the general who had visited the hospital with his little daughter a few days earlier. She needed treatment for a minor ailment, but it was clear that the general's reception had not been as courteous and respectful as expected. He was sitting in the outpatients' waiting room when I arrived and he was fuming. I asked him to bring his daughter into my office, to try and quiet him down.

Easier said than done. No sooner had he sat down than he blew his top. 'I've had enough,' he said. 'I don't even have time to look after my family the way things are.'

I was surprised. We were strangers and talking to me like that could be fatal.

'And now you're preparing for a new war,' I said.

'What are you talking about? No one is going to fight. There is no leadership apart from a former motorcycle messenger and a man who sold ice blocks in Tikrit.'

The general was alluding to Ali Hassan al-Majid, Saddam's cousin, and Izzat Ibrahim al-Douri, Deputy Chairman of the Revolutionary Command Council.

'How on earth can you expect the army to fight under such men?'

Barzan made no comment.

'But I think the greatest tragedies will occur after, not during, the war,' I continued, and reminded him of what I had witnessed during the revolution and the fall of the monarchy on 14 July 1958, and how Abdul Ilah had been towed behind a lorry through the streets of Baghdad, strung up and dismembered by the mob. I reminded him too of the looting and bloodletting during that coup and the one that toppled Abdul Karim Kassem in 1963.

Barzan looked at me. 'Why don't you tell Saddam?'

'He knows.'

Two days earlier, Barzan's brother Watban had sent two of his prostitute girlfriends to my clinic in Mansour. They arrived with their bodyguards. One wanted me to reduce the size of her breasts, the other wanted me to do something with her buttocks: they were rather large.

'It's hardly the time for such things,' I said. 'This country is preparing for war.' Fuming, I sent them packing. The bodyguard phoned next day.

'The boss asks whether you might help the girls after all?'

'No.'

This was what had happened to him. Watban's life consisted now mostly of alcohol, belly-dancers and prostitutes. The same could be said of Sabaawi, Barzan's older brother, but he kept a lower profile.

I mentioned the story of Watban's two girlfriends to Barzan.

'I have always said that that man is hopeless,' Saddam's half-brother said.

He was even more depressed when he left.

Momentous symbolism charaterises Saddam's last and
unpublished novel: *Get Out! You Are Cursed*.

CHAPTER 18

The Author

The President concentrates on his literary
work. His opinion of Israel is unaltered.

Hamed Hamadi became Saddam's last Minister of Culture. Like
so many of the other big guns in Baghdad he too was from Tikrit.
He'd joined the Baath Party as a young student and had followed
the President through thick and thin all the way to the summit of
power. He was the President's personal secretary for many years,
and a very powerful man. His opinion of himself, as far as I could
see, was inflated beyond reason. He was never wrong and as stub-
born as a goat. However, he was a workaholic and to a degree
loyal to the President; he worked for Saddam night and day.

On 18 March 2003, two days before the bombs and missiles
once again started to fall on Baghdad, he was at his desk. While
other ministers and civil servants went to ground in anticipation
of the unavoidable American–British attack, the Culture Minister
stood his ground.

He was shouldering a heavy burden. The President had written a new book and it was Hamadi's job to proof-read and get it
printed before it was too late.

Saddam enjoyed writing. As problems both at home and
abroad piled up he devoted more and more time to his literary
work. Daily control of the country was left to his nearest and most
trusted supporters: Ali Hassan al-Majid, Izzat Ibrahim al-Douri,
Taha Yassin Ramadhan and Tareq Aziz, and in addition Abed
Hamoud. Unsuspected consequences, however, usually resulted

when the gang of four and the private secretary made their decisions.

The anniversary of the attack on the World Trade Center was marked with a service of commemoration at 'Ground Zero' on 11 September 2002. President George W. Bush and heads of state from all over the world were present together with the UN Secretary-General Kofi Annan. UN ambassadors had also been invited.

Said al-Musawi, Iraq's UN envoy, thought it prudent to ask the Foreign Minister in Baghdad, Naji Sabri al-Hadithi, for permission to be present. Naji Sabri passed the request on to Abed Hamoud who in his turn forwarded it to the gang of four. The answer was no.

As Foreign Minister and a long-time, experienced diplomat, this surprised and exasperated Naji Sabri. It did not take a great deal of imagination to see how the Iraqi ambassador's absence would be interpreted and how his failure to appear could be used in the growing PR campaign in Washington and London to justify a military attack on Iraq.

'I was at my wits' end,' Naji Sabri said.

Luckily, a few days before the ceremony was to take place in New York, he was called into Saddam's office. His place at the table was furthest away from Saddam. In Baghdad the twenty ministerial positions were ranked according to seniority. Naji Sabri had joined the cabinet only a year earlier.

During the meeting the Foreign Minister chose not to bring up the question of the commemoration service. That might provoke the gang of four and trigger off a flood of abuse from either Tareq Aziz or Taha Yassin Ramadhan. They were usually the ones who mowed down inexperienced ministers who dared call their decisions into question. Instead Naji Sabri wrote a note and sent it up to the President at the head of the table asking whether he might see him after the meeting. There he presented the ambassador's request.

'Of course he must be present,' said Saddam.

The gang of four were not consulted.

The President's literary debut came late in life, in 1999, with the fable *Sabiba and the King*. The book was published under the pseudonym 'Written by the one who wrote it', and was of course an immediate bestseller.

Not since the Sumerians of ancient Mesopotamia invented the art of writing six thousand years ago, had such a literary triumph seen the light of day. Reviewers in TV, radio and the state-controlled press fell over each other extolling the magnum opus.

Every department, directorate and public office was urged to order in bulk. The norm was one book per four employees. From the ministry of health came the decree that they expected Saddam's Centre for Plastic and Reconstructive Surgery to take seventy-five copies, to sell on to doctors, nurses and the 300 staff. Both I and the other seventy-four book-buyers in the hospital had, with all due respect, some difficulty in understanding the contents, as had Iraq's great poet, Abdul-Razzaq Abdul Wahid, when asked to write a full-length play based on the book.

The commission came from Latif Jassin, Chairman of the Baath Party's cultural committee and member of the country's powerhouse, the Revolutionary Command Council. 'Initially I hadn't a clue who the author was. But after a while Jassin admitted that Saddam had written *Sabiba and the King* with a bit of help from his friend, the press secretary Ali Abdallah,' Abdul Wahid told me one day.

The poet, who now lives in Paris, struggled to unravel the President's tortuous and long-winded language and complicated train of thought. He said that, with a bit of goodwill, the book might be interpreted as a sort of self-examination, where Saddam – the King – discusses the many pitfalls and temptations of power and authority with himself and his own conscience, expressed through the beautiful and devoted young woman Sabiba.

'But it was very difficult to make any sense of what he wrote,' said Abdul Wahid.

The next book, *The Safe Fortress*, was, if possible, even more difficult to digest. It was published one year later and distributed in the same way as *Sabiba and the King*, i.e. in huge print runs, which in turn were loaded onto central and local authorities, hospitals and public offices whether they wanted the book or not.

The subject matter was the importance of improved solidarity in Iraqi society, but the President's well-meaning message probably passed unnoticed; the advice was confused and incoherent.

However, this time too, the reviews were rave.

'We do not know who the author is but this is a well-written and thought-provoking narrative. For eternity, it will shine a beacon of light on Iraq's rich literary heritage,' one of the critics wrote.

No doubt all this praise whetted the appetite of the unknown author. After a break of only six months he was on the market again. Again the hospital was required to buy seventy-five copies. *Men and Town*, was the title of the new work. Like the two previous books it was characterised by a lot of tedious detail and muddled thinking. But to be perfectly honest, what the author published in the autumn of 2002 was not completely uninteresting. Saddam's stories from his childhood and adolescence, growing up in wretched circumstances outside Tikrit, paint a frank and truthful picture of the illiteracy and poverty he fought his way out of. The world should not forget the social and economic backdrop he describes – his extreme poverty – when trying to understand why the dictator and his cronies developed as they did.

'I learnt,' writes Saddam, 'that I could trust no one with regard to my own safety. To survive I had to be on the lookout all the time.'

The President's last book, the one Hamed Hamadi sweated to proof-read only forty-eight hours before the American missiles were dispatched and the bombs started to fall in March 2003, was keenly anticipated in the Iraqi press. There was still speculation about the unknown author and I read that the critics were waiting with bated breath for the new literary masterpiece: *Get Out! You Are Cursed*.

Saddam comes straight to the point. Not much imagination or empathy is needed to understand who he wants to throw out, and on whom the curse rests. In the preface he tells us about an evil and deceitful people who lived near Syria two and a half thousand years ago. They were hated by all with whom they came into contact. According to the author there was obvious relief over the whole region when King Nebuchadnezzar, who arrived from Mesopotamia with his army, managed to round up the tribe and drive them on to Babylon as his slaves. But Nebuchadnezzar should never have taken the Jews with him to Mesopotamia when he attacked Jerusalem and destroyed Solomon's temple.

The Iraqi President was in no doubt that it was precisely these slaves who played a decisive role when the Persians, under Cyrus, captured and occupied the one-time mighty kingdom more than 2500 years ago.

'The plotting of the Jews and Persians led to the fall of Babylon,' he says in *Get Out! You Are Cursed*.

I do not know whether Saddam hated Jews. He never spoke disparagingly of them. He was not like his uncle and foster-father Khairallah Tulfah, who in the seventies distinguished himself by publishing a pamphlet: 'God should have abstained from creating three things: Persians, Jews and flies'.

The creation of the state of Israel in 1948 and the to him shameful defeat of Arab countries in the subsequent wars in the Holy Land had left an indelible mark on Saddam's psyche. He never really came to terms with the Arab countries' inability to match the political and military might of Israel and drive the intruders away from the land they had stolen from the Palestinians. Israel's existence and the fate of the Palestinians was an open festering wound, to him and to so many, many other young Arabs who grew up at that time.

When I was a young student at secondary school and later at university I believed in the ideas of pan-Arab nationalism: that we Arabs could break the colonial powers' dominance in the Middle East if only we stood together. Having lived in the darkness which was the Ottoman Empire for many hundreds of years, and escaped out of it, we now glimpsed the end of British and French influence in this part of the world. We were full of optimism.

We were betrayed. First the European Jews threw our Arab brethren in Palestine out of their towns and villages and put them to flight, then the Israelis inflicted a catastrophic military defeat on the Arabs. Our pride was shattered; the feeling of powerlessness is still strong.

*

In April 1993 I was invited to take part in a large medical congress in the USA. I went to Jordan to get a visa but at the consulate of the American embassy I was told it would take between two and three weeks for the visa to come through. The congress would by then be over, so I decided to stay in Amman with a few artist friends instead.

One day we visited a tourist restaurant in Umm Qays, on the mountain plateau north of the Jordanian town of Irbid. From our table we could see all the way to the south end of the Sea of Galilee. Along the foot of the precipice below us a valley separated us from the occupied Golan Heights. I looked straight down on to a number of farms.

'They belong to Jewish settlers,' my friend explained.

This was the first time I had been so close to the Holy Land of which I had heard so much. I spotted several settlers and their Palestinian farm workers going peacefully about their business, side by side. My thoughts drifted back to 1948 when, as a young boy, I ran around the streets of Baghdad and bid goodbye to the soldiers on their way to the Palestinian front. I thought about all the strikes and demonstrations I had attended as a student, protesting against the Arab countries' weakness in the face of the Zionist intruders.

I felt bitterness mixed with sorrow and humiliation as I enjoyed the beautiful landscape displayed in front of me.

I wanted to run away and hide. I held fast on to the armrest, so fast that I felt as if it almost became part of me. Chairs and their relationships to human beings became the theme for my next exhibition of paintings in Baghdad.

In Iraq, as elsewhere in the Middle East throughout history, the Jews have on the whole lived as an integral part of society in natural harmony with Christians and Muslims. But developments in Palestine destroyed this peaceful oriental coexistence and in time made it impossible for the Iraqi Jews, about 120,000 of them, mostly in Baghdad, to stay in the country.

Between fifteen and twenty thousand Iraqi solders went to the Holy Land: the largest single contingent from any Arab country. Their mission was to crush Israel, nip it in the bud, after David

Ben-Gurion had declared the Jewish State an entity on 14 May 1948. But the results were not much to write home about. They suffered one military setback after the other, like all the other Arab forces.

Scapegoats were required and no one was better placed to be cut down in the heated, defeatist atmosphere than the Jews themselves. They were systematically bullied and pestered. Their freedom of movement was curtailed, many were court-martialled and imprisoned, accused of and condemned for spying for the Zionist state. They were denied jobs in many parts of the civil service and public administration and to cap it all they were banned from many academic professions. In the course of just a few years Iraq's Jews disappeared to Israel. They were welcomed with open arms in Tel Aviv. In Baghdad the government was obviously glad to be rid of them, but they were sorely missed by their local communities.

In the neighbourhood where I grew up a Jewish shopkeeper ran a little ironmonger's and furniture shop. He was honest and upright, loved and respected by all, not least by those who had little money to spare. Most things could be had on tick and he even cancelled debts when they could no longer be honoured by those worst off. He was a good friend of my father and his son and I were best mates. We cried when the family left Iraq.

A few Jewish families resisted the state-sponsored bullying and all the encouragement to settle in Israel. On the whole they lived in peace and respect. In 1969, however, immediately after Saddam had been appointed Deputy President, seventeen alleged spies stood trial, were sentenced to death and hanged in Baghdad. Eleven of them were Jews.

The court case fuelled the strong anti-Israeli sentiments which characterised the Arab countries after their disastrous defeat at the hands of Israel during the Six Day War in 1967. The executions were also an indication of Saddam's uncompromising stance vis-à-vis the Jewish state.

There was no room for manoeuvre in Saddam's vision of Israel. He never made a speech without attacking the 'worldwide Zionist conspiracy' and always encouraged holy war in Palestine.

The Israeli air force attack on Iraq's one and only nuclear power plant did not help matters. The attack no doubt shattered the dream of developing an atom bomb. The Scud missile attacks on Israel during the first Gulf War in 1991 were a small consolation.

When the Palestinians rose against Israeli occupation of the Gaza Strip and the West Bank in September 2000 it came as no surprise that the President supported the families of suicide bombers and fallen activists with considerable sums of money.

However, it is not true to say that Saddam hated the sight of Jews, as has been claimed in many books and articles. When Uday shot his uncle Watban in August 1995 one of Europe's most prominent orthopaedic surgeons, Professor Alain Gilbert, got him back on his feet. During the time he was at Bin-Sina with his French colleagues one of Saddam's bodyguards came into my office.

'Is it true that one of the French doctors is Jewish?'

'Yes,' I said, 'and he is outstanding. I have known him for more than twenty-five years.'

When Saddam came to visit his brother the following day I briefed him about the Jewish surgeon.

'You know I have nothing against Jews as long as they do not occupy Palestine's soil,' the President said.

Nor did he mind that a laser machine I had ordered from the USA was made in Israel. An ardent soul on the President's staff discovered the origin of the machine and asked me why I had picked that particular make, 'Coherent', I remember was its name. I told him it was the best available but so as not to get into difficulty with Saddam I would mention the matter to him.

'I couldn't care less where the thing comes from, as long as it's the best available. Change the label at the border and we'll avoid any tittle-tattle,' was the President's comment.

One of my most able medical students, Zafir Dawoud, came from one of the Jewish families who chose to stay in Iraq. When he had completed his studies, the ministry of health wanted to appoint him as orthopaedic surgeon to a hospital outside Baghdad. I wanted to keep him at the Saddam Centre for Plastic and Reconstructive Surgery. To make sure he was not moved I mentioned Dawoud's quite exceptional ability and qualifications one day I was talking to the President. I did not make a secret of the fact that he was Jewish.

'They are clever,' Saddam said. Dr Zafir continued to work in al-Wasiti hospital from that moment on.

On 17 February 2001, the Iraqi news agency INA announced the construction of a new people's army, the al-Quds Army. Two weeks later our television screens showed radiant volunteers reporting for weapons training in Baghdad and around the provinces. The goal was to recruit between six and seven million Iraqis, trained by experienced Iraqi officers. Israel's neighbours were asked to open their borders to welcome the army when it arrived to turn out the Zionists.

A poverty-stricken and exhausted Iraqi populace did not know whether to laugh or cry when this Fata Morgana rolled across our television screens.

Saddam's opinion of the Jewish state hit home one evening in February 2003, when I was invited to dinner at the home of Fatiq al-Safi, the landowner who was one of the very first Baath Party members and who had for many years been the President's honest and intimate conversation partner – that is until Saddam broke off all contact in 1987. That was the time Fatiq told Saddam that the people's praise was mere window-dressing; they were playing to the gallery.

Barzan, Saddam's half-brother, had also been invited. We talked of course of the impending war. Hans Blix, head of the UN weapons inspection team, had just delivered a fresh report to the UN Security Council in New York. The deliberations and signals from the USA and Great Britain left no doubt as to where it was leading.

'The problem is Israel's security,' said Barzan. 'I've tried time and again to get my brother to understand that the world has changed and that we will be internationally completely sidelined if we can't find a solution that we, the Americans and the Israelis can live with. But I might as well be talking to the wall.'

As Iraq's UN ambassador in Geneva he had been approached

in 1989 by an Arab diplomat who conveyed Israel's concern over the large amounts of weapons Iraq had accumulated during the Iran war. The diplomat had signalled Israel's interest in opening a secret arbitration channel to explore the possibility of negotiating some sort of peace agreement between Baghdad and Jerusalem, either over or under the table.

Barzan contacted his brother in Baghdad who reacted as though he had been stung by a wasp. Minister of Culture Hamadi was dispatched to Geneva in record time, carrying a letter to the UN ambassador. Saddam wrote that the suggestion reminded him of the infidel tradesmen who tempted the Prophet Muhammad with money if he would halt his proselytising. 'The Prophet, peace be upon Him, answered that if they gave him the sun in one hand and the moon in the other, he would never let up converting the infidel.'

'The President has made it clear that he never wants you to make suggestions like that in the future,' Hamadi said.

But Barzan tried anyhow. After the Gulf War in 1991 he was on leave in Baghdad and visited Saddam. 'I told him that it was not in Iraq's interest to portray Israel as our chief enemy, that we needed to keep a low profile and maybe even change our political attitude vis-à-vis Israel completely. The President flew into a rage and told me to keep my bloody mouth shut.'

'You are too influenced by Western thinking. You need to be mentally rehabilitated,' was the advice he gave Barzan.

The evening round Fatiq al-Safi's dinner table was a protracted one. In the end Barzan could only shake his head over his half-brother's unbending opinions about Israel and Palestine's futile rebellion against the occupation, but he was extremely vocal and sarcastic about the new army, the al-Quds Army, established to free Jerusalem.

'The President boasts that it comprises six million able-bodied volunteers and that they're ready to go to war in the Holy Land. But we all know that this army is just a joke. I've written to Saddam and told him that if even five thousand of the six million who have volunteered are ready to fight, this would be a great surprise and an even greater step forward. But he won't listen. He chooses to listen to all the hypocrites and liars around him who tell him that Iraqis from all walks of life are queuing up to join the toy army and how happy they all are that at last they're receiving weapons training, which of course is just a big lie.' He was utterly exasperated.

Barzan may have done little more than shake his head at Saddam's stubbornness over the Israeli question that night, but on several occasions over many years he repeated that a peace settlement with Israel would solve many of the international problems the regime encountered. 'My brother needs to admit the facts and sit down with the Americans and find some pragmatic solutions that Jerusalem will accept.'

I had a small suspicion that the man was no stranger to the idea that he himself might effect the necessary political about-turn, if he ever got the chance; and that during diplomatic conversations someone might have given him a more significant role at home than that of UN ambassador in Geneva.

In 1989, when I was briefly visiting the well-known Lemain clinic in Paris, the UN ambassador phoned me. He had gone to Iraq where his son Muhammad had bought a motorcycle, crashed and been injured. His jaw and femur were broken and Barzan asked me to return to Iraq as quickly as possible with two French surgeons whom I know and trust.

My excellent colleagues Dominique Le Veit and Sylvain Staub, who were working at Lemain, accompanied me to Iraq. Having done all we could for him in Baghdad we returned with him and his father to France. Muhammad was admitted to a clinic outside Paris and while he was there Barzan had time to inspect some colour photographs of himself taken in Geneva. There were more than twenty portraits taken from various angles and in different poses, and they were blown up to thirty by forty centimetres. I remarked that he looked good in several of them.

'One day you can have one,' he said.

People other than Barzan also tried to get Saddam to change his mind about Israel. On 2 May 1994, when UN sanctions were really starting to bite, the President's son, too, was implicated in a secret diplomatic push. It originated in Egypt and Raouf Boutros-Ghali, brother of the Secretary-General Boutros Boutros-Ghali, was the mediator through a Kurd politician.

The signal to Saddam via Iraq's Olympic committee, ruled over by Uday, was straightforward: if Baghdad would make peace with Israel, Egypt would suggest to the USA that the sanctions be lifted.

But Saddam's answer, in the shape of a top secret note to Uday two weeks later, was forthright.

> It has become clear that the communication we have received from our Arab brotherland is yet another attempt to muddle our relations with the Zionists. It is nonsense to believe that we will change our attitude towards them should they choose to help us out of our problems. To hell with them and the damned Arabs who encourage such policy. That door is closed. I have nothing against Boutros-Ghali's brother coming here to talk to me about sanctions, but the condition is that he does not discuss the Zionist lobby's initiative with us at any time.

Zafer Muhammad Jaber, Uday's friend and private secretary, gave me the note.

The old, estimable Bedouin Abraham is the main character in *Get Out! You Are Cursed*. His three sons are killed in battle but they all leave a son behind, Isaac, Joseph and Mahmoud. The three grandsons move in with their grandfather and it is their life and development that we follow in Saddam's last work.

Isaac is a miser and a scoundrel who always behaves deceitfully. He wears a small piece of cloth on his head.

'Why is it so small?' Joseph asks.

'Because a hat is expensive,' Isaac answers.

Joseph and Mahmoud come out of it a bit better. They are industrious, honest men who only want the best for their grandfather, the tribe and the Bedouin society around them.

The work is dripping with symbols; none of them difficult to decipher. The climax approaches when Isaac leaves Babylon and

settles in 'a country to the west of the Dead Sea'. Not unexpectedly he teams up with a greedy Roman governor who supports
him through thick and thin. The two make sleazy deals at the
expense of honest people, and make so much money that they
build two big and tall towers to store all the money and gold they
have acquired.

'It's a good thing we've safeguarded our treasure,' says Isaac.

But something dramatic happens on the last pages of
Saddam's book. Isaac and his governor discover that the tower
has been attacked and burnt by a group of intrepid Arab resistance fighters who die in the flames, crying, 'God is great, God is
great.'

The chief of the governor's guards breaks out into praise, and
shouts: 'May God have mercy on the Arab martyrs and may He
curse the infidel.' It strikes Isaac, who starts to cry, and his business partner, that what they are witnessing is the start of a
never-ending problem. The Martyrs of the Tower have become
examples to follow.

Minister of Culture Hamed Hamadi never got to publish
Saddam's last work, the war overtook him. Having finished the
final proof-reading and noted in the margin that the book was to
be printed without delay, he found there were no longer any civil
servants left to do the job. Their priorities were now their families.
The printers too had disappeared. Saddam's literary effort was
therefore lying on Hamed Hamadi's desk when Baghdad fell on
9 April.

When the ministries were looted the manuscript and the
Culture Minister's scribbling and corrections were found by
someone who knows a friend of mine.

Saddam Hussein al-Tikriti, President of Iraq 1979–2003.

CHAPTER 19

The Caliph

Baghdad falls, yet again.

The sixth of April 2003 was to be my last day in the service of Saddam. The American invasion force had already been observed in Baghdad's suburbs and the international airport outside the capital captured; the first American planes had landed.

I was on my way to a twenty-four-hour shift at Bin-Sina. The President's private hospital was still functioning in one of the wings of the large Kazimiya hospital in north-east Baghdad. We had been moved there for reasons of security.

For the last twelve months Khairi Benoosh had been Bin-Sina's director; a brigadier with a military-medical background. Like so many who occupied Saddam's key positions he too was from Tikrit.

Dr Benoosh was not a bad director, however. He was highly qualified in his own field and administratively he ran a tight ship. He was not popular within the President's circle of intimate friends: they thought he was too soft with his employees.

'I have instructions from the highest authority,' he said when I reported for duty. 'You can't leave Bin-Sina. You must stay until further notice.'

I quickly realised what was going on. Saddam wanted me if he was forced to leave Baghdad.

'That's OK,' I said, 'but I'll just have to drop in on my mother. She's nearly ninety and not at all well. She'll need food and medicine if I'm to stay here indefinitely.'

As usual Dr Benoosh was easy-going. 'OK,' he said. 'But be quick.'

The seventeen days that had passed since the war started had not been easy. My most important task was to keep al-Wasiti going. As the person in charge, everything rested on my decisions. I therefore moved into the hospital and slept in my office where I had stocked up with water and tinned food.

Luckily almost the entire staff – doctors, nurses and ancillary workers – reported for duty; only a few stayed at home. We had been through wars before and thought this one would be short-lived.

No extraordinary initiatives had been put in place to prepare us for the American and British attack which we all knew would come. Before the war against Iran and after the invasion of Kuwait clear emergency directives were issued. But not this time. The regime had obviously fallen apart long before the American planes and cruise missiles had left their bases.

Not even Baath Party members appeared to have made preparations to fight. International news media indicated that Saddam and twenty to thirty of his closest collaborators would be removed from office and tried for their criminal activities. The remainder of the administration would be maintained, with the police, peace and order upheld and the status quo would continue after the occupation.

The news was eagerly seized on by those affected. There was little or no fighting spirit evinced by the officers and soldiers of the Republican Guard or the Special Republican Guard who I met and spoke to. Everyone was fed up with corruption and misrule and dreamt of a better day tomorrow.

Che sarà sarà.

I was on a twenty-four-hour shift at Bin-Sina every fourth day. But the Kazimiya hospital was on the other side of Baghdad, far away from al-Wasiti. The distance between the two was about thirty kilometres and thanks only to my good and fearless chauffeur, Ismail Muhammad Kaabi, was I able to get from one to the other, and survive, in the difficult driving conditions that prevailed during those days.

It was never possible to predict explosions en route. We tried to steer clear of the roads where we knew communications centres, military camps, ministries and other public buildings which represented obvious targets for American and British bombs and missiles were situated – but it was not always easy to find alternative routes.

One morning, en route to Kazimiya hospital and Bin-Sina, we passed, as usual, the area's telephone and communications centre. Fire and smoke rose from the ruins. American bombers had scored a bull's eye just a few minutes earlier. We zigzagged between pulverised and burnt-out cars; not everyone had found an alternative route that morning.

But our main problem was visibility. Some idiot had decided to cover Baghdad in smoke to impede American precision bombing. Trenches had been dug over the whole town, filled with heavy oil, and set on fire. The smokescreen caused endless collisions and accidents. Asthmatics and people with respiratory illnesses were suffering badly. When a heavy dust storm hit large parts of Iraq on 25, 26 and 27 March, many succumbed. The combination of explosions, smoke, dust and sand was intolerable, even for healthy people. It was hell on earth.

On 29 March Barzan came to Bin-Sina to talk to me. He was accompanied by two heavily armed bodyguards. I was very surprised: it was extremely risky to move about outside owing to heavy fire from anti-aircraft artillery and machine guns.

'What'll be the outcome of this war?' he asked.

'The regime is finished and the possibility of stopping the war before the Americans and British reach their target is zero,' I said.

Barzan thought the same. 'Have you seen the President lately?' he asked.

I hadn't. Rumours were circulating that he had instigated a meeting with the top brass of the Revolutionary Command Council and with ministers two days before the war broke out. He appeared calm and relaxed, and Abed Hamoud, Taha Yassin Ramadhan and Izzat Ibrahim al-Douri would, in customary fashion, have assured him that the patriotism and fighting spirit amongst the armed forces was at its zenith and that American and British aggressors would be beaten back.

Since then no one had seen Saddam. His movements were, as always, unpredictable and secret.

'I'm convinced that he's aware he can't win this war. He'll have made plans to go to earth, rather than fight what he knows is a superior force,' I said to Barzan.

Barzan looked desperate. He appeared to be on the brink of a mental breakdown. 'We could have avoided all this,' he said. 'I've told him repeatedly that he has to start being realistic about the world situation and forget the Palestinian question and get some sort of agreement going with America and Israel. But he would never listen to me. On the contrary, he banned me and others from even mentioning the subject.'

Barzan said he would return in a couple of days, but that was the last time I saw and spoke to Saddam's half-brother.

Half an hour after having left with his bodyguards, six missiles hit the military intelligence centre, only five kilometres from the Kazimiya hospital. The explosion was so strong that the sheet roofing over us collapsed.

Shortly after midnight I heard rumbling and the strong drone of engines. I peeped out of the window from my third-floor room and counted at least ten cannons, armoured personnel carriers and tanks stationary under the trees round the hospital. Whoever gave orders for this must be an idiot, I thought.

Three hours later I thought my last hour had come: ear-shattering explosions surrounded all the hospital walls. I was alone on duty with one other doctor the night of 30 March. The rest of the staff must have disappeared before the bombing and the military vehicles under the trees started to arrive. They knew what to expect.

The problem for me and my colleague was that we were not familiar with the layout of the large hospital. We groped our way down to the basement while the building shook and whatever was loose above us came tumbling down. We found a storage room and took cover. But there was only one door in the room and as the bombing continued we reasoned that it would be wiser to find a place less confined if the hospital wing was hit.

We made our way up to the first floor and sat in the corner of the outpatients' waiting room. The windows were glassless. The panes had long gone, blown out by the air pressure from nearby bombs.

How come, I thought, that we Iraqis always find ourselves squeezed between greater or lesser despots in Baghdad and forces from outside who want to get rid of them and occupy our country.

The loud bangs continued and the intense flashes of light unremittingly tore the darkness in tatters. From the cradle of civilisation in Mesopotamia to the Sumerians teaching the world to read and write five or six thousand years ago, that squeeze and that tyranny have run like a red thread through our entire history. In such a context, Saddam's regime, his megalomania, the internal strife, brutality and cruelty, were maybe not all that special.

Nor was his fall.

Dawn was approaching and the bombing petered out. I went to the exit to have a look. Twisted scrap metal was all that was left of Saddam's missiles and tanks. I could only admire the American precision – it had saved my life – but nor could I stop wondering what that mangled war matériel had cost Iraq. How well we could have spent the money elsewhere.

At the end of the turbulent shift at Bin-Sina I asked Ismail to drive me home. The trip through Baghdad was a tour through a ghost town. The streets were empty bar a few Republican guards here and there; abandoned everywhere were bombed-out tanks, armoured personnel carriers and military lorries. Military intelligence HQ was burning. Trees were blackened, their burnt branches resembling the ribs of shattered, charred skeletons.

My house was intact but the windows were smashed. There didn't seem to have been any looting.

At al-Wasiti hospital the deputy director told me that the head of East Baghdad's secret police had moved into the hospital with his staff while I was at Kazimiya. The police chief feared that his own HQ would soon be targeted. I was furious. It would put all our lives in jeopardy if the newcomers were seen walking in and out of the hospital with their weapons. My fear was that al-Wasiti might be mistaken for a military compound; it wasn't unreasonable, smaller mistakes had been made.

But I could do nothing. The police were asked to stay in their rooms. That very night their office block, near al-Wasiti, was flattened during a raid. They thanked their lucky stars.

On 4 April rumours were flashed round that there was heavy fighting near the international airport, not far from Hay al-Jihad and my house. Ismail and I went to see if it was reasonably whole and undamaged. Baghdad's streets were deserted and more ghostly than ever.

All the windows had been blown in, the curtains were flapping. Ismail and I tried to block them up with cardboard and cartons but I knew it would not be long before the neighbourhood descended like vultures and emptied the house of furniture and carpets, stove, fridge, radio and TV and anything else of value.

I had no illusions left.

During the afternoon Saddam showed himself in al-Mansour, near 'The Union', the monument which had been unveiled in April 2002. He was surrounded by a few bodyguards but appeared tired and depressed.

Some commentators speculated whether in fact it might have been one of his many 'doubles'. But it was Saddam himself. In my opinion his 'doubles' were a figment of the imagination. Neither I nor any of my fellow plastic surgeons in Iraq have had anything to do with altering someone's face to look like the President. I would have known about it, being a member of his medical team.

I never returned to Bin-Sina. I had finished with Saddam. I owed him nothing; certainly not having to follow him into exile. I had never been a member of the Baath Party or any other party. Saddam had once asked me why I didn't join the party.

'I don't like to view my country through a keyhole,' I said. 'I like to look at it through an open door.'

Nothing bound me to him, his family or his desperate gang of followers who were now about to lose power and be held responsible for their actions over the last thirty-five years. I had carried out my work as a doctor at Bin-Sina and amongst his family circle to the best of my ability and I had no doubt pleased him with my sculptures and paintings, but my conscience was clear when I now turned my back on him.

I asked Ismail to drive me to my sister's place and then told him to save himself. My sister lived in the al-Khadra district and my elderly mother was with her. I reckoned the President's body-guards were unaware of my sister's whereabouts.

On 7 April the Republican Palace and its associated complexes of offices and buildings were under American control.

On 8 April nearly all the bridges crossing the Tigris and the greater part of Baghdad were controlled by the invasion forces.

I lay low during the last days before the regime fell. Towards midday on the last day someone banged on the door. It was my cousin Fawzi Farman Bashir. He was in bad shape, and could barely walk. His hair and beard were long and unkempt; but he was alive. I could hardly believe my eyes when I embraced him.

Fawzi had been taken by the Mukhabarat three months earlier. Intelligence officers in plain clothes came for him and after that he never knew where he was. We had all feared the worst. Fawzi had persisted in his blunt criticism of the regime after he opposed Taha Yassin Ramadhan and was imprisoned in the wake of Nazim Kazzar's attempted coup in 1973. When Saddam freed him a year later he went to Paris and took a doctor's degree in agricultural economics at the Sorbonne.

Having returned home he continued to test the boundaries with his dissenting views. He lived for, and believed in, a democratic and secular Iraq, void of despotism and corruption. He was imprisoned again in 1994 but let out after two years. This last time however, he nearly lost it all.

'I was accused of having organised an opposition group planning to topple the regime. They'd decided to execute me for treason. Then the war came and saved me – in the nick of time,' he said.

Fawzi was initially taken to Mukhabarat's torture centre in Harthia in al-Mansour. Here he was beaten senseless with an iron rod. The soles of his feet were whacked with a cane. When the American bombing commenced he was moved to another of the intelligence service's prisons. But this prison too was an exposed target for American bombs and he was moved yet again, this time to '17 July' police station, three hundred metres from my sister's house in al-Khadra. Earlier that day all the policemen had fled and left the prisoners to their own devices. The mob moved in to loot and freed the prisoners. Helped by a plain-clothes policeman he had managed to make his way to my sister's house.

Fawzi was bursting with enthusiasm when we settled round the kitchen table. He was now sixty-six years old and as soon as he had recovered from the strains and stresses of the last months he wanted to form a secular, socialist political party.

'Surely it should be possible, with the help of other decent, honest and educated Iraqis, to build up a democracy.'

I was not quite so optimistic. It is easy to mouth the word democracy but I found it difficult to fathom how a liberal, pro-gressive democracy could take root in a country where so much hate, lust for revenge and brutality has flourished throughout its history. Our country needed forgiving leaders who would exercise humanity. That would be the first step along the road if the dream of a viable democracy were to become a reality.

'Where do you find those sort of people today?' I asked.

'I'll try, no matter what.' Fawzi said.

I remembered a story told me some years earlier by a medical colleague in Baghdad. He had one afternoon been strolling along the bank of the Tigris with a friend, a visiting professor from England. In front of them a boy, no more than ten years old, was also walking along. The boy seemed suddenly to see something down near the water, and as the two professors watched, he picked up a heavy stone and dropped it down the bank. A scream was heard, and my colleague rushed forward, to see a dog, its hind legs both broken, in agony on the river side. The boy walked on as if nothing had happened. The poor dog had been sleeping in a little cleft in the bank, away from the sun. The English pro-fessor looked at my colleague, tears streamed down his cheeks.

I had witnessed such examples of cruelty many times in Iraq. Most often perpetrated against one another by my fellow men. Sometimes for reasons of so-called bravery, sometimes just through plain aggression. At yet other times, as with the young boy, for no obvious reasons at all. At that moment I felt the path to true democracy – where all Iraqis could live together decently, peacefully – would be a long one.

On 9 April it was all over. An American tank was on hand to help pull down the large statue of Saddam on al-Fardous square.

I set off for al-Wasiti. In front of the gate a large mob had collected, preparing to loot the hospital. Luckily an American journalist friend from the *New Yorker*, Jon Lee Anderson, was there to interview me and he rushed off to the nearest American tank commander to persuade him to despatch soldiers to protect us. That saved al-Wasiti.

The orgy of looting broke all barriers. Wherever the mob got a chance, anything and everything of value was stolen. There is some evidence to confirm the claims of eye-witnesses that looters were enouraged by Coalition and other Arabic-speaking soldiers. At the Yarmouk and al-Kindi hospitals the patients were dumped on to the floor and their beds stolen from underneath them. It was the very same mass-psychosis operating as when Imam Hussein's surviving relatives were picked clean by howling people in Kufa on their way to the Caliph Yazid in Damascus. 'If we don't rob them someone else will.'

Al-Wasiti was filling up again, but we were not primarily dealing with victims of war. Now we were mostly treating thieves shot by partners in crime or other robbers, or who had been wounded fighting house-owners or businessmen defending their earthly goods.

The mortuary quickly overflowed.

I remember a twenty-two-year-old who was brought in following an exchange of fire with a fellow thief. He was dead on arrival, and in a little while his father and mother came to the hospital. They wept and wailed – naturally so – then a nurse found $150 in the pocket of the deceased and handed it to the father. The mother started to rant and rave and a fight broke out between the couple. The nurse, unable to restrain them, summoned an American officer who happened to be present. He relieved the father of the money, and, in the manner of Solomon, divided the parcel of banknotes in two. They left the hospital, happy to have found a solution, their son forgotten.

I was informed that my house in Hay al-Jihad had been plundered. En route home Ismail drove me to al-Fardous square. Iraqis were spitting on the demolished Saddam statue; some were stamping their feet on the toppled dictator's face.

Baghdad's last Caliph, Mustasim, was the world's richest man when the Mongols invaded in 1258. The streets overflowed with blood and the waters of the Tigris ran red following the weeks of massacres. Figures are vague but most recognised historians believe that over a million Iraqis were butchered.

Legend recounts that the Caliph was thrown into a dungeon while Khulagu, Genghis Khan's grandson, made a survey of the incredible riches which Mustasim and the other Abbasid Caliphs had amassed during the golden age of Islam, from the year 750 to the Mongol invasion. By and by the Caliph grew hungry and Khulagu served him a meal on plates of gold – but the food was pearls and precious stones. Before Mustasim was killed – he was rolled into a carpet and trampled to death by horsemen – Khulagu visited him down in his dungeon.

'If you had only spent a quarter of your riches on your soldiers, I would never have been able to invade Baghdad,' he said.

On al-Fardous square only the legs of the copper Saddam statue were left on the pedestal. I wondered whether he, who was so fond of reading, had ever read Henry Wadsworth Longfellow's poem on Khulagu and the Caliph.

I said to the Caliph, 'Thou art old,
Thou hast no need of so much gold;
Thou should'st not have heaped and hidden it here,
Till the breath of battle was hot and near,
But have sown through the land these useless hoards,
To spring into shining blades of swords,
And keep thine honour sweet and clear.
Then into his dungeon I locked the drone,
And left him there to feed all alone,

In the honey cells of his golden hive;
Never a prayer, nor a cry, nor a groan,
Was heard from those massive walls of stone,
Nor again was the Caliph seen alive.

PART FOUR

Enclosure

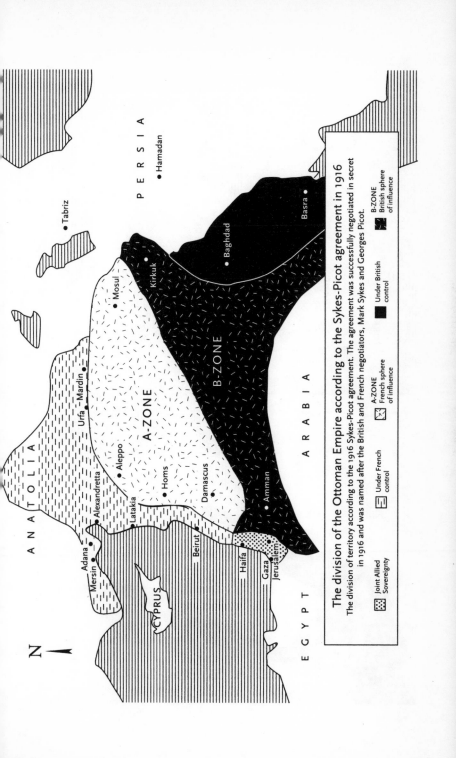

The division of the Ottoman Empire according to the Sykes-Picot agreement in 1916

The division of territory according to the 1916 Sykes-Picot agreement. The agreement was successfully negotiated in secret in 1916 and was named after the British and French negotiators, Mark Sykes and Georges Picot.

Joint Allied Sovereignty

Under French control

Under British control

A-ZONE French sphere of influence

B-ZONE British sphere of influence

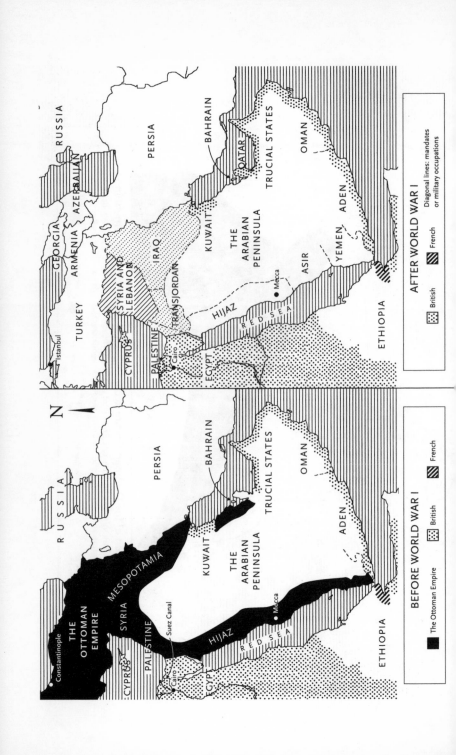

BEFORE WORLD WAR I

The Ottoman Empire · British · French

AFTER WORLD WAR I

British · French · Diagonal lines: mandates or military occupations

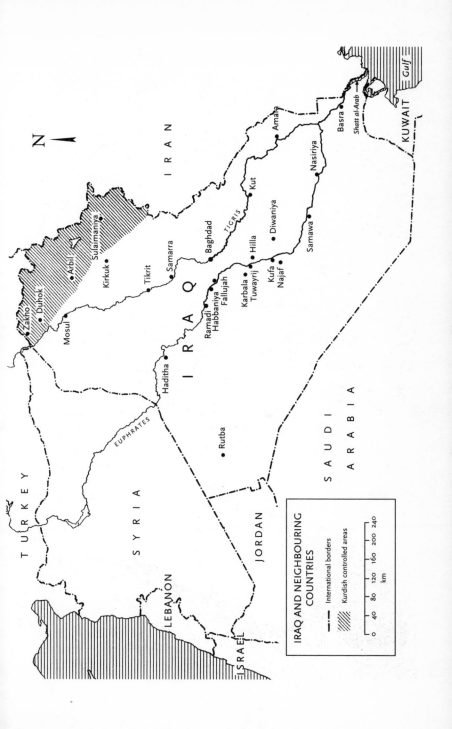

IRAQ AND NEIGHBOURING
COUNTRIES

---·---·--- International borders
///////// Kurdish controlled areas

km
0 40 80 120 160 200 240

SUMMARY OF HISTORIC EVENTS

c. 5000–3000 BC	Sumerian civilisation develops in Mesopotamia – from Greek *mesos* (between) and *potamos* (river), 'the land between the rivers', i.e. Euphrates and Tigris. Towns are built, irrigation systems established and the art of writing is invented.
c. 2300 BC	The Akkadians conquer Sumeria. Babylon is founded near the Euphrates.
c. 1950 BC	Elamites and Amorites conquer Babylon. King Hammurabi codifies the law.
c. 1600 BC	Hittites and Kassites subdue a large part of Mesopotamia. Hittites forge weapons and horse-drawn war-chariots of iron.
c. 900–670 BC	The Assyrians rule Mesopotamia.
c. 629–539 BC	The Chaldeans establish a new kingdom in Babylon and construct the Hanging Gardens. King Nebuchadnezzar (604–562 BC) brings the Jews to Babylon as slaves. Develops money and banking practices, judicial systems and science, in particular mathematics and astronomy.
539 BC	Babylon falls. The Persians, under their King Kyros the Great, conquers Mesopotamia.
330 BC	Alexander the Great conquers the entire region.
138 BC–AD 636	The Persian Arsakid and Sassanid dynasties succeed Greek rule and dominate the region.
637	The Arabs subjugate the country and introduce Islam.
750	The Abbasid dynasty comes into power.
762	Baghdad is founded by the Abbasid Caliph Abu Jaafar al-Mansour
800	The Islamic Empire stretches from Iran to

	Africa with Baghdad as its capital. Baghdad is a town of approximately one million inhabitants and becomes a centre for culture and trade.
1258	The Mongols invade, plunder and destroy Baghdad. The Abbasid Caliph Mustasim is executed and the inhabitants massacred.
1405–1508	Turkic-Mongolian chieftains invade Mesopotamia. More plunder and massacre.
1534	The area is conquered by the Turks. Up until the First World War Mesopotamia consists of three provinces under the Ottoman Empire – Mosul, Baghdad and Basra.
1914	The Turks throw their lot in with Germany and Austria/Hungary after the outbreak of the Great War. Great Britain lands an expeditionary force in Basra to protect the Persian oilfields.
1916	In secrecy Great Britain and France enter into the Sykes–Picot Agreement about the division of Ottoman territory in the Middle East after the war.
	The Grand Sharif in Mecca, King Hussein of Hijaz, rebels against Turkish rule. His son, Prince Faisal, leads Arab guerrilla soldiers in battles against the Ottoman forces. T. E. Lawrence and weapons from Britain come to his aid.
1917	British forces conquer Baghdad.
1918	The Ottoman Empire crumbles.
1920	The League of Nations decrees that the three Ottoman provinces, Mosul, Baghdad and Basra, become a British mandate renamed Iraq. Uprising against the British military rule is brutally put down.
1921	Prince Faisal is elected King.
1922	Anglo-Iraqi treaty signed. Great Britain's dominance of the country is assured.
1927	Oil is found in Kirkuk. This confirms the geologists' theory that 'Iraq is floating on petroleum'.
1928	American-British-French-Dutch oil consortium is created to excavate and produce oil in Iraq.

1932	Iraq gains its independence.
1933	Faisal dies. His son, Ghazi, is crowned.
1934	The first of seven military coups in the next five years takes place. Ghazi retains his crown.
1934–35	The export of oil takes off and adds enormously to the country's wealth.
1937	Saddam Hussein al-Tikriti is born on 28 April. Date and year of birth are uncertain.
1939	King Ghazi is killed in a traffic accident. His three-year-old son, Faisal II, becomes King. Faisal's uncle, Abdul Ilah, takes over as regent until his nephew's coming of age.
1941	Pro-Nazi officers attempt a coup. The royal family flees to Jordan. British troops intervene and overcome the rebellion.
1948	The state of Israel is established. Iraqi, Syrian, Jordanian and Egyptian forces suffer severe military defeat during the acts of war that follow.
1953	King Faisal II succeeds the regent, Abdul Ilah.
1955	Iraq and Turkey establish the Baghdad treaty on defence cooperation in case of attack. Great Britain, Pakistan and Iran join the treaty.
1956	Egypt's President, Gamal Abdul Nasser, nationalises the Suez Canal. Great Britain and France intervene militarily but are obliged to withdraw their troops following strong American condemnation. Nasser is seen as a hero in the Arab world.
1958	Faisal and virtually the entire royal family are killed in a military coup. Iraq's strongman through many decades, Prime Minister Nuri al-Said, is killed. Iraq becomes a republic under the leadership of Abdul Karim Kassem.
1959	Iraq withdraws from the Baghdad Pact. Bloody street fighting between Communists and pan-Arab nationalists in Mosul in Northern Iraq.
1961	The Kurds in Northern Iraq demand autonomy and rebel once again.
1963	Abdul Karim Kassem is toppled and executed. Abdul Salam Aref becomes President of an

administration in which Baath Party members
dominate.
Saddam Hussein returns to Iraq from Egypt.
The Baathists are slowly pushed out and Aref
takes sole charge.

1966   Abdul Salam Aref is killed in a helicopter crash.
His brother, Abdul Rahman Aref, becomes
President.

1967   Arab forces suffer new painful defeat during the
Six Day War against Israel where the Israelis
capture and occupy the Golan Heights, Gaza
and the West Bank of the Jordan, including East
Jerusalem.

1968   Baath Party gains control. General Ahmed
Hassan al-Bakr becomes President and Saddam
Hussein his deputy and right-hand man.

1970   Saddam Hussein negotiates a ceasefire with the
Kurdish rebels and promises far-reaching
autonomy.

1972   Baghdad and Moscow enter into a friendship
treaty. Iraq nationalises the oil industry.

1973   The torturer Nazim Kazzar attempts a coup but
fails.
The Yom Kippur War between Israel and Syria
and Egypt results in an international oil crisis
and a large increase in oil prices.

1974   The Baath regime uses the increase in oil
revenue to build hospitals, schools and roads.
The standard of living in Iraq increases and is
now one of the highest in the Middle East.
The Kurds rebel again. The Iraqi government
has not adhered to the agreements from 1970.

1975   Iraq and Iran sign an agreement about the
disputed boundary river Shatt al-Arab. The
agreement does away with the conflict between
the 'sister nations'. The Shah in Tehran stops all
money and weapons delivery to the Kurds who
are forced to give up their guerrilla war in
Northern Iraq.

1978   The death penalty is introduced for political
activity outside the Baath Party.

1979	President Ahmed Hassan al-Bakr withdraws. Saddam Hussein gathers all power into his hands and executes political rivals.
1980	War against Iran. The Shatt al-Arab border dispute is blamed.
1987	Saddam Hussein's cousin, Ali Hassan al-Majid, leads the special forces who in the course of two years kill between 50,000 and 100,000 Kurds in the mountain areas of Northern Iraq. He is given the nickname Chemical Ali after the village of Halabja is bombed with nerve and mustard gas.
1988	Ceasefire between Baghdad and Tehran. About 150,000 soldiers have been killed and 750,000 wounded. Iraq is on its knees economically. Saddam's oldest son Uday kills the President's valet.
1990	Iraq invades Kuwait. UN Security Council demands withdrawal and introduces sanctions against Baghdad.
1991	Under American leadership an alliance of thirty-two nations throw the Iraqi soldiers out of Kuwait. Saddam's military defeat is total. The coalition forces halt their advance when the sheikhdom has been freed. Shia muslims rebel in the south and the Kurds rise in the north. Government forces crush the rebels. Saddam accepts a Security Council resolution which demands the obliteration of all weapons of mass destruction. He also accepts the right of inspectors to control observance of the resolution.
1993	USA attacks public buildings in Baghdad with missiles. This is a reply to an alleged attack on President George Bush in Kuwait.
1994	The Kurds, who have been granted limited autonomy following the Gulf War, start a civil war.
1995	Saddam's son Uday shoots his uncle Watban Ibrahim al-Tikriti in the leg with an automatic weapon.

The President's sons-in-law, Hussein and Saddam Kamel, flee to Jordan with their families.

1996   Hussein and Saddam Kamel return to Baghdad. They are shot and killed.

Large sections of the Iraqi population suffer and live in abject poverty due to economic sanctions. Saddam finally agrees to cooperate in the oil-for-food programme. The export of oil can resume and the income be spent on food and medicines.

Kurdish leader Masoud Barzani invites government forces to advance on Kurdish autonomous areas. They help Barzani put the rival Kurdish leader Jalal Talabani and his guerrilla soldiers to flight.

Attempted assassination of Uday, the President's son, in Baghdad.

1998   Tense situation between UN weapons inspectors and Iraqi authorities who no longer cooperate. Inspectors are withdrawn.

USA and Great Britain carry out Operation Desert Fox: bombing and missile attacks against targets in Iraq.

2001   Terrorist attacks on 11 September speed up a political process in USA which demands regime change in Baghdad.

2002   US President George W. Bush and Great Britain's Prime Minister Tony Blair insist that Saddam Hussein is hiding weapons of mass destruction and consequently is a threat to world peace. War preparations are initiated.

UN weapons inspectors return to Iraq towards the end of the year.

2003   George Bush: 'In Iraq a dictator is building and hiding weapons which will enable him to dominate the Middle East and threaten the civilised world – that we cannot allow.' He is supported by Tony Blair.

War breaks out and Saddam's regime is toppled. No weapons of mass destruction are found.

ACKNOWLEDGEMENTS

Many people have helped me with this account from a painful and difficult epoch in the long and proud, but also bloody history of Iraq. First of all my friends and acquaintances in Baghdad who have opened up and told me many of their own stories of what they saw, heard and experienced before and after Saddam came to power. The majority have been named in the book and I owe them a debt of gratitude for their contribution. A special thank you to my close friends former Foreign Minister Dr Naji Sabri al-Hadithi, former Deputy Foreign Minister Dr Raid al-Qaysi, and to the late ambassador Nizar Hamdoon. Also to my wife Amel, my daughter Amina and my three sons Sumer, Tahsin and Muhammad; without their patience and moral support this book would never have come to fruition. Lars Sigurd Sunnanå wants to thank his wife Unni and his son Lars Magne for their advice, assistance and tolerance during the writing of the book, most of which was written whilst staying with Sheikh Hassan bin Muhammad bin Ali al-Thani in Doha. His Arab hospitality to us both has been unlimited.

INDEX

SH stands for Saddam Hussein